How to Bring Up a Child
Without Spending a Fortune

HOW TO BRING UP A CHILD WITHOUT SPENDING A FORTUNE

Lee Edwards Benning

DOLPHIN BOOKS
DOUBLEDAY & COMPANY, INC.
Garden City, New York, 1976

To J. R.

who challenged me to budget a baby
and taught me that babies are cheap
at twice the price

HOW TO BRING UP A CHILD WITHOUT SPENDING A FOR-
TUNE was originally published in hardcover by David McKay Company, Inc. in 1975. The Dolphin Edition is published by arrangement
with David McKay Company, Inc.

DOLPHIN EDITION: 1976

ISBN: 0-385-11513-x
Library of Congress Catalog Card Number 75–25436
Copyright © 1975 by Lee Edwards Benning

DESIGNED BY LAURENCE ALEXANDER

Foreword

A WORD ABOUT THE DOLLAR FIGURES . . .

All costs are based on either government statistics or industry computations and cover the expense of raising a child to age eighteen in an average area IF YOU WENT OUT ON ONE SPREE AND BOUGHT EVERY ITEM YOU WOULD NEED FOR THE NEXT EIGHTEEN YEARS. In other words, these are not projections and do not include built-in hedges against inflation. Thus, you should consider these figures only as guides to the very least you will get away with . . . and as such, you can pat yourself on the back every time you come close.

P.S. The $43,240.64 total of expenses for that child does not include the dollar-value of your own and your husband's work (estimated at over $121,400) nor the lost earning power you give up by staying at home (as little as $30,000 or as much as $69,000). Add all these together and the total cost of that child is between $194,640.64 and $233,640.64.

Acknowledgments

It is the generous spirit, who, when brought among the tasks
of real life, hath wrought upon the plan . . .

Wordsworth

It is those generous spirits—the dozens and dozens of them—
whose help I must acknowledge:

My husband, Arthur E. Benning, Sr., who read and proofed and
edited, then reread and reproofed and reedited, devoting every Saturday and Sunday morning to my book for months and months. And
among all the comments that this father of four made, one I treasure:
"I never knew it took so much to be a mother."

My mother, Edna S. Edwards, who gave me my first instructions in the fine art of mothering . . . and who cheerfully baby-sat
whenever the going got rough. My father, Albert I. Edwards, who
insisted on my becoming a home economist. He also did several
charts, and much of the proofreading. My sister, Joan E. Klein-
dienst, who introduced me to that best of budget-savers, hand-
me-down clothes. Keep 'em coming, please!

And that relay team, Liz to Al to Judy to Phil to Judy to Al to
Liz to me, in which the whole idea of budgeting your baby was
first planted.

My friend, Gertrude Neal, D.E.E., who came to my house and
my rescue time after time so I had more time.

That great sisterhood of women who gave me their secrets,
suggestions and encouragement, my friends, the mothers: Patricia Day-
ley, Margaret Doherty, Carolyn Dunn, Irene Freyler, Carol Josel,
Mary Price Lee, Carol Molnar, Helen Packert, Mary Rhode, Sandra
Van Amburgh, and many more, especially Anna D. Seymour, who
graciously and generously shared her expertise and knowledge as a
mother of five with a bewildered mother-to-be.

I owe much to the time and knowledge that doctors gave so freely
to me, especially Alexander Randall IV, Franz Vossenberg, Paul

Gyorgy, Kristine Knisely, Winslow Tompkins, Richard Schwarz, Cortez F. Enloe, Jr., William Krogman, Richard Hein, Paul Honig, Thomas E. Shaffer, Elmer Macht, the late Merle Miller, and my friend the dentist, John K. Reimer, D.D.S. There were also the doctors H. T. E. Hertzberg and Robert A. Stewart, the nurses Loretta Phillips, Julie Donohue, and Mabel Forde (who is also a professional midwife), the pharmacists Albert St. George and Robert Hoover, to name only a few.

Then there are those in government, people who really take the idea of being public servants seriously: Lucie G. Kressa, Dr. Francis Magrabi, and Jean Pennock of the Department of Agriculture; C. Warren Devereux of the Bureau of Standards; Susan McIntosh Ralph, staff economist of the Commission on Population Growth and the American Future; Elaine Besson and Walter Johnson of the Bureau of Product Safety, Children's Division; James Bryant and Nancy Bernstein of Amtrak; John V. Lester of the Social Security Administration. The staffs of H.E.W. Commissioner Caspar W. Weinberger . . . of Sen. Richard Schweiker (Pa.), especially Vivien Mitchell . . . and of Sen. Charles Percy (Ill.), especially his legislative aide, Stuart Statler. At the local level, having the Wissahickon Valley Public Library nearby was like having my own personal research staff, thanks to the efforts of Marjorie Smith and others.

Thanks, too, should go to Elizabeth Scott, Wilma Sim, Marilyn Steinberg, Thelma Shenkman, Prof. Mary Carter, Bill Lowery, Bruce Douglas, Charles (special thanks to you) Farley, and you, too, James E. Jeffries, Eddie Miller, and John Rieff. And to Addie Ryan, Bob Spain, Alvin Field, Maribeth Cuccinelli, Norman Germany, Barbara Hulse, Harry Carroll, Orien Ried, Jerry Carasick, Conrad Levinson, Robert J. Mullen, Richard File, Carroll Stoner, Daniel Kushner, Jim Buchanan, Jean Coventry, Rosemary Giesy, Donna Winnett, Mrs. Alfred G. Robinson, Mrs. Oscar Stonorov, Joan Miller, Mrs. John Scott, Beatrice B. Szalai, Ruth Livesey, William V. Driscoll, Franklin Kolyer, Jesse Hutton, Paul Sykes, Gerry A. McCormick, Joseph Rizzuto, Eugene Dubois, Marilyn Ellman Frankel.

On the financial side, these gentlemen were most helpful: Theodore Robertson, Frank X. Gillespie, Edward Madara, Robert A. Waldron, Harris Aller, Jeffrey Adams, Arthur J. Sconig, Calvin S. Drayer, Jr., Alan Jay Josel, and the gentleman who handles the Benning legal problems, whom we prefer remain anonymous.

On the corporate and institutional level, I wish to thank National Institutes of Health, National Institute of Infant Services, American

Paper Institute, Childbirth Education League, La Leche Society, Guild for Infant Survival, National Association for the Education of Young People, Association for Childhood Education International, American Footwear Industries Association, Institute of Life Insurance, Pennsylvania Insurance Department, Prudential Insurance Company, Insurance Company of North America, Pennsylvania State University, Cornell University, University of Pennsylvania, Valley Forge Presbyterian Nursery School, Charlestown Playhouse, Kimberton Farms School, Swamp Creek Valley Nursery School, Ravenhill Academy, Colorado Springs Montessori School, St. Christopher's Hospital, Booth Maternity Center, Thrift Drug Company (Division of J. C. Penney), Blue Shield/Blue Cross, KYW Radio, *The New York Times*, The Philadelphia *Inquirer*, *The Evening Bulletin* (Philadelphia), *American Druggist*, *The Farm Journal*, *Consumers Report*, *Consumers Bulletin*, *The Home Finders Directory*, *Time*, *Newsweek*, The Fidelity Bank, Philadelphia Electric Company, Philadelphia Gas Works, Bell Telephone Company of Pennsylvania, Singer Sewing Machine Company, Dy-Dee Service, Inc., Scott Paper Company, Gus File, Inc., Simmons Furniture, Creative Playthings, Childcraft Education Corporation, Johnson & Johnson, Gerber Products Company, Heinz U.S.A., E. I. duPont de Nemours, Simplicity Pattern Company, Ross Laboratories, Health-Tex, Inc., Montgomery Ward & Company, Sears Roebuck & Company, Lord & Taylor, Saks Fifth Avenue, Greyhound, Eastern Air Lines, United Air Lines.

And then there are the two people besides my husband who made truly major contributions: Ruth Hunter, who wrought artfully upon it, and Narcie Lu Lord, who was more consultant, adviser, editor than just typist. Many were the pointed questions she asked, the right-on suggestions she made, the easily overlooked errors she caught.

Contents

How to Bring Up a Child
Without Spending a Fortune

Part I

Clothing

Exclusive of your maternity wardrobe and basic layette, experts predict you will spend close to $4,300, or 10 percent of the total cost of raising a child, on clothing. For the first three years, clothing purchases will be dictated by your child's rate of growth. When growth slows down, costs stabilize and remain at the same level throughout the preschool period.

At six, you join the back-to-school rush as the need for school clothes adds to your clothing bill. Breathe a sigh, costs stabilize again . . . and remain relatively stable until the twelfth year. At this last step before teens, increased activities and peer pressure add to the growth-needs to cause another upward spurt.

For girls, growth will practically stop—at least upward—during the period between twelve to thirteen. However, a growing fashion consciousness, social activities, and physical maturation take up the slack a lack of growth makes in your budget. Boys will continue growing at a relatively fast rate beyond age fifteen, and some degree of growth can continue on into their twenties.

Sixteen heralds another clothing spurt for both sexes as fads have their way, and then the transition is made into adult-type activities and adult-type clothing.

Chapter 1

Born Mother Naked

What will your baby need in the way of clothing to see him through the first three months? Well, you could get by with two dozen diapers, three gowns, and three yards of cotton flannelette. And, depending on the weather, maybe just the diapers would be enough. However, neither you nor I will ever settle for so little when there's so much more recommended by every magazine, pamphlet, baby ad, neighbor, friend, father, grandmother—you name it. So, why fight city hall? Let's throw all the lists together into a list to end all lists . . . and then take it apart, item by item:

THE EXPERTS' RECOMMENDED BASIC WARDROBE WITH
REPRESENTATIVE COSTS*

4 to 6 shirts ($2 to $9)
4 to 6 gowns or kimonos ($4.50 to $33)
2 to 4 sacque sets ($5 to $24)
2 summer sleeping bags ($3 to $8)
2 winter sleeping bags ($10 to $18)
3 to 4 stretch coveralls ($6 to $36)
4 to 6 receiving blankets ($3 to $24)
1 shawl ($5 to $12)
4 waterproof panties ($1 to $5)
2 to 3 pair booties ($1.50 to $7.50)
2 to 3 pair bootie socks ($1.50 to $3.00)
1 bunting or outdoor suit ($5 to $25)
4 rompers, creepers, sunsuits, coveralls (depending on season)
    ($12 to $60)
1 dress with slip and/or 1 suit with jacket ($3 to $20)
1 coat with bonnet ($6 to $25)

* Exclusive of diapers; see "At the Diaper Station," Chapter 15.

2 sweater sets ($6 to $15)
2 pair crib shoes ($6 to $18)
2 pair crib socks ($1 to $2)
2 bibs ($1 to $2)
1 brush and comb ($1 to $12.50)
2 diaper pins (25¢ to $1)
1 diaper bag ($4 to $28)
1 pacifier (25¢ to $1)?

What will all this cost you? As little as $88 if you bargain-hunt, or as much as (are you ready?) $388. And that's not shopping at Neiman-Marcus, either—just at a local middle-class department store. Recovered from shock yet? Then get ready for another. Sixty-five percent of those items will have to be replaced in three to six months, depending on the initial size clothing you buy, and then again at nine to twelve months. It depends on how fast your baby grows. The average baby doubles its weight in five months (from seven to fourteen pounds) and triples its birth weight in one year. He also grows in length an average of eight inches the first year. Fortunately, that rate of growth slows to five to six inches the second year and even less the next. Otherwise, few could afford to keep a baby clothed or fed.

Do you really need to spend even the $88 for your initial layette? Of course not. In fact, you can clothe your baby more than adequately for between one-third to one-half of that. And without skimping on quality or shortchanging baby.

How do you do it? First of all, purchase all garments in the six-months of "up to eighteen or nineteen pounds," or Medium-size—three different ways of buying the same-size garment. Only for a premature baby should you buy any garments in size 0 or "New-born." Since there is no way of predicting prematurity, you can't buy those in advance, anyway.

Second, be realistic. The first several months are going to be devoted to the two of you learning about each other, not visiting neighbors or having play sessions. The clothes you need must be easy to care for . . . and you need enough of them so that you are not constantly doing laundry. If you want to spend your money on frilly playclothes or dress-up coveralls or knitted treasures, go ahead. But buy them in big sizes, such as nine to twelve months or twelve to eighteen pounds.

Third, recognize that certain items are eminently giftable. If you choose to buy them yourself, save the sales slips so you can return them later if you have too many duplicates.

Fourth, multiple births mean multiple layettes. The only way to hedge your bets if twins are common in your family is to buy your entire layette at a store that has a "double the babies? We double the layette—at our expense" policy.

Now let's pick that list apart.

Shirts
Of cotton knit, they come in long-sleeve, short-sleeve, or sleeveless styles . . . either as pullovers or front-opening wrap styles (they fasten closed with ties, snaps, or zippers—avoid the latter, they're more trouble than they're worth and cost the most). The front-opening shirt is the safest bet since it is easier to put on, for both mother and baby, than the pullover. Babies object strenuously to over-the-head styles. In addition, when putting such styles on, you have only one hand to use. The other must support your baby's neck and head. Moreover, inexpensive shirts may not have enough "give" built into the neck opening to fit over your baby's head. The long-sleeve style is the least versatile of the three, since it can only be used during truly cold weather. Of the other two, sleeveless or short-sleeve, a case may be made for either, just ask your husband and then abide by his decision. (It'll be one of the few decisions he'll make on baby's clothing.)

The point is do you really need either one? Yes, babies have traditionally worn such shirts, but is tradition a good reason for spending as much as $9 on shirts every three months for the first year or so? It *was* in the days when houses were poorly insulated and fireplaces or stoves supplied heat, but unless your home fits that description today, you can forgo the shirts. Yes, I know baby's feet will feel cold. All babies have cold feet and cold hands . . . all the time. It's the result of an immature circulatory system, not the lack of a shirt. In fact, it would take more than one shirt or two to make his extremities warm. You'd have to bundle him up as if for outdoors. Which is why many doctors, such as Frederick Rutherford, M.D., author of *You and Your Baby* (New American Library, 1971), recommend either a shirt or a nightgown, not both . . . and that in "a room temperature of 70° F. day and night for a very new baby. After the first few weeks, 65°–68° is better."

If shirts are not needed for warmth, why else are they used? For protection during the summer. They can help absorb perspiration and keep flies off baby, not to mention sunburn. Of course, gowns or kimonos will do as well. What else then? They have little tabs to which the diaper can be pinned to keep it up. But those tabs have a disadvantage as well. When pinned to the diaper, they act as a wick, drawing the urine up into the shirt. The result is that every time baby is changed, the shirt must also go. This means more of baby must be washed, and, of course, more laundry must be done more frequently—one of the things we said we wanted to avoid.

RECOMMENDATION? No shirts for the first six months, or until baby is beginning to crawl. Use a kimono instead.

Gowns or Kimonos

They're not the same thing. Although made of the same material (seersucker, cotton flannelette, knitted jersey, terry cloth, or synthetics) and of approximately the same length, twenty-four to twenty-seven inches, gowns are the closest thing to a straight-jacket that you can buy for baby. They have a placket opening, which means baby must be stuffed into it feet first like potatoes into a sack . . . or that long, long gown can be put on over baby's head, which baby hates. The bottom, either permanently stitched closed or made with an optional drawstring, encloses baby's feet and keeps them covered, preventing free kicking. The long sleeves with convertible mitten cuffs prevent little hands from accidentally scratching their face . . . and deliberately exploring their surroundings . . . or blissfully thumbsucking. Did you know that some babies are born with calluses on their thumbs? Did you know that some dentists believe that insufficient sucking can create orthodontic problems? Maybe you should rethink your ideas on thumbsucking.

What's a kimono? A negligee for a baby. It opens all the way down the front, has no drawstring or stitched-in closing at the bottom, and fastens only at the top with either ties or snap fasteners. The latter are more convenient since they won't knot when wet, but ties allow for expansion and longer wear-life.

One of the main advantages of the kimono is that the opening can be either in front or in back. The baby determines that. If he likes to sleep on his stomach, as 90 percent do at first, the opening would be in front, with the kimono spread apart to keep it away from the wet diaper area. If baby either starts out on his back or switches to the supine position later, the opening will be in back and thus underneath him.

Moreover, with the kimono, unlike the gown, you have easy access to the diaper area and thus need not undress baby every time you change him. With kimonos baby remains drier, he isn't unnecessarily handled, and life is easier for mother. The larger-sized ones can also be used later as bibs or smocks.

RECOMMENDATION? At least six kimonos, eight preferable. Look for attractive prints, they cost only pennies more, if anything, and will take your mind off the fact that you're being so practical. Cotton flannelette can be used all year round, is absorbent and withstands repeated launderings well. Seersucker for the summer does not hold up as well.

Sacque sets

What's a sacque? Back in 1745 it was a long, loose gown of considerable fullness that women wore over a hoop skirt à la Martha Washington. It hung from the shoulders and was heavily gathered in back, with long folds of material hanging down to the floor. In front, the sides did not come together but were parted to reveal the underskirt. The front edges were trimmed with lace or ribbon.

Today, the description is much the same, except that the sacque has shrunk in length until it more closely resembles a bolero than a gown. A sacque set includes the bolero and plastic-lined panties in a matching material, plus a bonnet and/or booties and/or receiving banket—all of cotton or lightweight synthetics. It is a gift item with a capital G. Sacque sets look cute on some babies, horrid on fat ones. There is nothing a sacque can do that some other garment can't do as well.

RECOMMENDATION? Don't buy.

Sleeping Bags

Also known as "blanket sleepers." These come in summer† and winter weights, in cotton blends and synthetics. The amount of

---

† A summer sleeping bag is nothing more than a zip-front gown with a sewn-in bottom rather than a drawstring. It is basically a waste of money to buy one.

warmth they provide depends on the thickness, not the weight, of the fabric. *Consumers Report* rated acrylics as the warmest but least absorbent, thermal knits as the thinnest and most absorbent, blends as a happy medium. My experience has been that the absorbency of the acrylics is more than satisfactory when combined with adequate diapering underneath—and the acrylics stay the softest after repeated washings without using a fabric softener.

The sleeping bag is your answer to the restless baby who won't stay covered once he has started sleeping through the night. Rather than tieing baby or blankets into place—a dangerous thing to do—you zip baby into his blanket, and as he moves around, he takes his blanket with him.

If you buy what's known as a "grow sleeper," you can count on getting at least a year's wear out of it, maybe more. Like the regular sleeping bag, the grow sleeper has no legs, but it has a triple hem so that it can be lengthened to accommodate your growing baby. Optional darts at the shoulders can be let out in case your baby does much of his growing sideways. The bag section is cut wide to allow baby to kick as he pleases, so much so that some children are able to climb out of a crib while wearing one.

Although you won't need one until the baby's started sleeping through the night, anywhere from six to twelve weeks of age, it's a good idea to have a sleeper on hand. What should you look for? *Metal zippers!* Although the synthetic ones allow you to free jams easily, they have a disadvantage you'll quickly discover once you start using them. They tend to stick when saturated with urine. "Tend to?" Why, I once had to use a pliers to pull one open. And of course, the sticking will occur when speed is of the essence and you are the most frustrated.

The zipper, in either case, should be a two-way one, openable from top or bottom, depending on whether you plan to take the baby out of the sleeper or just want to change the diaper. There should also be a snap or button-fastened flap at the top to prevent nimble fingers from getting at the zipper and opening the bag.

RECOMMENDATION? One sleeper now, preferably a grow sleeper—though more expensive, it will wear twice as long. Then, another sleeper in size one year. No more. The wise mother will prevent falls by switching to sleepers with legs between twelve and eighteen months.

Stretch Coveralls

These are knit suits that cover the baby from head to foot. Most have long sleeves, but short sleeves are available. A parade of snaps march down the front to the crotch, then branch out to go down both legs so that you can open the lower half of the garment to change diapers. The cheaper the suit, the fewer the snaps. As a result, where the branching occurs, gaposis also occurs and the diaper shows through. Not very satisfying aesthetically, but baby doesn't know that.

The beauty of these suits is that they stretch and are not quickly outgrown. Some can see six months of duty at a time. And they fit fat babies and skinny babies, short babies and long babies equally well. Of all the clothing created for baby, these seem to be the best yet. (The blanket sleeper ranks next in my mind.) Unfortunately, nothing's perfect, and these have one drawback: it's necessary to use waterproof pants under them to keep baby from becoming wet from neck to toe. This in turn can cause diaper rash. So, use these suits with caution, especially during the first three months.

Because they have so much "give" built into them, they have become the perfect baby gift (no pun intended). And most gifters know it. So don't stock up on them, especially in the small size. And if you get any that fasten up the back (the cutest ones do) return them or give them away or save them for doll clothes—squirming babies and back snaps don't mix.

RECOMMENDATION? Buy one for taking baby home from the hospital.

Receiving Blankets

I'm not sure where the term "receiving" originated. Nevertheless, these approximately 36"×36" squares of lightweight fabric can be handy. From spring to fall, even longer in a warm bedroom, they can serve as blankets. If made of cotton flannel or a cotton synthetic blend that would be equally absorbent, they make good bath towels—larger and softer and thirstier than the usual towel.

You'll need several of them, but don't buy any until you see how many you get at showers or as gifts; remember, they come in those sacque sets. Moreover, they're easy to make. All you need is a yard of 35" or 36" wide cotton flannelette (haunt the remnant counters for the best buys). The cut ends may be hemmed by hand or machine, or simply pinked (to pink with a regular scissors, just cut a series of notches ¼″ deep, one adjoining the other, the whole of one edge). If possible, reinforce the pinked edge by running down a row of machine stitches ⅜″ from the edge. But this is not absolutely necessary. Later these blankets are great for doll babies or dish towels or polishing cloths or stuffing quilted animals.

RECOMMENDATION? You'll need three to use as blankets, one as a bath towel. Wait until the last minute to buy. The homemade ones are the prettiest.

Shawl

This can be crocheted or knitted in an open-work design to give the effect of lace. Or it can simply be a square of fine, lightweight wool with a fringed edge. Traditionally, a shawl is what you wrap the baby in to take it home from the hospital. And that's the only real purpose a shawl serves. It is not warm enough to do duty as a crib blanket . . . nor sturdy enough to be used and washed daily. Nor is it strong enough to serve the purpose of a "Lovey" or drag-around-the-house blanket such as Linus uses in the comic strip. (That's something you hope your child won't do, but he probably will. Some won't. I don't know why. I only wish I did so I could pass the secret on to you. I suspect from talks with friends that never propping the bottle in the crib has something to do with it. The crib and its blanket don't become a substitute source of warmth and affection, a surrogate mother.)

Back to shawls. They are obviously unnecessary, another of those very eligible gift items. But if you must be traditional—and if you can afford it, I'm all for it—either get the shawl while you're pregnant and use it for yourself, or after the baby is born, appropriate it for yourself.

RECOMMENDATION? If budgeting, be antitradition. If you buy one and also receive one as a gift, return one.

Waterproof Panties

Don't get the "rubber pants habit." Too frequent use of waterproof pants will cause that bugaboo and nightmare of every mother—diaper rash. How? Because such pants keep the baby's bed dry and the baby wet—and you aren't alerted to the fact that your baby is wet and needs changing. I don't mean that every time baby wets, he must be changed instantly. But, the longer the diaper stays on him, the better the chance of ever-present bacteria breaking the urine or urea down into ammonia, the prime cause of diaper rash.

Do you remember the days before the advent of spray oven cleaners and the self-cleaning oven? Those were the days when you'd put a dish of ammonia in the oven at night so that by morning the fumes would loosen baked-on spills and burns. What do all those grease-cutting all-purpose cleaners have in common? They proudly announce they contain ammonia. Now, if ammonia can do that to stubborn stains, imagine its effect on baby's tender bottom. So, don't give that old devil diaper rash a chance, avoid waterproof pants like the plague, in the infant stage at least. Again, here's one place where you can avoid or create problems of your own free will.

Obviously, there will be times when you'll need to use those pants in the interest of a dry lap for you, such as when bringing baby home from the hospital. So, what do you look for in such pants? There are pull-on and snap-on styles, the latter usually found in that ubiquitous gift box, the sacque set. The advantage of the snap-on is that they're easy to put on, just like a diaper. And the snap closing automatically supplies ventilation. On the other hand, unlike the pull-on styles, they're quickly outgrown. Pull-on styles can have stitched or heat-sealed seams. The former cost more than the latter, but except for the very low-priced pants (under 50¢), both wear about equally well. The leg openings should be the cause of your greater concern. Bound openings are less irritating than ruffle-edged ones, but in case of ruffles, the softer the better.

The most important thing to look for with pull-on pants is that they have air holes for evaporation of moisture; otherwise, the pants will act as a steam bath and cook baby's skin.

The el-cheapo styles are fine for occasional wear, but will not withstand many launderings before tearing and defeating your purpose. Thus, if you are going to use waterproof pants, you would be wise to spend at least $1 a pair if you wish to get by with just a few pair that will be washed frequently. One manufacturer actually guarantees his pants to last six months without deteriorating . . . and for me, they did.

RECOMMENDATION? Only one pair in small or medium size

for first three months, and three pair for the next six months. On sizes, better to go too big than too small, because tight leg and waist openings can impair circulation.

Booties and Bootie Socks
They're cute, they're dainty, they make delightful sachets for your drawers, but are totally unnecessary indoors and just barely necessary outdoors. Besides, the &*@%& things won't stay on, nohow! Bootie socks? They're just one more thing to buy and are not needed under booties, which are soft and gentle to baby's skin as it is. But if you have a winter baby, you're sure to get at least one pair of booties as a gift as part of a sweater set or one of those good old sacque sets.

RECOMMENDATION? Use the bootie money to buy something for yourself, like a lavender sachet for your lingerie drawer. Booties don't warm cold feet, they just hide them.

Bunting
What is it? A luxury for most. It's a form of outdoor garment that comes in either one-, two-, or three-piece styles. The one-piece style covers baby from head to foot; it's a sleeping bag with an attached hood and cuffs that convert into mittens. The one-piece is most popular because it is easy to get into, out of, and to sleep in. The two-piece garment consists of either a full-length suit or short jacket, both with attached hoods; in addition, there's a separate, pillowcase-like bag that baby goes into, jacket or suit and all. The three-piece outfit is basically the same, but has a bonnet rather than an attached hood.

Are you lost? Don't worry about it. If you don't receive a bunting as a gift (I received four, two of which were really practical— they had to be *dry-cleaned!!*), you can use a sweater and cap and a blanket designed for outdoor use. Or, make use of your winter sleeping bag. All you need to do in cold weather is add a cap and some mittens.

There's one other style—it's called the convertabag snowsuit. If you zip it one way, it's a sleeping-bag style. Zipped another way, it develops legs and becomes a snowsuit. Don't worry about this one either, because you'll get a written set of instructions with it— which you'll need.

RECOMMENDATION? No bunting if you're budgeting; otherwise a washable one-piecer is a good choice.

Rompers, Creepers, Sunsuits, etc.
This covers a whole gamut of clothes that are unnecessary until your baby is crawling around and needs protection for his knees. That will be somewhere around eight to nine months. Buy after the baby is born. See following chapter for hints.

Dress with Slip and/or Suit with Jacket
Got lots of money? Buy one of each, just in case. But realize that either is about as necessary to the average new mother as having the fifth reunion of your high school graduating class held at your house on the day you and your new heir come home from the hospital. However, of all the clothes available for babies, these are the hardest to resist. And after all, the baby does have to look nice for his first pictures, right? So, if you're only human, this is as good an area to splurge in as I can imagine. Just don't go overboard. Lovely things can be found for under $10. Truly nice ones for under $5. You don't have to spend the $20 to $25 that many stores ask. Select the outfit by weight (not "Newborn" size, although in some cases weight and size markings may be identical) for the baby to wear home from the hospital. While you're at it, remind Daddy to stock up on color film for that great day. (Did you know the average proud parents of a first baby spend more than $75 for film the first year?)

Coat and Bonnet
This is pure luxury . . . and an expensive one at that, for such sets under $10 are few and far between, with those for $35 to $40 far more common. They are not easy to put on and require some kind of covering for the legs, whether it be tights or leggings or the use of a blanket over the top.

Sweater Sets
A set can be comprised of sweater and bonnet and/or booties as well as knit diaper covers (known as "soakers," and not to be used because they're too hot and frequently too tight) plus other accessories. These again are typical gift items and should be regarded as such.

However, here is an item that you might want to make yourself, especially during the last trimester when you're glad for an excuse to sit down and stay put. If so, make your sweaters cardigan-style (babies hate pullovers, remember?) and knit them in sizes one, two, or three years, with the emphasis on the latter two. Why? Because it's after the baby's a year old that you'll make the greatest use of sweaters—just the time when you don't have the time to knit them yourself.

As for colors, go strong! You'll be so sick of shower yellow and watery green and safe old white followed by petal pink or barely blue, that you'll cheer olive green and purple plum and real red. Besides, dark, bright colors don't show dirt and stains as fast as their pastel cousins. And baby will like the colors—the brighter, the bolder, the better.

Be sure to check the stretch in the neck of any pullovers you receive as gifts. I received a lovely turtleneck, lovingly handknit, and it wouldn't go over my newborn's head. The average newborn's head will be twelve to thirteen inches in circumference, with the distance from head to chin about one-quarter of his entire length. Of course, when he's fully grown, his head will be much smaller in proportion, only one-eighth to one-tenth of his height. But for his first two to three years, his head will be disproportionately large . . . and its size must be taken into consideration in buying clothes. More on that in Chapter 2.

RECOMMENDATION? Don't buy sweaters if you can avoid it; knit only one small one, concentrate your efforts on larger sizes.

Crib Shoes and Socks

Some people will do anything to make a fast buck. How a non-walking, much less noncrawling infant could have a need for shoes is a mystery. What's more, did you know one pediatrician has put forth the premise that properly fitting crib shoes can cure colic? As my own pediatrician said, "He's probably right—*if* the colic is caused by improperly fitting ones."

Nine out of ten babies are born with perfect feet, but within the next ten years, four of those nine babies will develop defective feet. And of the five that make it through the first ten years without trouble, only one will graduate from high school without foot problems.

Unless there is a medical reason, one that a doctor points out and prescribes for, I do not believe any child needs to wear shoes until he's walking. And even then, the shoes need only be used when the child is outside walking on hard surfaces like pavement. Walking on sand and grass barefoot is the healthiest exercise for growing feet. You know how you discover new muscles in your own feet after a day of walking or running on the beach. A baby, moreover, needs to kick his feet and wiggle his toes; that's the only way he can prepare the muscles for weight-bearing later. (For more on shoes, see Chapter 2 for sizing, Chapter 3 for buying.)

RECOMMENDATION? Do not buy shoes before the child's tenth month unless your doctor gives you a *medical* reason for doing so.

So much for clothes. Diapers will be covered in depth in "At the Diaper Station," Chapter 15, for the number and style you buy will depend on how you're going to handle the entire diapering situation.

What about accessories?

Bibs

For the first three months, if you're using cloth diapers, use one of those instead of a bib. It covers most of baby, it is easy to launder (the diaper service will do it for you, for example), and one is always on hand. Besides, until the child can hold his head erect, a bib is awfully hard to fasten with only one hand. And there's a way to avoid using a bib even after that. See Chapter 5.

Don't use costly disposable diapers as a bib, buy the biggest you can find. A kimono worn back to front does an excellent job. Its advantage is that you protect more clothing from food stains and can use a corner of the bib to wipe dirty faces, and thus save having a washcloth or towel on hand. The plastic-backed bib is a mixed blessing: it does a good protecting job, yet does not take kindly to frequent washings.

Brush and Comb

A possible baby gift. An excellent thing to suggest that poor, anxious, "let me do something for the baby" Daddy buy while you're convalescing in the hospital. Why wait till baby's born? Because inexpensive brush-and-comb sets come only in pink or blue.

Those that do equally well for either gender cost more, at least double.

There's another reason for waiting until baby's born to acquire this item. Some babies don't need it. They're born without hair. Some of the hairy ones start losing their hair before they've left the hospital. Most will lose it sooner or later, so wait until sooner or later to spend the money. Then, too, you might be surprised and receive a sterling silver one as a present. It makes a marvelous complexion or fingernail brush for you later.

Diaper Pins
If you can find them, outsize, regular safety pins are as good a bet as the plastic-capped diaper pins you find in baby stores. Why? Because that plastic head gradually wears away; then one day those "safety-grip, never-open, permanently locked" locks don't stay locked anymore. Therefore, you can plan on each of these plastic-and-metal pins having a life expectancy of about two months, even less during the baby's first three months, when diapers are changed most frequently. So when you read about authors who pooh-pooh checking a crying baby for an open diaper pin, you know they were writing back in the days of preplastic pins. Today, it's one of the first things to check because a prematurely opened pin is going to happen to you, and more than once, too.

If you really search, you may be able to find special pins with metal slip-on caps that will really stay closed. If you can't find those but have $5 to $10 to spend, you can get a pair in sterling silver.

RECOMMENDATION? Always have four diaper pins on hand. Two on the baby and two just in case. See Chapter 15 for diaper-pin maintenance.

Diaper Bag
Unless you're a collector of oversize handbags or go in for shopping bags, this will be an absolutely, positively, definite must-have. If you can afford it, this is one place to go mad, to splurge like crazy, to worry about appearances. Other than the fact that it should be able to hold about a half-dozen diapers, a bottle or two, plus toys, washcloths, etc., the only other requirement is that it

look chic. It does not have to be plastic-lined or insulated, if you follow directions in Chapter 17 for traveling with young children.

Lady, once you start carrying a baby (the equivalent of lugging around a ten-pound sack of potatoes), at the same time hauling along a handbag and carrying a diaper bag, you'll soon decide something must go—just about as fast as your maternity clothes got packed away in the attic. And that something? The handbag. So turn your diaper bag into a handbag, too. Shop your heart out. Go to exotic baby specialty stores and get the one that converts—I kid you not—into a car-bed! How about a fisherman's wicker creel or a beach bag from a sporting goods store? In the luggage department you might find a handmade, tapestry-covered satchel from Portugal. Use your ingenuity. You've been so practical up to here, you deserve a little splurge. After all, you've saved more than $300 so far, haven't you? (Use the fact that you didn't buy [insert your own list here] to justify the expense to yourself and your spouse, who may see the bill.) Besides, you can continue to use your nondiaper-bag diaper-bag later—for trips to Portugal maybe.

Pacifier

You're either a "no child of mine will go walking around with a plastic plug in his mouth" type or an "I'll try anything if it'll only stop the yelling" type. Me, I'm not going to take sides. But I do suggest that if you should decide to switch from the former position to the latter at 4:30 A.M. with no twenty-four-hour drugstore within a thirty-minute drive, it might be very comforting to know that hidden under the third pile of sweaters on the left in the next to the bottom drawer is a pacifier.

After all, they cost less than 50¢, and nobody can force you to use one. To avoid the "plugged look," break off the outsize ring; it'll look smaller. However it is important that the mouth guard be bigger than his mouth. That's to prevent his choking on it. The more expensive ones you buy will be ample in this regard primarily because the government is now regulating the manufacture of pacifiers—and it costs more to make them to government specifications than the old way. So, be wary of the cheap ones— they may possibly be dangerous in more than just this respect.

For a dollar or so more you can get a specially designed pacifier on the market that's supposed to protect your baby's mouth and tooth formation . . . and not cause protruding teeth and expensive braces later on, although it has not been proven that pacifiers cause these to begin with. Anyway, it has one problem that has not been ironed out yet. Many mothers who have used it claim that it doesn't pacify. Babies don't like it.

A word to the "I'll try anything" type. If you're going to use a pacifier, buy two. Once the baby learns to rely on it and loses it, he'll be as frantic as a cigarette smoker with an empty pack going through ashtrays looking for long butts. Not an appetizing argument for using a pacifier? Well, when was the last time you saw somebody light up and take a deep drag on a pacifier?

Chapter 2

The Facts of Sizes

This is the land where manufacturer A's size 2 is identical to B's size 3 and to C's size 1; where T stands not for Tall nor for Toilet-Trained but for Toddler, which is not to be confused with Tot, which is a synonym for a child who wears any size under 8; where the same size terminology is used by pattern makers and ready-to-wear producers, although the sizes aren't the same; where in the past the only way to beat the size game was to "Buy for today, not for tomorrow; for only tomorrow will you find out that what you bought today won't fit tomorrow." (Translation: So what if the size 5's are on sale but the 4's aren't. Unless your daughter wears a 5, you're out of luck because you daren't buy ahead for fear it won't fit.)

Confused? Join the group. Which, by the way, includes many manufacturers and sellers of children's clothing. In fact, the Mail Order Association of America was responsible for the first standardizing of clothing sizes. And that was back in 1945. Using measurements made during the 1930s, the U.S. Bureau of Standards proposed a Recommended Commercial Standard for the sizing of apparel for infants, babies, toddlers, and children. When presented to interested producers, distributors, and users for written acceptance, only the knit underwear industry accepted and approved the standard.

Since then many other manufacturers and sellers have come to use it, but in every case the action was—and still is—completely voluntary. As a matter of fact, the written acceptance form used by producers, distributors, purchasers, and testers to show they will abide by the commercial standards includes this statement: "We reserve the right to depart from it as we deem advisable."

"Do manufacturers depart from it?" you ask. Do they? You know it. And for many reasons. Let them speak for themselves:

"Today's children are bigger than the recommended sizes."

"The forms [like your own dress form] supplied us and the rest of the industry aren't the same as the government's requirements."

"We surveyed mothers and found they didn't want such constricting sizing."

"You ask the government; even *they* aren't satisfied with their current standards." (I did, and they aren't. C. Warren Devereux of the Bureau of Standards hopes to get industry-wide agreement on sizes. The question is, when?)

All of these are in their own way perfectly logical and legitimate reasons for deviating from those outdated, okay-for-1945 standards. The problem is that not everyone deviates . . . and they don't all deviate the same way, as you'll see from charts on pages 30 and 31.

Thus, in an effort to try to clue-in the consumer as to which garment will fit which child, the industry usually labels its garments either by age (three months, twelve months, four years, etc.), or by weight (up to eight pounds, twenty-three to twenty-seven pounds, thirty-three pounds), or by size-span (S-M-L), or any combination of these. However, company after company, manufacturer after manufacturer, buyer after buyer will tell you that height is the one, the only criterion in buying clothes. Yet height is the one measurement most often omitted on labels. That's why more knowledgeable manufacturers emphasize height, sometimes by itself, sometimes in conjunction with age, weight, etc.

Age-sizing is the one common denominator to all sizing, also the most unreliable. Age-sizing is done either by month (three months, thirty-six months, etc.) or by year (one-half, one, six, etc.). Few if any garments will not contain some indication of age—and not one of those indications is worth two cents to you in terms of buying a garment. Granted you know to the month or the week or the day the age of your infant. What you can't know is whether the garment you're looking at was designed for a child twin to your own . . . or three inches shorter . . . or six pounds heavier. "Well, then," you ask, "why do manufacturers bother to use age-sizing?" Good question. I wish the answer were equally good. Because (*a*) once it was valid; (*b*) they have to use something; and (*c*) your fellow mothers are flattered by it.

You see, most mothers believe age-sizing is accurate. It pleases them to know that their three-month-old baby is wearing a six-month-sized garment, or that their three-year-old is so tall for his age that he's wearing a 5 or 6. There would be a great many less self-confident mothers if all sizes were downgraded to reflect the fact that most three-month-old babies, for example, belong in present six-month-old sizes.

Is this farfetched? Not at all. Let me demonstrate. Our youngest at birth was twenty-one inches long (tall?), and by the end of three months, he was twenty-six inches tall, which meant, according to the Montgomery Ward size chart, that he was at the very end of the limit for Ward's six-month size.

Did I suspect something was amiss with the sizing? Not for a moment. I loved it. I was proud of my son's stature. I felt that I had done an outstanding job of bringing forth an exceptional baby and then nurturing him well. The size clothes he wore were living proof that I was a good mother. And if this happens to other mothers, too, maybe age-sizing should stay; in a psychological sense it will be providing some sort of service.

Weight-sizing is relied upon by a great many manufacturers as well as by many stores with house brands. And for children under one year of age, weight-sizing is highly accurate because the child is growing more weightwise than lengthwise (doubling his birth weight, for example, by five to six months and tripling it by one year). After that, weight is only a factor in relation to height. Only the child heavy for his height should have his clothes bought on the basis of weight. The tall, lean child must have his clothes bought on the basis of height.

In England they have a golden rule for buying clothes. Babies by weight, toddlers by height. It's memorable, it's beautiful, it's simple—but it no more takes care of the short-fat and the tall-skinny child than does our system. The interesting thing about the Britons' golden rule is that it fits our size buying better than theirs (in terms of getting the best fit, because we have more sizes available).

Speaking of height and weight, the pattern people will tell you that weight—not height—is most important in selecting a pattern since the easiest alteration to make on a pattern is that of lengthening it. Are you ready for this? Of all measurements given on a pattern-size chart, the only one missing is weight. Height's there, but not weight.

Size-spanning (S-M-L) is, as one manufacturer told me, "a

great big one-hundred-percent cop-out!" It's an attempt to fit the greatest number of children with the fewest number of garment sizes.

Here's what actually happens when you buy a size S, for example. You quickly discover it's a bit too big for your child—not a wrong-size-too-big, but a slightly-sloppy-too-big. Soon, the garment fits much better because the child's grown into it; then, gradually it becomes more and more form-fitting. So you buy an M. Now history repeats itself. The M is too large at first, then . . . but you know what happens.

The point is that a more accurate description of a size S, which is supposed to fit a size 2–3, is a 2½ . . . an M (4–5) a 4½ . . . an L (6–6x) a 6½. This means a perfect fit for the child of a wealthy, fastidious mother who could buy first a 2, then an S, then a 3, then a 4, then a M . . . if you get the picture.

For the rest of us, size-spanning is one way to beat the cost of living, but only if you don't mind somewhat less than perfect fit. Instead of buying regular sizes, buy size-span. So what if the S, for example, is big on the true size 2 . . . and small on the true size 3? You're saving yourself the cost of buying two separate sizes when you buy one size-span. Savings like that are not to be sneezed at.

It should be pointed out that although, according to my chart, Sears is the only store to have S-M-L-XL in its Infants clothing, other manufacturers do too. In Toddler and Children's clothing size-spanning is extremely common. I just couldn't include every variation in every chart.

CLOTHING CLASSIFICATION

The U.S. Commerce Department's Bureau of Standards classifies clothing in four size categories: Infants, Babies, Toddlers, and Children. Which is about the only thing the entire clothing industry agrees on—except those that don't agree that there's a difference between infants and babies.

Infant Sizing

A baby at birth can weigh between twelve ounces and twenty-two-and-one-half pounds, with five to twelve pounds the normal range;

while in length, seventeen-and-one-half inches to twenty-two-and-one-half inches is the normal range.

Although the medical profession classifies children under the age of one as infants, and *all* children under the age of three as babies, the clothing industry does not. They will happily manufacture two garments in exactly the same size but label one "Baby" clothing and the other "Infant." Yet there is a difference. One that makes lots of money for some stores.

In these stores, those two same-size garments would be segregated—one being stacked up on counters for mothers to inspect—the other being sequestered in drawers or in storerooms, out of sight and out of touch of all but the helpful, hard-selling, grandmother-type clerks dressed in white. Here is where many new mothers-to-be go to buy their layettes, and where their friends go to buy gifts . . . and where sometimes a premium dollar will be charged for the same garment selling for less elsewhere in the department.

Now don't get me wrong, in some cases there is a difference between the two garments other than their location within the store: one might be of printed flannel and the other a solid color, one might have a lace (one-eighth inch or less) edging around the bottom, the other just a rolled hem. In terms of fit, of style, and of purpose, the two are virtually the same, with the less expensive, less fussy one the more utilitarian and a better buy.

A wise shopper should compare the garment she's considering with others in the store. Remember while you do so that the six-months size is the first practical size out of the zero-, three-, six-, nine-, twelve-months sizes.

Baby Sizing

For a baby, you buy by weight, and you buy big. At no other time in a child's life will he/she grow as rapidly. Here is one of the few periods that absolutely demand, for your budget's sake, that you buy "grow-into" clothing. As was mentioned in the chapter on the layette, your incentive still is to keep the wardrobe as simple as possible for every day and every night.

More and more stretch outfits should be supplanting gowns and kimonos—but don't discard the latter, especially the larger sizes. A kimono, size twelve to eighteen months, can be worn backward

as a full-length bib, and finally as a painting smock for a child
approaching the age of three. What I'm trying to say is, Don't discard clothes that may possibly be used later—or, was it a man
who outgrew his regular jacket who discovered the bolero?

To understand what differentiates a baby-size from the next
category, Toddler, you must understand something about the
growth of a baby. Using the Recommended Commercial Standard
measurements as a guide, you can see the trend in baby's growth.

Age	3 mos.	6 mos.	12 mos.	18 mos.	24 mos.	36 mos.
Leg length*	7¾″	9⅛″	10½″	11⅞″	13¼″	14⅝″
Trunk length	10½″	11⅜″	12⅜″	13¼″	14⅛″	15⅛″
Difference between length of trunk over length of leg	2¾″	2¼″	1⅞″	1⅜″	⅞″	½″

Total leg growth between 3 months and 36 months was 6⅞″ (14⅝″—
7¾″)
Total trunk growth during this exact same time: 4⅝″ (15⅛″—
10½″)

In other words, a baby starts out with her legs less than 75 percent as long as her torso . . . but her legs grow faster than her
trunk until there is just a half-inch difference between them. At
this point you have a Child, not a Toddler. From then on, her legs
will completely outstrip her trunk, and she will eventually become
the long-legged beauty for which America is famous. "But," you
ask, "if a baby automatically becomes a Child, where does Toddler come in?" Good question.

Toddler Sizing
The 2T's, and 3T's, and 4T's you see refer to Toddler. And what
does Toddler mean? *Non*-toilet-trained. So, what's the big deal?

* More precisely, inseam length (distance from crotch to floor). Inseam
is more accurate here because trunk length is measured from the crotch to
the lowest cervical vertebra in the back of the neck.

After all, babies aren't toilet-trained either. Why, then, do we need another size range especially for non-toilet-trained children? For one thing, because some mothers want their children to look and act older than they are. Therefore, T-sized clothes are designed with more style and "sophistication"—if you can use that word with children's clothing. But some mothers want their babies to stay babies as long as possible. They'll prefer baby-type clothing—cute clothes with frills and animal motifs and pastel colors—the whole gamut of devices stores and manufacturers and mothers use to make a child seem more like a baby, at least up to size thirty-six months.

But there is more to it than that. Again using the government's trend-revealing figures, here's what Toddler sizes show about your child's growth in this stage:

Age	1T	2T	3T	4T	5T
Leg length	11½"	13⅛"	14⅞"	16⅝"	18⅜"
Trunk length	13¼"	14¼"	15⅛"	16⅛"	17⅛"
Difference between trunk/leg or leg/trunk length	1¾"	1⅛"	¼"	½"	1¼"

Notice the race between the trunk and leg lengths. Somewhere around the 3T or thirty-six-inch mark, the trunk loses its race to stay ahead, in terms of size, of the child's legs. Instead, the legs catch up and overtake his trunk so that by size 5T there's a sizable difference between the two, and your child's growth pattern has been set for life.

The other difference between babies and toddlers is reflected in the walking ability of the toddler. Surprise! The walker is shorter than his non-charging-around identical twin brother. The difference, according to T. Berry Brazelton, M.D., comes from the fact that upright posture causes vertebrae to settle. A vertical child could be as much as one inch shorter than when he was horizontal.† This change is reflected also in toddler sizing.

(Did you know you're taller in the morning than in the afternoon because during the day your vertebrae have settled?)

† See charts on pages 28 and 29.

Children's Sizing or Little Girls' and Boys' Sizing

It's still a unisex deal, at least for sizing, right through this size range. We've already determined that the difference between a baby and a toddler is in the relationship, proportionately, between trunk and leg length. So what's the difference between toddler and child in terms of measurement? N-O-N-E! Not according to government measurements.

There is, of course, a difference between garments: (*a*) Toddlers' clothes are wider through the waist and hips to allow for diapering; (*b*) some Toddlers' clothes, but not all, have snap-open inseams and crotches to allow for easier access for diapering; (*c*) Toddler *girls'* clothes are one-half to two inches shorter than a Child's size ready-to-wear, and two inches shorter than a Child's size pattern. Boys' clothing, which is determined by leg length, not fashion, is exactly the same length in Toddlers' and Children's garments.

However, the pattern industry makes its Children's patterns one-half-inch wider through the shoulders as well as longer in the bodice than in Toddlers' patterns.

One other note about Toddlers' clothing, in terms of size. That diaper allowance through the middle can add up to an extra one-and-one-half or two inches—a big asset in terms of the chubby child, who may or may not be toilet-trained.

As for Children's clothing sizes, there are three things you should notice besides the fact that both Children's and Toddlers' clothing will fit the same child. The first is that although there are five T sizes and seven Children's sizes, not all manufacturers make all sizes (sound familiar?). Many skip the 1 and 2 sizes, concentrating on the upper sizes. Some who concentrate on the upper sizes manage to ignore size 5 while doing so.

The next peculiarity in Children's clothing sizes is the 6x. According to Montgomery Ward, a 6x and a 7 are synonyms for the same size, but according to most manufacturers a 6x is actually a transition size, a size in between 6 and 7, a size 6½. One mother put that transition idea another way, "When your baby graduates to a 7, he's no longer your baby—he's a child." Postponing that graduation and prolonging babyhood is the whole purpose of the 6x.

The third peculiarity is that at the same time some manufacturers are making boys' and girls' clothing more childlike, other manufacturers are aware that the lean, lithe, lanky figure so prized in cowboy movies and at model agencies begins to make its appearance during this size range.

For this reason, some Children's clothing—as you'll note on the size chart—is divided between Slim and Regular, without Heavy. Whether it's because there are no pudgy children, or because it is diplomatic to ignore that fact, whatever the reason, it's not until the next size range that Husky, Chubby, and Chunky rear their evil heads.

Clothes for Older Girls and Boys

There are no government standards for these sizes, and they are not really needed. At this age, it is not only possible, but also a good idea, to take your child along and try clothes on or against him/her. Check for width of shoulders and hips. Bust and waist don't become important until puberty sets in for girls. Even then, feminine clothes are sized according to hip. Check for length at waistline and at hems of slacks, sleeves, jackets, skirts.

If you can't take your child along, take some statistics with you. With older children, height determines size, weight determines proportion, whether Slim, Regular, or Chubby. With teen-agers, the opposite is true. Weight determines size, and height determines proportion, whether Petite, Short, Average, Regular, or Statuesque/Tall.

Other measurements that you will need are:

NECK: around the base of a boy's neck, used with older boys in buying shirts.

CHEST: used to determine underwear size for boys and girls; shirts, blouses, sweaters for girls; jackets, pajamas, sweaters, suits for boys.

WAIST: for underwear bottoms for boys and girls; for skirts, slacks and shorts for girls; for slacks and jeans for boys.

HIP: for tight dresses; or if more than six inches difference between waist and hips on young and preteen, more than ten inches difference for teens, use when ordering skirts, slacks, and shorts, too.

INSEAM: distance from crotch to one-and-one-half to two inches above floor, used when ordering boy's pants.

Comparative Clothing Size Chart, By Height

As was true of the weight chart, this chart again shows how the same child could wear five or more different sizes (see the child who has hit the 1-yard mark). This is the chart to use for everything but baby and infant clothing and slim or regular children's sizes. To use this chart, find your child's height on the top line, then read down to the appropriate category of clothing to determine the size irregularities and options you might have.

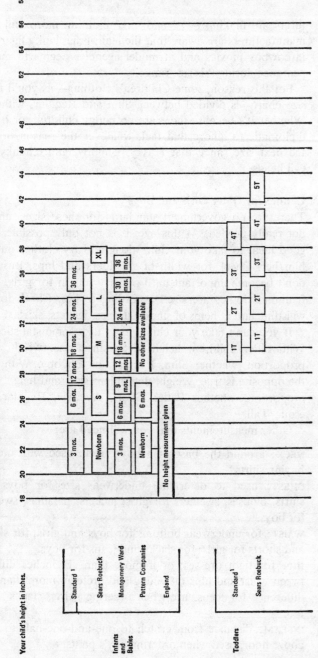

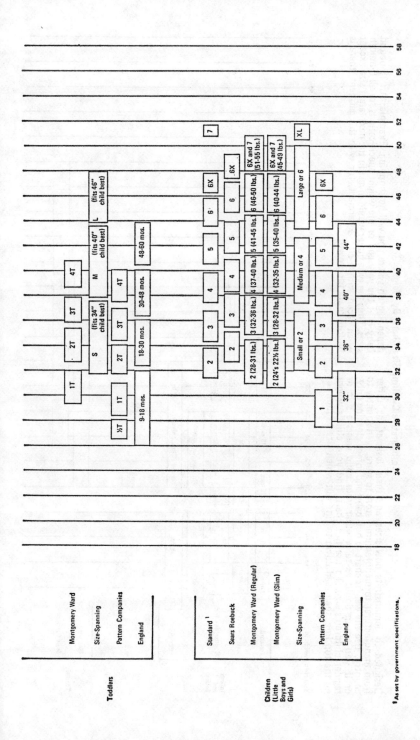

Comparative Clothing Size Chart, By Weight

Designed to demonstrate how sizes, and their designations, differ from manufacturer to manufacturer, store to store, even country to country. Use the weight chart to buy baby and infant clothing only, or if you are in doubt as to whether your child wears a slim or regular children's size. To use this chart, find your child's weight on the top line, then read down to find out which size to look for depending on where you will be shopping. Example: An 18-pound baby is at the very end of the weight specifications for all 6-month sizes. Thus the wise buyer would invest in the next larger size except when faced with a size S garment, for with this garment, there is built-in room for growth.

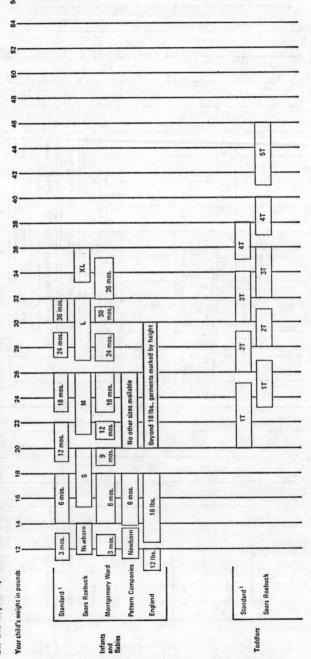

Your child's weight in pounds	12	14	16	18	20	22	24	26	28	30	32	34	36	38	40	42	44	46	48	50	52	54	56

Infants and Babies

- Standard[1]: 3 mos. | 6 mos. | 12 mos. | 18 mos. | 24 mos. | 36 mos.
- Sears Roebuck: Newborn | S | M | L | XL
- Montgomery Ward: 3 mos. | 6 mos. | 9 mos. | 12 mos. | 18 mos. | 24 mos. | 30 mos. | 36 mos.
- Pattern Companies: Newborn | 6 mos. | No other sizes available
- England: 12 lbs. | 18 lbs. | Beyond 18 lbs., garments marked by height

Toddlers

- Standard[1]: 1T | 2T | 3T | 4T | 5T
- Sears Roebuck: 1T | 2T | 3T | 4T

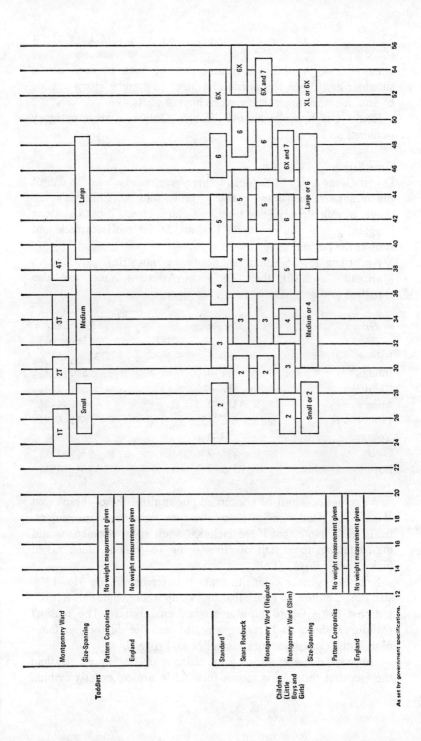

As set by government specifications.

SLEEVE LENGTH: measure from center of back of neck across shoulder and down to outside of elbow; continuing along outside of arm, measure to wrist; use when buying shirts.

Heave a sigh, we're almost through. Only one more category remains:

Shoe Sizing

Do you wear a size 8? So does a three-year old. He's at the end of the Infant size range and ready to move into the Children's size range, having already gone through Babies. Hey, I'll bet I've done it again, gotten you confused, I mean. So let me backtrack and start at the beginning.

According to the American Footwear Industries Association's Maribeth Cuccinelli, their Technical Assistant, shoes are also classified into groups:

Group	Size Range	Foot Length (in inches)
Babies	0–5	$3\frac{29}{32}$–$5\frac{19}{32}$
Infants	5½–8	$5\frac{3}{4}$–$6\frac{19}{32}$
Childrens	8½–11	$6\frac{3}{4}$–$7\frac{19}{32}$
Misses	11½–2	$7\frac{3}{4}$–$8\frac{29}{32}$
Little Gents	8½–13½	$6\frac{3}{4}$–$8\frac{13}{32}$
Youths	1–3	$8\frac{19}{32}$–$9\frac{1}{4}$
Girls	2½–9	$9\frac{3}{32}$–$11\frac{1}{4}$
Boys	3½–6	$9\frac{13}{32}$–$10\frac{1}{4}$

We're not going to be concerned about all of these—aren't you glad?—but I did want to show you how sizing overlaps and repeats itself. Note that if we included adult sizes, Womens would duplicate the upper half of Girls sizing (6–9) but Mens would pick up after Boys left off.

Note how gender begins to make a difference in the 8½–13½ size range. Note also how Misses picks up where Childrens left off, but that Little Gents duplicates Childrens entirely. The reason? Children's shoes tend, styling-wise, toward the dainty and feminine; Little Gents are more masculine and rugged.

However, nomenclature in shoe sizing is of less importance than the fact that shoe sizing moves forward in a nice, orderly fashion starting with size 0, equalling $32\%_{32}''$, and continuing with an interval of one-third of an inch between whole sizes.

Wouldn't it be loverly if here, at last, we would find one, and only one set of sizes? Dream on, because the facts are otherwise. The "American Size Stick" (which is the proper name for the industry's size scale) when placed against the measurement charts of both Sears and Montgomery Ward reveals that: NO TWO MATCH. The industry's size 0 is Sears' size 2, which is Ward's size 3.

To make matters even more interesting, the size chart enclosed in Sears baby shoes does start at 0, but that 0 is three-quarters of an inch smaller than the size stick's . . . and all the rest of the sizes are also off by at least one-half inch . . . and the Sears' enclosed size chart does not match Sear's own catalog chart.

On this basis you might think you could work out a formula to determine what size regular shoe you would buy if you were buying Sears' or Ward's shoes before, and vice versa. Right? Wrong. Comparing actual shoes shows that some non-Sears' and non-Ward's shoes are identical in sizing to either Sears' or Ward's.

To complicate matters, there may be variations within a single size made by one manufacturer, just as there are differences within the mail-order houses' lines. Why? "Because," explains Norman Germany, of A.F.I.A., "although the same wooden last may be used to make two shoes, the amount of give inherent in the shoe-material will determine the size."

What do you do about the shoe situation? See the next chapter.

Chapter 3

Cost Cutting from Head to Foot

Actually, cutting costs starts from the ground up, for it is in the area of footwear that you'll find one of the major expenditures you'll make for your child.

Shoes

The magic word here is "Don't Buy!" Don't buy booties, as noted earlier; they won't stay on, and anyway, you'll get some for gifts. And don't buy them to keep your baby's feet warm—the cold's an internal problem not an external one.

Don't buy crib shoes to keep baby's feet warm either. All they do is keep you from knowing whether your youngster's feet are cold. Besides, they only hamper your child's efforts to get to his feet and walk around. And, if you aren't buying booties and crib shoes, you won't need socks either.

The savings are really beginning to mount if you consider that many experts say that up to eight months, a child needs a new pair of shoes every month, then almost every month (figure every six weeks) until eighteen months; from eighteen months to thirty months, every two to three months (with three months more logical), from thirty months to forty-two months, every four to five months. At this rate, we're figuring on something like twenty pairs of shoes—in the first three and a half years alone.

And that's if your child owns only one pair of shoes at a time, which is not recommended by shoe people, you can bet. They'll tell you that from the time a child starts walking, he needs two pairs of shoes so that he can wear one while the other airs out. So now we're talking about more than forty pairs of shoes, not counting the special-weather-wear footgear you'll probably end up with:

snow boots, rain boots, sandals, beach shoes, dress shoes. Do you have any idea of what that means in the way of money? Between $160 and $200 if you never spend more than $5 per pair, which many times is not possible to do. Add to that expense the cost of socks, and you can see why "baby needs new shoes" is often used as justification for a raise.

So how do you beat this major money drain on the budget? The best and easiest way is to do a "don't buy" on shoes for the young baby. But your mother or your mother-in-law or your favorite aunt—one of them is going to have a royal conniption, especially once your child is walking.

Well, hold out as long as you can. Quietly explain that external rotation (foot turning out) is a self-correcting thing, just as knock-knees and bow-legs are also self-correcting in most cases by the age of ten. Admit that once upon a time that wasn't so, back in the days of rickets, caused by a lack of vitamin D, but hasten to add that you're seeing to it that he gets his vitamin D. Remind them that almost 90 percent of the human race doesn't wear shoes in childhood.

When they persist, as they will, hint that the pair of shoes might be a welcome gift. If that doesn't work, you're going to have to invest in something—a pair of slippers maybe—for use when the older generation is around. If the psychological warfare continues, give in. Although wearing shoes won't do the baby's feet any good, the wearing down of your nerves won't do you any good either. So what next?

Buy the cheapest shoes you can find. I'm not kidding. Go cheap. At the early ages a child won't give his shoes enough wear to outwear one of those advertised "strong as iron . . . long-wearing . . . durable," etc., shoes. Sneakers will do fine. So well, in fact, that many pediatricians who once frowned on sneakers have begun recommending them. That's because they're so soft and flexible, your child's foot molds them and not vice versa. About the only thing you have to watch for is roughness of interior stitching. Sometimes, it can cause an irritation on your child's foot, although rarely so when socks are worn.

Have you heard the sage advice about secondhand shoes—that they must never be worn by another foot? As one expert put it, "That's just a figment of someone's imagination; however, to be truthful, the shoes have to be in pretty good shape. Not great shape, just pretty good shape."

What about size? Won't the marking on the inside of the shoe be long gone? Right you are. Of course, sometimes the size is printed on the back of the shoe on the heel, and frequently it is molded into the design on the sole of the shoe or branded under the instep. Check for it. Not there? Well, no matter. As with most things, a specific size in shoes is only a general guide. Trying them on your child is the only way to get a good fit anyway.

But there *are* shoes, indeed, that must never be worn by another child—and those are orthopedic shoes. Never, never, not even if you think your child has the same problem.

Okay, so you haven't found any secondhand shoes for your child—or, and this is more likely, you just can't buy that idea, at least for his first pair. What then?

Off you go to buy a pair of shoes . . . taking your child with you. His presence is especially necessary if you're going to buy the expensive kind of shoe that comes in five different widths, twelve different kinds of lasts, etc.

How do you make sure the shoes fit? Well, not by asking the child. He doesn't know for sure and can't say anyway. The salesman, however, will thumb the toe of the shoe knowingly, squeeze the ball of the foot intelligently, maybe slip a finger inside the shoe at the instep, humming, and uh-huhing the whole time. Well, I've got news for you, he doesn't know whether the shoe fits or not either.

EXPLANATION: The toe thumbing is meant to determine how much space there is between the longest toe (it isn't always the big toe, you know) and the end of the shoe. And how long should that be? Take your pick of answers. The Children's Bureau of H.E.W. says "it should be half an inch longer than his foot," while Pennsylvania State University's Extension Service booklet says, and *in italics* to emphasize the importance of its statement, "Buy shoes one inch longer than the child's foot."

Take your pick. But do take these other two factors into consideration: If the toe box is reinforced or hard (which it is in about 85 percent of all shoes), it's difficult to push it in enough to give an accurate reading; secondly, when a strange man starts pushing down on your child's foot, the child may react as so many do and curl his toes back, again giving a false reading.

The finger in the instep is a test of the space between the heel and the ball of the foot. If the finger goes in, that's good, not bad. However, if the heel slips up and down easily, that's bad, not good.

The squeezing of the instep is an attempt to determine the width of the shoe—supposedly, if the foot gives, there's foot-ball room. Again, the flexibility or nonflexibility of the material will have something to do with this—and whether or not the baby keeps his foot flat. But the truth is that for the first eight years the foot will *always* give. That's because the bones in the foot are not fully formed yet. In fact, at the age of six months a baby's foot consists of small lumps of gristle surrounded by soft, fatty tissue and no bones. It isn't until the age of two that bones even begin to form, and some of the midfoot bones won't appear for another two years. When they do, at age four, there will be large amounts of space between bones, and much gristle instead of bone. It will take another four years for that gristle to become bone, and not until the child is sixteen to eighteen years old will his feet be fully formed and fully grown.

It's easy to understand why children, having such moldable, malleable feet, can wear ill-fitting shoes without complaint, short shoes without noticing it, the wrong shoe on the wrong foot without limping. Again I repeat, the greatest service you can do your child's feet is keep them unshod for as long as possible. If you can't do that, encourage him to kick off his shoes in the house. It'll keep your furniture cleaner, too.

Things were different years ago when shoe stores often had small x-ray machines that allowed you to see whether or not the shoe fit—but x-rays are dangerous, so the machines went. The next development was a clear, plastic, simulated shoe. When put on the child's foot, it enabled you to see the actual fit. But it was expensive to make in all the vast variety of sizes needed (because the sizes are not all the same, remember) and believed unsatisfactory in terms of sanitation, too. So the plastic shoe went the way of the x-ray machine, and once more, we're in the dark about the fit of the shoe.

THESE SUGGESTIONS: You do the fitting and testing yourself. The child is more comfortable with you, and you have an investment to make in terms of money and your child, which the salesman, who may have been hired only a week ago, doesn't. You know how your child walks (that he walks on the inner surface of his foot and toes out at first, as a child should) and so will notice the variations in his walk with these shoes.

AS TO THE SHOES THEMSELVES: No patent leather, it doesn't breathe. Suede looks funny after a rain. White? You know who's going to do the polishing. Cheap, washable shoes don't wash well —and frequently end up a different size. Light color? That's asking for trouble. Buckles look cute, are irritating for fathers to put on, have a tendency to come apart at the stitching, sometimes require the punching of new holes to let them out.

The darker the colors the better. Leave fashions to adults— pointed toes, heavy, cloggy soles, heel-less shoes and slings don't belong on a child's foot.

Mail-order shoes are money-savers, once you've bought a satisfactory first pair. Same-fabric shoes can be bought one size larger in the event of a sale—but not two sizes.

Laced-type shoes always have laces that are too short, especially for tieing in a double-bow that won't come loose. Ask your salesman for a longer pair to replace the ones in the shoes. Frequently, you'll get an extra instead and at no extra charge—because manufacturers include extra laces in shipments.

Frequent washing of laces really won't take the gray away, but it will weaken the laces. Soaking your laces in bleach whitens and weakens them more . . . enzyme soaking is safer but results are grayer, and remember ecology . . . and a combination of the two equals total disaster and disintegration. Colored laces are a better bet. An even better idea is to replace old laces frequently at a cost of about a dime a pair. It's an inexpensive way to forestall the breakage problem and give an old pair of shoes a new shot in the arm in terms of appearance.

In cold winter areas, a pair of warmly lined boots is preferable to the shoes-galoshes combination. They're easier to put on, they keep the foot warmer, and they cost less than the combination. Lined boots may well be the first pair of shoes your child can put on and take off at will. And that's worth their weight in early training. However, *stretch-type* pull-on-over-the-shoe boots are available—and although expensive initially, can be worn longer than the single-sized ones, which is an advantage in areas where the bad weather starts early in the fall and lasts until the following spring. In a short-bad-weather area, the stretch boots won't pay off. Certain shoes—like sneakers, suedes, and soft-soled—don't get on well with boots.

OTHER HINTS: Mark the right (or left, it makes no difference—just be consistent) shoe on the heel with an indelible marker or nail polish so that everyone in the family will know which shoe is which. Otherwise you may—and this happens to everyone—find you've put the right shoe on the wrong foot. Dads are especially good at making this mistake because the smaller the shoe, the less easy it is to tell one from another. Some mothers spray white shoes with hair spray to keep the polish from coming off—a damp cloth removes the spray when time to repolish.

SIGNS A NEW SHOE IS NEEDED: Walking out of the shoes doesn't mean they're too big; it means they're too small. Redness around the toes—on top or at either side—means shoe is too short or too tight. Irritations under the laces means the shoe is laced too tight. Blisters on the heels—the heel's too loose (line its inside with chiropody felt, available at dime, drug, and department stores).

Socks

The cheapest socks are all the same style, all the same color—white and unsized stretch ones. Why? If they're all the same color and style and you lose one, so what, you've still half a pair that can be paired up with any of its mates, including the mate to the one that gets a hole in the heel or a run in the sole. And the matching on laundry day is so easy this way. Why else white? They don't make black. And only white goes with everything—important to the fashion-conscious. Besides, it can be bleached semiclean.

As to stretch socks, they can be worn through two or three shoe changes, so they pay for themselves many times over. How many to have? At least one pair, preferably two pairs more than the number of days between washings. If you wash every week, you'll need eight or nine pairs of socks; a two-day-a-week washing schedule means five to six pairs of socks. Nylon socks are strongest, cotton most absorbent, acetate and rayon poor bets.

Tights

These are a fashion item and should be considered as such. They are not a satisfactory substitute for pants on cold days because they're no warmer than your own long stockings are. They run; even those whose manufacturers say they won't, do—or get gaping holes. They're baggy on the wrong legs. They're always falling down on small legs. And surprise!—on fat legs, too. And they're hard to find in the right size.

To be fashionably right, you should have an assortment of tights to go with the child's various outfits, in different colors, in different designs, and so on. Oh, one other thing: on a non-toilet-trained child, a wet bottom can mean wet tights if you use disposable diapers that are not—and shouldn't be—watertight around the legs. With rubber pants, tights can soak up urine through the air holes, or can add to the diaper-rash problem by keeping the air out.

UNDERWEAR

Shirts/vests and pants/briefs
But not body suits and leotards, which are fashion items, not necessities. Your first concern, underwearwise, will be the tops, since diapers will still be covering the bottom until your child is between two and three and even three-and-one-half or four.

After the first year, snap side openings won't be available, and you'll have to graduate to either T-shirts and tank tops for boys, or low-cut vests and tank tops for girls. That is if you're going to do the gender bit. Otherwise you'll choose from undershirts that cover lots, or undershirts that cover not so much, remembering as you do that girls' underwear (of which there is usually less available) can cost more because of its "fancy trimmings" than boys' plain styles.

The advantages of the various styles? The T-shirt is warmer than others during cold weather because it covers more, is more protective sunburnwise than the others for the same reason, can be used in place of other tops during warm weather and thus saves your buying more outer tops.

Advantages of the tank tops and low-cut sleeveless vests? Nothing quite so clear-cut as the other, except that during hot weather they are cooler when worn under other tops. They're "better than nothing" for those mothers who feel modesty training should start young. "They're cheaper because there's less material in them," you say. Nice idea, but fabric doesn't determine cost. There's another reason, which has to do with putting them on. Your child won't fuss as much putting either of these styles on because they go on fast, without covering the eyes for very long. In that respect, you can also buy vests and T-shirts with lap-shoulders, a means of overlapping material across the shoulders without having a normal shoulder seam. When worn, the lap-shoulder undershirt looks as form-fitting as the others; but as it is being put on, the overlap enables the neck opening to expand three to six inches, making the battle of the over-the-head easier. And the lap-shoulders cost no more than the regular ones. However, they're not available in other than Babies' and sometimes Toddlers' sizes.

Which brings us to fibers and fabrics. Cotton is used totally or in a blend in all undergarments. It's needed because of its absorbency. When blended with acrylics or polyesters, it feels softer, looks better after repeated washings, and has better shrinkage control. These blends are also more expensive than 100 percent cotton.

More important to you as a consumer is how that cotton is fashioned into an undergarment fabric; in other words, which knit is used: interlock, flat knit, or rib knit. Interlock (which looks like rib knit, but is identical on both sides of the fabric) is the best, the most durable, and the finest—but I don't know any brand that has it in children's sizes. Besides, using interlock knit for such a garment would be like using filet mignon as the meat in a spaghetti sauce.

Flat knit is lighter in weight than either of the other two, and once was less expensive, but no longer. Today, it's the labor involved in making a garment that determines its cost, not the fabric. Flat knit has one other quality that should be mentioned—it stretches more in width than length compared to rib knit. It is the type of knit used when the label doesn't say what kind of knit is used.

Because of its desirable light weight, flat knit is sometimes treated by a process, according to *Consumers Bulletin,* such as Pak-knit®, a size maintainer. This negates at least one advantage of flat knits—the sideways stretch, something a mother of a chubby child needs.

Rib knit is more elastic and more durable than flat knit—the elasticity is of importance, the durability not so much so. However, a flat knit shows its age very early, a rib knit usually does not. Rib knits also go over the head easier than flat knits, and according to the Benning durability tests, which involve normal washings after normal wearings by a normal Benning, rib knits don't give up as easily as flat knits do.

When buying children's underwear tops, look first for rib knits, then for construction details, such as reinforced seams, hems at bottom and at sleeves, and last for the style you want at the best price, regardless of whether it's a boy's or a girl's style. During the toddler period, children should be wearing the unisex look anyway; it's more practical for adults-to-be who need to master small motor and large motor skills alike. Fussy, frilly, feminine clothes they don't need on a day-to-day or even week-to-week basis.

Panties (briefs)

Usually a child outgrows diapers and graduates to special training pants. Training pants have multiple layers of fabric in the crotch, and although boys urinate forward and girls backward, 99 percent of all training pants are unisex. And only those layers of fabric stand between you and disaster.

If you insist on waterproofing, you might want to look into reversible training pants, plastic on the outside, terry cloth on the inside. Terry side in, regular pants; or terry side out, as waterproof pants over diapers. Certainly if you need to buy new plastic pants at a time when you think you're going to start toilet training, these make sense to buy, and are not that expensive either.

For those of you who do not insist on this requirement, go for the greatest number of layers possible (and of course, no cotton-something blends, which have less absorbency) and keep your fingers crossed. You should also invest in one or two plastic pants to put over these in case you're going out; toilet training will never work if you keep putting the child back and forth into pants and then diapers during the daytime. Nighttime is another story.

Once your child is toilet-trained, you may wish to move him or her up to real panties or briefs. In case of a boy under three, don't bother. I don't mean that he should be kept in trainers, I just mean he does not need fly-front or taped-fly briefs. Plain no-opening-in-the-front pants will do fine for as long as he can't manage the zipper on his outer pants. He'll do what most boys do and just push his pants down in front. So keep the pants plain and save money.

As for girls, I see no rationalization for spending the outlandish prices—would you believe $2.50 and up for a pair of lace-trimmed pants—for underwear that can be had for less. Spend the difference on panties for yourself; your husband will appreciate it more, and your daughter won't know the difference. Also, band-leg (no elastic at the leg opening) panties will wear longer than those with elastic—the elastic will either become worn or too tight.

Once your daughter starts wearing dresses and slips a good bit of the time, at around age five, you'll have to bow to the inevitable and put her in scoop-necked vests. Boys between three-and-one-half and four will be ready for flies in their briefs; or let me put it another way, when they start wearing size 5s and 6s, pulling down becomes more difficult and it's time to learn the adult way of doing things.

P.S. Move all of that timing up if you send your child to nursery school. Nursery school bathrooms dictate conformist underwear.

P.P.S. Bikini panties and hip-hugger briefs and bra-length vests are premature fashion aberrations. They have no function other than to convince me that some mothers have problems. Did you know that more bikini bathing suits are made in sizes 3 to 6x and more SOLD than in all other sizes from 7 to 14? And do you know why? Because mothers choose the small sizes; their size 7–14 daughters are more modest.

Slips

Avoid frills and rosebuds, they cost extra. Go for permanent press, avoid acetates. If you get a very plain A-line style, you can easily add a ruffle later to lengthen it. Waistlines have no business in little-girls' slips; they only shorten their wear-life. In this connection, you might want to know about "lights"; these are short, approximately hip-length, slips or camisoles for use under see-through blouses when worn with slacks. They cost as much or more than vests, not quite as much as slips; however, anyone who can afford see-through blouses for young children needn't worry about spending the money on lights.

Pajamas

By the time you read this, it will be impossible to buy a pair of 3–6x pajamas that are not flame-proof, thank goodness and thank your government. However, until your child is toilet-trained, summer and winter blanket-sleepers are for you. They keep the bed drier, your child warmer (remember, as urine evaporates it acts like the beads of water on you after a shower, drawing heat from your body and cooling it—that's why a summer shower's so refreshing. Not so with sleepy children). Blanket-sleepers have another advantage, if you buy properly—they have built-in house slippers and bathrobes. Once the blanket-sleeper is no longer practical, you can buy what you want—pajamas with feet or pajamas without feet.

Only don't buy two-piece pajamas that snap together at the waistline. Children and laundering cause the snaps to be outgrown too fast. Also, the snaps can be mighty uncomfortable to sleep on.

Bathrobes

Avoid. Get your child dressed as soon as he gets up. Bathrobes for boys are made to look like men's and they cost a pretty penny . . . are outgrown before showing any wear . . . and in houses with adequate heating, totally unnecessary. And if it's really cold, reach for a cardigan. One of yours, for example, with the sleeves rolled up.

Slippers

A necessary evil, I guess. Usually, they're the result of impulse buying because "they look so cute with the elephant's head on each toe." Look for stretch slippers or slippersocks. They'll stretch your money the most. Try not to buy otherwise. But good luck. I swear I won't, but I do . . . and he swears he'll wear them, but he doesn't. So who am I to talk?

OUTERWEAR

Stretch Suits

Use as long as possible, usually until your child is crawling. Then overalls, jumpers, coveralls. The concept here is not to impede the crawler yet still keep the clothes on. At this age, you'll discover the song "no hips at all" is 100 percent accurate. Your child is just one big belly, caused, naturally enough, by the immaturity of the abdominal muscles to hold it in. So don't hope to suspend clothes from it.

A dress is an abomination to try to crawl in—put one on and try it yourself.

Difference between coveralls and overalls? The amount they cover. Coveralls are the precursor of the 1970s jump suit, a full-length suit with a zipper from neck to mid-abdomen. The difference between a baby's and an adult's coverall is that with a baby you have to practically take the whole thing off to change the diaper, not just drop it to the waist. For this reason, it'll pay you to look for coveralls that have snap-open inner legs and crotches.

In fact, forget those charming, cutesy animal motifs on the knees that are supposed to do something—protect the knees, protect the garment, or protect the floor—and look for crotches with snaps.

Overalls

Come in two styles: one basically a sleeveless coverall; the other a pair of slacks with a bib front covering some of the chest. The sleeveless coverall is buttoned or snapped closed at either one or both shoulders. It's one of the fastest-outgrown garments you can buy since there's no let-out room built in at all.

Now the bib-front, which comes up letter-high in front, has no back till you get down to the waist. The two straps crisscross in the middle of the back before coming over the shoulders and fastening to the bib.

The longer the straps, the longer your child can wear the garment; it's the length of the straps that determines when the garment is outgrown for 90 to 95 percent of all children. Buy it, sew a series of additional buttons to the straps, and then just keep buttoning one button lower to allow for growth.

The straps also have a disadvantage: they slip and droop and fall over the shoulders, driving you madder than the child who never seems to be bothered with them. The solution? (1) cross the straps, as usual, at midback. Then twist and twist together until they're too snug to slip off—which sometimes leaves nasty red marks on the back, (2) use something, a rubber band, a safety pin, a paper clip (it doesn't work too well), to hold the straps crossed together at midback, (3) look for shirts that have shoulder tapes (like your lingerie tapes) under which the strap will go and then be securely fastened in place; (4) use that extra set of diaper pins to make a loop at the shirt shoulders for the straps.

Tops

For under those overalls. Don't buy blouses and shirts. They have no give built in to allow for growth. Go for knit tops. Sorry, you won't find any rib knits, but you can find interlocks—their stretchy qualities mean that you can put your child into a size too large and find he looks rather rakish, not at all waifish.

However, the first tops you'll probably buy will be those with snap shoulders so as to ease the battle-of-the-head. Watch out, in the case of mass-market, competitive manufacturers, that they have not skimped elsewhere to pay for the snap shoulders. Like in the length of the shirt.

When buying tops, you have two concerns. First, the sizes of the garments, which vary all over the lot, remember—a hazard that can only be overcome by bringing the child or one of his old garments with you. Second, the neck opening. You won't have to worry about whether the top will fit over your child's head if you find any with zippers—but in most cases they're not available. And when they are, they cost extra—like a dollar or more over the cost of the same garment zipperless. Of course, you can always put your own zipper in if you know how to sew knits; if you do, put it in front, because a zipper in the back often irritates a child's short, pudgy neck.

Don't sew? Can't afford prezippered garments? Join the crowd and invest in a cheap, cheap measuring tape. When you go to buy a knit top or knit under-T-shirt, pull the neck opening as far apart as possible between two fingers. The next part takes a little dexterity: Holding one end of the tape measure between your thumb and the index finger within the garment, pull the tape measure from one end of the neck opening to the other to determine just how wide that neckline will stretch.

What'll you find? Well, I have before me three different size-6 shirts, by three different manufacturers, ranging in price from $1.28 to $2.60. For the sake of this comparison, the cheapest will be called A, the next B, and the most expensive C.

Although all three are exactly the same style, no two are identical in any measurement, especially in neck opening:

A—17 inches
B—18 inches
C—23 inches

A remarkable difference, eh? So what if that C is narrower in the middle, shorter in sleeve length, narrowest across the shoulders and most expensive? It's the only one that will go over a size-6's (21"–22") head.

Speaking of head sizes, Montgomery Ward were the only ones —of *all* the mail-order people and big-name manufacturers— willing to divulge their *minimum* neck openings for each size garment. They say, *minimum* opening for a 6 or 6x top should be twenty-three inches.

Ward's other minimums are:

0–12 months	20½ inches
18–36 months	21 inches
3–5 size	22 inches

Barbara Hulse, head designer of Simplicity Patterns, gives slightly different measurements for head openings, but then her pattern sizes can't be compared to ready-to-wear sizes. (More on that in Chapter 16.)

Newborn	19 inches
Up to 6 months	20 inches
Toddlers	22 inches
2 to 6x	22 inches
Girls	22¾ inches

Why so much emphasis on neck openings? Because it is here that many women are defeated in their attempts to save money, by buying tops on sale that won't go over the child's head. You will also find that difficulty in putting one of his own tops over a child's head is the first sign that he's graduated to another size.

Tops become more and more important immediately beyond the crawler stage, when you'll want to move into separates that offer you greater versatility plus ways to escape the fact that children are messy. The mother of a rough and tough child may find he's slopped up his clothes, so they look disreputable long before they're outworn.

The following may keep your child's tops from looking like vomitable bibs:

1. Never buy solid-colored pastel or medium-intensity colors; stick with deep red, navy, forest green, dark brown for solids.

2. If you can't find the right solid colors, go for stripes. Somehow the horizontal, variegated lines break up big spots, and only the small, not so glaring ones show.

3. One-hundred percent cotton, non-permanent-pressed, can be bleached until spots are removed and then dyed another color.

4. Terribly spotted overshirts can be worn as undershirts under dark colors.

5. Nobody notices spots and stains like you do. If you have nothing presentable for him to wear, put whatever you have on him and send him off to face another mother's inspection. If she does notice the spot—and most won't, being more worried about who's going to bash whom over the head first—she'll probably heave a deep sigh of relief and say to herself, "Thank god, there's another messy kid around."

Pants/Slacks

If your child is the neatest eater and drinker of them all, but a mud-pie maker and a tripper over his own feet, you may choose to ignore the suggestions on tops and apply them instead to slacks. In any case, you will probably find that slacks wear better and stain less than tops. You also may find that you go through two sizes of tops to one of pants. Therefore, go for whatever you like—prints, stripes, solids—in slacks, recognizing that you'll need about half as many of those as you have tops. Which is all fine and good except that below a size three or in non-fly-fronts you have mostly a choice of solids, solids, and solids. So, go for dark solids or at least strong-colored solids—no whites, no pinks, no powder blues, no yellows, no mints, please.

At last he's toilet-trained, and you're in the market for the snazzy ones—the flares or the stove-pipes or whatever the fashion at the moment is—your little man is growing up! Only he isn't. He can't handle that sign of masculinity, the fly—either the zipper, or the snap opening, or the button opening. It's all beyond him (which is why some manufacturers stitch in fake flies—at an extra charge, of course) but he's saved by the elasticized back (sometimes known as boxer pants).

Or is he? You see those little loops—two to the front and one to three to the back—they're for a belt! And "little men" can't work belts any better than snaps or buttons. So save your money. Remove all the belt loops from pants to free your child to do his best to be toilet-trained under the frustrations of the clothing put on him. Besides, you save the cost of the belt or belts. After all, you have to have black for pants with black in them, and brown for all brown prints. A navy one? Of course, for the blue jeans.

And since belts come in even sizes, you're going to have to replace those belts too frequently. Sounds terrible, that replacing, doesn't it? Well, it's not—fortunately children in the 3–6x group are flattening, skinnying out, so a belt at this age might last longer than a belt for a size seven- to eight-year-old. Feel better? Good. Now I'll tell you that children's belts can and do cost more than $2 and frequently more than $3.

To a mother, pants are pants, and the same is true of little boys —those under the age of three. On or around his third birthday, pants divide into: pants and POCKETPANTS! It can happen overnight . . . usually it takes a week or so, but when it happens, plain pants are *verboten,* outlawed and tantrum material.

Solutions? Open the side seams of his present pants and insert pockets, put patch pockets on the front of his pants—fortunately pocketpantslovers don't much care where the pockets are—or begin buying pocket-pants before the need arises.

Suits

They cost a fortune, and I mean a fortune. As much as you spend for a dress or probably more. Like $40 or more. Best advice I can give you is to get these in a resale shop—they're often only slightly worn, because children grew out of them so quickly. And the real advantage of separates begins to make itself felt when you discover that your son is a size 4 from the waist down, but a 5 from the waist up, or vice versa.

Short-pants suits are a different story, however. Short pants can be worn longer than long pants because the waist and hip measurements stay much the same from one year to the next. So before disposing of a short-pants suit check to see if you can salvage the pants. You may be surprised to discover the pants fit, and nicely.

Better yet, if you're going to do the dressed-up bit, stick with separates. Buy the pants and check them before you buy another pair, buy the jackets as you need them to match the pants. *But don't attempt to use a short-pants suit in cold weather—knocking knees will tell you and the world that it's no good.*

Dresses

The simpler the dress the better. Frequently the money you're paying for a dress, hoping that it will guarantee quality fabric and workmanship, is paying for imported French knots and bobbin lace, embroidery and appliques. All this is fine if you're looking for a special-occasion dress, of which few if any children need more than one per size. Regardless of your neighbor's stares, most churchgoers will be as understanding of less frilly clothes as any good churchgoers should be.

In order to fit all-sized children, those dresses made with waistbands usually have elastic in the back and half-belts to boot. Any dress with any other kind of waistband is a dress with a built-in obsolescence feature. Not so with waistband-free A-lines. The sleeveless A-line that's too small across the shoulders can have armholes enlarged so it can be used as a pinafore; the A-line that's too short can have an underskirt added to convert the dress into a tunic. What I'm trying to say here and elsewhere is that the fewer landmarks, built into a dress, that have to be outgrown, the stronger your budget.

WINTER

Raincoats

I happen to be a sucker for yellow slickers (they cost surprisingly little, way under $5) for rainwear, but I also happen to know that an umbrella is never outgrown. So much for rainwear.

Dress Coats

These are among the most expensive clothes you can buy. For example, there's an English tailor who comes to America once or twice a year to make dress coats-to-measure for certain children, as he did once or twice for John F. Kennedy, Jr., when he wore a 3–6x. Have you any idea how much these cost? A bundle.

Of course, this must be mitigated by the fact that the fabric is the best, it wears like iron; the sewing is impeccable, with double-stitching wherever reinforcing is necessary; and the styling has been proven by over forty years of only the best children wearing it. Too bad wearers can't stop growing, so they can realize the full advantage of such workmanship. Lucky for you, they don't; so such coats can be a real steal at resale shops.

Your best bet for everyday wear? Depends on your weather outlook. But in most regions, a hooded, warmly lined jacket will do just fine—especially one with knit cuffs to keep the heat in.

Snowsuits

Heating experts will tell you that one-piece styles keep the heat from leaking out at the waist. Mothers will tell you that they're easier for the mother to put on and the child to take off. But only your weatherman can tell you if there will be enough cold weather to justify its price.

If you have an on-and-off type of winter, you might want to forgo the snowsuit proper and find yourself another arrangement: such as a jacket and a pair of lined pants that might be water-proofed by your dry cleaner or with the spray from the sporting-goods store.

If you should decide to go the one-piece route, I suggest you look for zippers. Zippers at the cuffs, zippers at the waistline, zippers at the bottom of the pants. As many and as long as possible. And don't, whatever you do, try to snowsuit a child with a fire engine in his hand or a pair of rubber-soled shoes on his feet.

If you should choose the two-piece route, remember this: Two-piece snowsuits are made for children who wish to make angels in the snow, not for children who have to make pee-pee in the snow. When Nature urges, the cooperative child comes inside. Off comes the scarf, the hat, the gloves, the jacket, the sweater, the pants—sorry! too late. Getting those suspenders undone undid him. What I don't know is why if you can trust a child to wear a pair of slacks every day of the week without benefit of suspenders, why then can't he be trusted to wear a pair of suspenderless snowpants for three hours one afternoon?

Sweaters

Buy cardigans, not pullovers. They allow the child an opportunity to adapt to the temperature of his surroundings. Buying more than two cardigans—which naturally will be machine-washable, or at least washable, and in dark, hide-the-dirt-colors—is to be frowned on from a savings point of view. Frankly, many mothers would think one to be perfectly adequate. I agree if your heat's perfectly adequate and not antiquated.

Hats, Winter
With a hooded jacket, there is no need for a hat. Without that, I suggest a helmet—it's a hat and turtleneck-sweater top all in one, and the latter takes the place of a scarf. No helmet hat available? Do the best you can and wrap the scarf around the outside of the coat, not the inside, tying it in back to make sure the throat's well-covered.

SUMMER

Shoes
I prefer terry-lined sneakers to sandals—it's better for the stubbed toes. If you do the sneaker bit, sponge out the insides occasionally with vinegar, or witch hazel, or any other astringent you might have—that keeps "stinky feet" not so.

Bathing Suits
No tops are needed for any little girl who wears a size up to 6x. But those little pre-training-pants briefs make fine bathing trunks. Didn't buy any? Do now, especially if your child will be swimming frequently. As for small boys, fancy crotch supports aren't necessary yet, so don't buy an expensive bathing suit for that reason. Around age five, a built-in athletic supporter is a good idea, if your son does any diving, jumping, or belly-flopping.

Bathing Suit Toppings
Use a bath towel (standard, large, jumbo, or beach size), fold crosswise, and make a horizontal slit for a neck opening—this makeshift coverup will do a very nice job of soaking up swimming-pool water. An idea suitable, depending on the towel size you use, for any age child—even a teen-ager.

Shorts
For those apt to be crawling, have crawled, or are likely to crawl —those children below the age of two—shorts should not be in their future until they do most of their perambulating on two feet. Then you can look over the old long pants you have to determine

the ones that will cut down easily. If possible, don't bother to hem them, just fray them.

Generally
In hot weather, protect your child with the most absorbent, lightweight, least cumbersome clothing possible—and stop worrying about appearances.

CLOTHING IN GENERAL
—OR, HOW TO BEAT THE HIGH COST OF . . .

1. Find a friend or relative who'll pass along outgrown clothes. This is the cheapest way to get the more expensive items—the coats, snowsuits, suits, Sunday-best dresses—because these will still have many good years left in them.

2. Search out clothing outlets specializing in children's clothing, look for thrift shops and resale shops (the latter will have the best clothing, and at the highest prices, because these are consignment clothes, not donated clothes).

3. Keep track of major department-store sales days (the once-a-month special sales usually fall on the same day of the month, such as the first Tuesday or second Monday), and plan your shopping around them. Normally, it is store policy to have sales items in each department, thus you can count on something being for sale in the infants department, toddlers, etc. Special-sale promotions frequently feature national brands, but they're often seconds and irregulars. However, the irregularity is never in the overall garment (its sizing, for example, or being off-grain) but in slubs in the material or defects in workmanship. It's cheaper for the maker to sell such a garment for less than to try to spend time correcting the faults.

4. Fall and spring annual sales that feature preseason merchandise are the time to stock up on expensive items needed shortly; the end-of-the-season sales are the times to stock up on items needed eventually.

5. Discover mail-ordering. It's the most convenient way to shop when you're tied down at home with baby. And mail-order stores have sales just as the regular stores do, except theirs are usually preseason sales rather than clearances. Unfortunately, deciding to shop through Sears, for example, is easier said than done. Before

you can get a catalog, you have to buy X number of dollars worth of merchandise through the catalog. If you don't have a catalog, try to borrow a friend's catalog and order from it. However, once you've made that purchase, you can usually count on getting your first catalog; then, continued purchases guarantee your receiving future catalogs.

Montgomery Ward, another giant among mail-order businesses, also requires that you make regular purchases to ensure receiving future catalogs. But to get your first catalog, all you have to do is write your local catalog house or store, and if they're all out, you can write to one of the regional offices, the address of which you'll find in the Appendix on pages 310–12.

6. Remember that in children's clothing, it's not the cost of the goods, but the cost of the labor that makes a real difference in price. So, if you're prepared to reinforce seams, check findings for possible failure, perhaps even secure buttons before they come off, you can save a great deal by buying poorly made merchandise in which the fabric is good, has been preshrunk, and is sanforized or permanent-pressed. The latter is especially important.

7. Although quality is always a good guide to buying, quality and high price are not always synonymous. For example, between 85 and 90 percent of all garments sold are of permanent-pressed fabrics; the balance is divided unequally between the highest priced garments and the lowest, with 4 to 10 percent in high-priced garments and 3 to 5 percent in lowest priced garments. As to price, in the last 10 years, between 75 to 80 percent of all garments for children have been sold in the $5 to $7 retail range. A comparison shopper for Sears told me that if you're shopping a store that specializes in higher priced merchandise than that, you can work out an average to determine how much you should spend. Example, in a store with dresses retailing from $8 to $22, the difference between the two ($14) is divided in half ($7) and one-half added to the lowest price ($7 to $8) to determine $15 as the optimum price for you to pay.

8. Separates are your solution to many problems: the many stages of growing disproportionately so that a child is all trunk or all legs, or the child who drips on his shirt or rips up his pant-knees. (Since this is so, before you throw out any garment, see if it can be cut down to a separate item.)

9. If you have a tomboy, buy the more ruggedly made boys'

jeans for her. Until fifth grade children are fairly tolerant of one another's clothing habits. After that, the girl wearing boys' clothes may be ridiculed by her female companions, unduly admired by her males ones—but the unisex look may change all this.

10. Peer-pressure will eventually outweigh your taste and the marvelous taste you've indoctrinated and taught your daughter. She will want to wear what her friends wear. This normally takes place around the first year of high school.

11. Growing boys resist all pressure and seem to be willing to remain slobs forever, even to the extent of wearing basketball shoes to church. However, what you can't do, a younger female soon will.

12. That takes care of outside wear, which people other than family see. Sleepwear and underwear are a different story. And sometimes the same one. Many children continue to wear their underwear to bed at night, under or in place of their sleepwear. The practice has certain advantages: summer sleepwear worn over an undershirt may mean you needn't buy heavy winter sleepwear. And the practice of boys wearing underwear in lieu of pajamas does save the cost of p.j.'s. For girls, you might adopt the short nightie idea (an old shirt of your husband's with sleeves removed makes a nice, soft, cheap, washable one).

13. Athletic supporters and bras are normally needed about the time puberty sets in. A girl will show obvious evidence, a boy won't, but at some stage his new swimming trunks will. Anyway, he'll probably take care of buying what's necessary. It's a milestone for him.

14. Sometime in high school, your children's feet will stop growing. Thank goodness that that normally happens not after, but simultaneously with a desire for, on the part of boys, different kinds of shoes . . . for girls, different styles of shoes.

15. Don't do as many mothers do and be so self-sacrificing that the child's wardrobe far outstrips his or her parents'. A child doesn't need a different outfit for every day. After the newness wears off, most children never even give a second thought to what they're wearing. And speaking of newness, hold some of your new purchases back for occasions special to you or to your child.

Part 2

Food

The costs of feeding your child could be as little as $9,000 or no less than $9,835. It depends on whether you breast-feed or not, and whether you have a girl or a boy (girls eat less after age nine). It will come close to 22 percent of the total cost of raising a child.

Young babies are gluttons, or so it seems. However, you are in for a surprise after age 2, when food requirements decrease as the rapid, rapid growth of the first two years slows down. Increased activity, especially larger motor activity, is one reason for the jump of 30 percent at age four. Costs will go up again, but only slightly, at age six, which will reflect a new item in your food budget: away-from-home meals and snacks; these can add on as much as 10 percent.

After six, you will find yourself living with a personal three-year plan. Every three years, food costs will soar, and you'll be amazed at the amount of food your child, especially a male, can eat. Costs will stabilize, you'll become accustomed to cooking larger quantities, and presto—another jump. It happens at seven, ten, thirteen, and sixteen. The one after that will either take place at college or be combined with earning a living—so, to a degree, you'll be spared at least the cooking of it.

Chapter 4

Nature's Dinner Bell

I will wager that you have already made, at least unconsciously, your own decision as to that most controversial of questions. Not whether to breast-feed or bottle-feed. Not at all. The question is whether to breast-feed, period.

Those who say, "Breast-feed? Me? You're crazy!" have no other choice but to bottle-feed since wet nurses are extinct, at least in America.

Those who say, "Breast-feed? Me? Yummy!" need only the telephone number of their local La Leche League to find out the how of doing it.

Those who say, "Breast-feed? Me? Well, I don't know," are the ones who can make an intelligent, logical, hopefully happy decision. And that is to feed the baby, by either breast or bottle. The method makes no difference to the baby. Unfortunately, the only one in a position to prove that is merely days old and unable to talk.

But that doesn't mean he lacks for champions. As William E. Homan, M.D., put it in *Child Sense,* a book long on medically sound common sense: "The pediatrician-author, the psychologist-author, the psychiatrist-author, living, dead, and neither, writing for the private publisher and for the government, have provided the American public with a mountain of 'facts' concerning the pros and cons of bottle and breast-feeding. But alas, the voice of the zealot, the missionary, and the reformer resounds through the land. In the twenty-seven 'authoritative' volumes before me, I do not find a single factual presentation of the controversy. Prejudice, emotionalism, evasions, innuendo, myth, and superstition bias each presentation according to the preconceptions of the author."*

Pretty strong stuff, eh? Well, wait until you see what he's talking about.

FACT OR FICTION: *Human Milk Is the Only Choice for Premature Babies.*

False. When faced with a choice, hospitals got better results with their premature and their sick babies on artificial formulas, in which the proportion of protein, fat, sugar, and calories could be varied to suit the baby's needs. The result? Mothers' milk banks went out of existence.

FACT OR FICTION: *Human Milk Is Safer than Formulas.*

Safer in what way? No formula is going to pass on anticoagulant drugs, contraceptive hormones, alcohol, nicotine, an oniony flavor —all things a mother can pass on to her baby through her milk.

On the other hand, no mother's milk will be contaminated by *strange,* disease-carrying hands, nor watered down until nutritionally inadequate.

The safety factor depends entirely on the user. How safe is safe to you?

FACT OR FICTION: *Sudden Crib Deaths Never Occur in Totally Breast-fed Infants and Rarely in Partly Breast-fed Ones.*

First, a word of explanation. Such deaths occur during the first seven months of life to more boy babies than girl babies. The baby is fine, no trace of a cold or illness, nothing. Minutes later, he's dead. Autopsies reveal nothing. This phenomenon claims as many as 20,000 babies a year. The cause of death is given as SCDS, Sudden Crib Death Syndrome. The experience is not as rare as we should all like.

Can you imagine the awful pain and horror every mother of a victim of SCDS must feel when she finds her dead baby? Can you imagine the guilty questions she will ask herself? Then, for her to be told that such deaths never occur in breast-fed babies, rarely in partly breast-fed ones . . . in effect, laying the cause of death, if she bottle-fed or even supplemented, squarely at her feet. What must she feel?

* Excerpted from Chapter 4 of *Child Sense: A Pediatrician's Guide for Today's Families* by William E. Homan, M.D., © 1969 by William E. Homan, Basic Books, Inc., Publishers, New York.

And all on the basis of a horribly cruel fiction. SCDS does occur to totally breast-fed babies. The SCDS people will tell you, "Breast-feeding does not prevent SCDS." The first case I heard of firsthand involved a mother of four. With the first three children, she had been unable to establish successful breast-feeding. Only with the fourth was she totally successful. And which do you think was the victim of SCDS?

FACT OR FICTION: *Cow's Milk Is for Calves, Human Milk Is for Infants.*

Fact! One-hundred-percent absolute fact. There is no question whatsoever that cow's milk per se is NOT a satisfactory substitute for human milk. For example, compare cow, goat, and human milk as to composition.

COMPOSITION OF MILK BY PERCENTAGES

	Fat	Protein	Carbohydrate	Ash	Water
Human	3.5	1.3	7.5	0.2	88.0
Cow	4.0	3.8	4.9	0.7	86.2
Goat	3.5	3.1	4.6	0.8	88.3

It is easy to see that for human babies to use cow's milk, it must be adapted. That's why diluting (to reduce protein) and sweetening (to increase carbohydrates) take place. In addition, the curd in cows' milk is larger and tougher than in human milk. But heat, either through pasteurizing or homogenizing, can break down that curd to increase the digestibility of the milk.

Raw milk, espoused by one zealot, besides being more expensive and possibly dangerous to health, is also less easily digested than its processed brothers. Evaporated milk, being concentrated, fortified, sterilized, is better than all three—and the basis for all do-it-yourself formulas.

Commercial formula makers, realizing the above, came up with their own version of this dictum on milk: "Cow's milk is for calves, evaporated milk is for cooking, and infant formula with iron is for babies up to twelve months of age."

And they do have a point. Human milk is deficient in iron. At approximately six months of age, a child's iron reserves are used up and his need for iron must be supplied from an outside source. Sometimes enough iron can be derived from a normal diet. But not often.

So, thank goodness for iron-enriched baby cereals and even iron-strong formulas. The trouble with such formulas, according to a public health doctor who has tried them on several hundred different babies, is that many children won't drink them. They don't like them. Then again, yours may revel in the taste. It's certainly worth a try.

FACT OR FICTION: *Studies Prove the Superiority of Breast Milk over Formulas.*

False.

FACT OR FICTION: *Studies Prove the Superiority of Formulas over Breast Milk.*

False.

FACT OR FICTION: *Studies Prove the Superiority of Breast-Feeding over Bottle-Feeding.*

False.

FACT OR FICTION: *Studies Prove the Superiority of Bottle-Feeding over Breast-Feeding.*

False.

Yes, studies are done. They put all the bottle-fed (no matter what formula) babies on the left, and all the breast-fed ones on the right. Then meticulous records are kept of whatever happens to babies in each group. The results? One study showed bottle-fed babies had four times as many colds and ear infections, eight times as much eczema, eleven times more hospital admissions, eleven times as many tonsillectomies, twenty times as frequent diarrhea, and twenty times greater incidence of asthma and hay fever.

Powerful, those statistics, aren't they? Yet no pediatrician that I have contacted will say tonsillectomies are caused by bottle-feeding; not even the advocates of breast-feeding say this. And when questioned about hospital admissions, they'll speak of birth defects, such as abdominal hernias and monorchidism. Exposure to infection causes colds and ear infections, allergens cause asthma and hay fever—but these factors are never mentioned.

As Dr. Fitzhugh Dodson says, in *How to Parent* (New American Library, 1973), "There is absolutely no scientific evidence that one method is better for infants than the other, either physically or psychologically. It should be strictly up to you to choose the method you prefer."

FACT OR FICTION: *Breast Milk Is Cheaper to Feed than Formula.*

False. "What?" you exclaim. "But it's free!" Free? Do you have any idea of what it costs to buy the raw materials to feed the machine that produces human milk? It could be as little as two quarts of cow's milk a day . . . or as much as an extra sixteen crisp slices of bacon per day (about three-fourths of a pound—but please, don't eat so much of that highly spiced food . . .) or three or four times as much lean meat per day as usual. Now that, in anybody's book, is expensive eating! Better than $400 extra the first year as compared to the $240 a non-breast-feeding mother will spend for formulas.

"Hold it!" you say. "I read somewhere that it costs only $65 to feed a baby cow's milk and $140 for dried milk." You're right, you did. It was in a news clipping or in a *Saturday Review* article or in *The Nutrition Factor* (copyright 1973 by The Brookings Institution). The figures were cited by Alan Berg, a nutrition planner, for (*a*) the first six months, not a year, and (*b*) for 437 liters (about 763 quarts) of cow's milk, which works out to a cost of less than 9¢ a quart, and for dried milk formulas about 77¢ a day. Neither cost is accurate here in the U.S.A., however, the former being about 300 percent too low, the latter at least 33⅓ percent too high. (See chart on pages 67–68 for costs you can expect to pay.)

You will note that no cost is given for breast-feeding. That's because "poor women in poor countries seldom get an enlarged diet during lactation. Generally, the milk is satisfactory for the infant even without extra food for the mother, but *the child's need is met at the expense of the mother's tissue.*" Italics mine, quote Mr. Berg's, tissue *yours.*

How can this be? Well, for one thing, you're not a cow. The cow can eat X number of pounds of alfalfa and come up with almost X number of pounds of milk, the human mother will produce about 40 percent less calories than she takes in. Explain? Gladly. If a mother drinks six glasses (eight ounces each) of cow's milk per day, she can produce three and three-fourths glasses (eight ounces each) of mother's milk. An accurate count would be to eat/drink 1,000 calories of food and produce 600 to 650 calories of mother's milk.

The unfortunate part is that drinking that quart and a half of cow's milk isn't the answer. It won't work. You can't put a cheap, under-par product in one place and, of itself and by itself, get a rich nutritional milk flowing out of two other places. Some way or other, your body has to get the nutrients to change cow's milk into mother's milk. If you don't supply those nutrients, the body will simply use whatever supply you happen to have on hand, thus you will lose a tooth, or become anemic, or suffer jaundice, or have receding gums. So long as there is a supply of minerals, etc., in your body, they will be utilized in the making of mother's milk. In order to supply those minerals, you need to eat the good things in life, in other words, the rich things in life, moneywise: lean meats, cheeses, eggs, raw fruit, raw vegetables. The fillers, like pasta and pizza, bread and bologna, they don't swing their weight in milk-production.

In order to keep some semblance of your eating within normal bounds, most mothers will take vitamin-supplements, or else use the concentrated diet foods like Slender with dried milk three times a day and then eat normally. In figuring out the costs of breast-feeding, figure out what those alternatives would cost you.

There are, to my knowledge, only two ways to describe the costs of human milk: expensive and more expensive, especially in this country!

What other choices do you have? Many.

Mother's Milk Banks

Human milk is not available in *most* parts of this country through mothers' milk banks. One nutritionist imported his from Italy. (Gina or Sophia?) If you choose not to breast-feed, you must rely on nonhuman substitutes.

Do-It-Yourself Formulas

These are normally the simplest, the easiest, the cheapest—but not the formula of a famous woman nutritionist, the costs of which are surprising. But the simple 1 can or 13 oz. evaporated milk/17 oz. water/2 T. sugar (or 2 T. corn syrup) formula is the one normally recommended by pediatricians. It is also, in the words of a teacher of pediatricians, "the one off which they make their money." The sugar usually needs adjusting. So every two weeks, back comes the mother with her babe to have the formula adjusted at the cost—in money—of an office call.

Prepared Formulas

These are milks modified for infant use, and especially altered to increase digestibility, the nutrient content, the fat/protein ratio, etc. Health-food nuts, and they are nuts in my opinion, resist these and denounce them because the manufacturers add sugar, vitamins, and minerals, they substitute fats, they balance the calcium-phosphorous level, etc., making use of all the knowledge of modern chemistry to prepare the closest approximation to mother's milk possible. Many of these people prefer the weird concoctions recommended by some that call for egg shells and Epsom Salts, the latter a potential, known poisoner of babies.

These commercial formulations are available four ways: as regular formula for most infants, formula fortified with iron for possibly iron-deficient babies, as plant-protein-based formulas for milk-allergic babies, and as low-calorie formulas for potentially overweight babies.

Regular Formula

This is the formula most babies can utilize well for at least the first six months. It is available in the most choices: powdered, which is cheapest; concentrated, which calls for an equal dilution with water, the most popular; ready-to-feed, quart size, the fastest-growing form, since it requires no work except to put in bottles; and ready-to-feed, prebottled. The last, although the most expensive on a regular basis, has a salvage value in terms of saving the bottles and using them again, which reduces the price of the pack by the cost of similar bottles. The prebottled also is worthwhile in terms of traveling, since there are no bottles to pack, no bottles to wash. Just use and dispose. Ecologists don't approve, but it is easier.

Formula Fortified with Iron

This is a formula you *may* choose to adopt at six months of age. At that time the iron reserves in your baby's body begin to give out and iron supplementation is necessary. The Committee on Nutrition of the American Academy of Pediatrics published their opinion in the *Journal of the American Academy of Pediatrics* that such formula would be worthwhile throughout the first year of life. For the next six months, however, their readers made the pages ring out with rebuttal. Most of this revolved around the question of unnecessary supplementation for the first six months and then the problems, tastewise, of switching over at six months when iron-supplementation is necessary. What it comes down to is that if you do not feed an unnecessarily iron-rich formula from the beginning, and at added expense, you *may* not be able to feed it later. The answer then, of course, is to go to vitamin drops.

Plant-Protein-Based Formulas

These are available in limited variations. They are for the baby who exhibits allergic tendencies to his regular formula and for the baby who *may,* depending on the family history, develop such tendencies. But I should point out here that, as the mother of an allergic baby, I would, if I had known or even suspected the fact, have put him on such a formula at birth. And hang the cost, which is not that much more.

If you should elect such a formula, be prepared for minuscule, pardon the simile, dandruff-size flecks in the formula. They come from the fact that plant protein does not go into supersaturated solution as easily as animal protein. As a result, there may be a very slight residue. This will be readily drunk, the nutrients absorbed, and the waste passed on with no difficulty to baby. It will, however, create havoc with the nipples of the bottles, and those nippleholes must be cleaned out with a toothpick after every use.

Low-Calorie Formulas

This is the commercial-formula makers' answer to the problem of multicell obesity, or the recognition that today's fat baby is not today's healthy baby, but tomorrow's fat kid. The child who is gaining too much weight, either at breast or bottle, is apt to find himself guzzling a low-calorie formula two or three times a day.

The idea here is that our pleasingly plump and horrendously heavy adult figures are not the result of lack of willpower on our part, but on the growth of fat cells, created by over-feeding after birth that won't reduce or reverse themselves. As a result, in the opinion of researchers on the subject, is is almost impossible for a once-fat baby to become and stay slim without constant, torturous diets.

Doctors know that overweight adults have much higher mortality and morbidity (death and illness) rates than those not obese.

An overweight child can also experience trouble, in terms of bone and joint problems, heart-lung complications, and emotional problems, especially in relation to the other kids. The "Fat Alberts" and not-so-slim "Slims" of this world carry a sign around with them that makes them a natural butt of jokes for kids who are generally more honest and less kind than adults.

Do your child a favor! Avoid those rolls of fat that used to signify a healthy baby but now denote the eventually unhealthy adults. Watch his weight, so *he* won't have to later.

FORMULA COSTS

		Per diem costs based on 1973 prices
Commercial Formulas		
Ready-to-feed, prebottled		
6 (4-oz.) bottles		$1.43
(Salvage value first two packs $1.80)		
4 (6-oz.) bottles		$1.54
(Salvage value first two packs $1.50)		
3 (8-oz.) bottles		$1.97
(Salvage value first three packs $1.80)		
Ready-to-feed, quart cans		
Iron-enriched		
By the can (1 day's supply)		
By the case (6 days' supply)	6/$3.54 or	.59
Regular formula		
By the can (1 day's supply)		.69
By the case (6 days' supply)	6/$4.10 or	.68
Allergy formula		.93
By the can (1 day's supply)		
By the case (6 days' supply)	6/$5.58 or	.93
Concentrate, to be diluted by equal amounts of water		
Iron-enriched		
By the can (1 day's supply)		.33
By the case (12 days' supply)	12/$3.96 or	.33
Regular formula		
By the can (1 day's supply)		.41
By the case (24 days' supply)	24/$9.00 or	.37
Allergy formula		
By the can (1 day's supply)		.53
By the case (12 days' supply)	12/$6.36 or	.53
Powdered concentrates (add H_2O)		
Regular formula		
1 lb. can (5 days' supply)	$1.53 or	.30

		Per diem costs based on 1973 prices
Home-made Formulas		
Evaporated milk, using your own water		.22
1 (13-oz.) can	$ .21	
2 T. sugar (1/16 of 1 lb.)	$ .01	
17 oz. water	—	
Evaporated milk, using bottled water		.31
1 (13-oz. can)	$ .21	
2 T. sugar (1/16 of 1 lb.)	$ .01	
17 oz. water (approx 1/8 of 1 gal.)	$ .09	
A woman nutritionist's concoction		
1 quart raw milk	$ .50	.50 plus
or		
1 quart yoghurt	$1.16	1.16 plus
or		
1 quart buttermilk and cream	$ .39	.39 plus
PLUS		
6 oz. boiled water	—	
3 T. milk sugar (lactose)	?	
1/2 shell of boiled (sterilized) egg	—	
1/16 t. Epsom salts	?	
1/4 t. vitamin C solution	?	

Now, in order to feed any of these formulas, or even to supplement a breast, more equipment is needed than Mother Nature has supplied. Like what? Like the following (amounts in parentheses are recommended quantities for breast-feeding):

Six to eight 4-ounce bottles (two or three). The easiest and cheapest way to get these is to wait until the baby is born. Then after each water or formula feeding, ask the nurse for the bottle. Most hospitals use prebottled water and formula. Once the bottle is used, it's disposed of, which is cheaper than sterilizing hundreds of bottles a day—so, the hospital will willingly give them to you—FREE! A word of caution: They'll also give you the nipple and the collar. Don't bother to save these. The nipple is made just strong enough for one feeding, and not strong enough for sterilizing. The plastic collars leak after sterilizing.

Another way to get these bottles is to wait for the free baby gift some formula makers offer mothers. This consists of one day's supply of prebottled formula. And the bottles will come in handy

whether you like the formula or not. If you're breast-feeding, you
may not be on the receiving end of this largesse. However, 4-oz.
bottles for supplementary feedings, juice, and water are available
on the market at 15¢ to 20¢ apiece.

Seven to twelve (two or three) 8-ounce bottles. You will probably
never need more than six in one day, but there is always the possibility that you'll break one. How I don't know. Mine seem made
of cast iron. The advantage of having extras on hand is to be able
to make two or three days' formula in advance. And don't think
you can't do that just because books written in the ice-box-age say
never to keep more than twenty-four hours' worth of formula in
your "ice box" to prevent spoilage. That was in the days of raw
milk when souring took place in twenty-four hours at room temperature. Today, because of bulk tanks, rapid refrigeration and
pasteurization, it takes regular milk and commercial formulas four
or five times as long to sour. Cost per bottle: 20¢ to 25¢.

Nine to fourteen (two or three) nipples.† Ahh, and now we come
to the great nipple controversy: the old-fashioned pyramid or
cone-shaped nipple versus the dome-shaped nipple with a round
chimney on top—if you get the picture. In other words, the new
nurser nipple or the old elongated one used when you were a
baby. How does Mother Nature stand on this topic? She makes
nipples that are long and protruding. The purpose? To put the
milk at the back of the mouth so that the tongue pressing the nipple against the roof of the mouth extricates the milk rather than
having to work as a conveyor belt moving the milk from the front
of the mouth to the rear and the throat. Nor does she make a nipple with but a single hole. Hers is a circle of holes, not just an
opening in the middle of a globe of flesh. So why ask your baby to
drink from a nipple with a single hole in it? Don't. Buy nipples
with three holes in them, or make two more fine holes (no more
than three total—it weakens the rubber too much) in the ones
you've already bought. That way the milk will not drip out but
spurt out under pressure—a much closer duplication of what happens in the baby's mouth with a human breast.

† Need more nipples than 8-ounce bottles since 4-ounce bottles still in use
for juice and water.

When buying nipples, watch carefully. The packages aren't always clearly marked as to the number of regular nipples inside. You may find yourself paying $3 a dozen instead of $2. The difference between the $3-ers and the $2-ers? The $3-ers make more claims for themselves: that they're anticolic insurance (which may or may not be true, but I'm giving them the benefit of the doubt), or that their shape is more natural (than what?), or that they're more durable. The latter is true. The question is, do you want two nipples that will get used one-third more frequently, or three nipples that will need washing and/or sterilizing only one-third as often?

If the type of nipple you want is not available (one-hole or three-hole) go for blind nipples. With the use of a heated needle, stuck eye-end into a cork, you can make your own holes. However, when you go for but one hole, you have the problem that the hole may be too large, and the nipple ruined. That's a budget breaker at a quarter apiece, even more for the nurser nipples.

If the thought of hot needles to nipples causes you concern, consider using a finely cross-cut nipple—but only for big, greedy babies. The opening and amount of milk released is controlled by the baby. When he sucks hard, the cross opens all the way up, and more milk is released. A gentle suck and the cross remains mostly closed.

Speaking of buying nipples, whatever you do, have an extra two or three on hand up in the corner of some cupboard for the day when the water in the pan in which you're sterilizing the nipples boils away and turns those rubber nipples into a glob of burnt nothing. Don't laugh. It's happened to me and millions of others, and chances are it'll happen to you. While you're throwing those burnt nipples away, you might as well throw the pan away, too; you'll never get it clean—not in a month of Sundays.

Nine to fourteen collars and discs (two or three). The collars are needed to hold the nipple in place when feeding. The disc fits within the opening of the collar *only* when the nipple is absent. If you leave it in place, you're going to have one frustrated baby.

The disc offers you a choice of storage methods for filled bottles. The normal way is with the nipple inverted and in place, and the disc on top of that. This works fine so long as the bottle is not being filled entirely full. When it is, the nipple is sloppy to remove and put into place for nursing. With the disc used instead, you keep the nipples stored in a dry place until needed. The disc comes out, the nipple goes on, and the bottle can be filled to the top.

The alternative storage method puts the nipple in place in feeding position (upright), but it must then be covered with a nipple cover (same price as the collar and disc set), otherwise the nipple wears out fast under frost-free conditions.

Remember, by tightening or loosening the collar on the bottle, you can change the flow of the milk. Don't ask me why, I never took physics. But it has to do with the speed of the displacement of the milk by air. And if that doesn't mean anything to you, you're in the same boat as I am. Who cares why it happens; all that's important is that it happens. Tighten the collar and the milk flow slows down; loosen the collar and the milk increases. It works!

Two (one) nipple brushes. They're cheap, and if you bottle-feed regularly, they get a workout and they wear out. If you don't believe me, buy one now and wait—in six months you'll be buying another one.

One bottle brush (one): If you get in the habit of rinsing out every bottle with cold water immediately after each feeding, you'll get by without a brush, maybe. But someday the phone will ring or something will happen, and the next thing you know, there's a ring of milk at the bottom of a bottle that's there to stay unless you have a bottle brush. Costs less than 50¢ and worth every cent, because they can also be used to clean out reusable peanut-butter jars, the gook at the bottom of vases, the glue at the bottom of your flour-water gravy maker.

Brushless bottle-nipple cleaner. A chemical compound that costs about 1¢ or more per pound to remove milk curds chemically. Cold-water rinsing and normal washing is cheaper. Chemically safer, too. For that matter so's a short boiling in water.

One nurser kit for under $10. Set: Six plastic bottle holders and caps, six nipples, no collars because the nipple fits over the bottle (and a determined nursing baby has been known to tug the nipple off—uggh! what a mess! avoid it by buying "nipple retainer rings"), a metal thing known as an expander, which you need to get the sixty-five plastic disposable pouch-type bottles into the plastic bottle holders. The advantage to buying the kit is that in effect you get the expander at a savings of $2. But be sure to double-check. Sometimes the sum of the parts is less than the cost of a kit. In 1973 an individual bottle with cap would cost about 50¢, the nipple about 30¢, the supply of plastic bottle for it 2¢ apiece. Thus, it would cost you better than $7 to buy the contents of the kit without the expander, which by itself costs $4 and up.

Remember, the nipple retainer rings are extra, under a quarter apiece.

The only things wrong with these nursers is that they have those newfangled pimple-topped, dome-shaped nipples, which we've already gone into. Also, it takes lots of practice to get the bags onto the expander and then into the holders. And they're not cheap. You not only have the initial outlay, but you also have to keep buying those disposable bags at 2¢ apiece.

However, many is the mother who swears by them, and you probably won't have to buy the kit anyway—some kind-hearted soul will give you one as a shower gift or baby present. In case you do get one and you decide you'd rather go the old-fashioned glass-bottle route, you'll find the plastic bottle holders make neat toys when combined with poker chips at the age of nine months, and those disposable bags have hundreds of uses. For example:

1. Put 3"×5" recipe cards in them and protect your favorite recipes from spills and splashes.

2. Use in lunch bags for such things as carrot sticks or celery, or pickle packing.

3. Keep cigars in them to keep them fresh.

4. Fill with frosting, cut a small hole in a bottom corner, and decorate a cake.

5. Fill with dirt and start seeds in them.

6. Use as savings banks (one for each coin denomination).

7. Store your good silverware individually in them to prevent tarnishing.

8. Roll clean stockings up in pairs and place one pair to a bag for a neater dresser drawer.

9. Use as tampon holders—two to a bag for in your purse.

10. Make novel pencil holders for school bags.

So save them.

The one great thing about these bags is *they eliminate sterilizing bottles.*

Which brings up the question of sterilization. Which is about as pertinent in this day and age as the use of ornaments on automobile hoods. Sterilization is an anachronism. Unless you have a well (and it should be checked semiannually), the water you drink is quite safe to give to your baby. It does not need boiling and more boiling and reboiling. As my own pediatrician, Alexander Randall IV, said when I discussed this with him, "Sterilizing simply isn't worth it. You're trying to kill bacteria that aren't even there. That's like killing flies with an elephant gun."

If for some reason you do choose to sterilize (and please do if you're feeding raw milk), the method most often advocated is terminal sterilization. In this, you prepare the bottles in toto and then stick them in a sterilizer; however it is more work and more trouble and more expensive than any other. And bottles that have participated in terminal sterilization have milk curds cooked on them. They are oh! so difficult to clean. Just as scrambled eggs leave a hard-to-clean remainder in skillets, so will there be a hard-to-clean coating inside these bottles. In order to do terminal sterilization you need a container that will hold the full bottles. This can cost anywhere from $5 to $25 or more depending on whether it is manual or electric.

Although most expensive, the latter certainly makes sterilizing easier. You wash the bottles carefully, fill them with formula, put on the collars and nipples, and stick the bottles in the sterilizer. Many have an automatic timing device and will shut off automatically. Others you'll have to turn off after thirty-five minutes or so. Let the bottles cool in the sterilizer, or remove them with rubber-tipped tongs, let them cool on the kitchen counter, and then refrigerate. But remember, the bottles are a mess to clean after use because of cooked-on protein.

But there's another way, a cheaper way than terminal sterilization. It's the sterilize-as-you-go method using the concentrated formulas on the market. To do this, you use your dishwasher to do the cleaning and sterilizing of the bottles as it does your dishes. Or, you stick the empty bottles in any handy pan that'll hold them while lying on their sides, then boil the dickens out of them, and when cool, allow to *drain* dry. No need to towel-dry them; this way they dry bacteria-free. At your leisure fill the bottles, making up a whole batch, and refrigerate immediately. Or at each feeding you fill a clean bottle half full of concentrate and add an equal amount of tap water and then feed. The latter method is good to know even if you decide to do it the easier by-the-batch way. Someday you're going to be caught short and will need a bottle in a hurry.

There are only two things to remember about saving your baby from harmful bacteria: Most bacteria won't grow (1) in a cold climate or (2) on a dry surface. So my advice to you is:

—Wash your bottles and nipples in soapy hot water.
—Let them drip or drain dry.
—Store upside down on a clean surface to keep the dust out.
—Fill with formula and refrigerate.
—And forget sterilizing!

You'll save time. You'll save money. You'll save aggravation. And your baby will be just as healthy as the one next door, maybe more so, because your baby's mother is going to have more time to play and care for her baby.

Chapter 5

Blender Babies

"Ah ha," you say, "now she's going to discuss making your own baby food." I wish you wouldn't jump to conclusions like that. Because I'm not. Not yet. Here, I wish to pass on a solution to a problem that has beset women since the first piece of horn was shaped into a spoon. Nancy Stahl, in her newspaper column "Jelly Side Down," probably described it as well as, or better than anyone:

PERILS OF SPOON-FEEDING

There are many marvelous joys in parenthood; spoon feeding a baby is not among them.

While giving him the bottle can be a beautiful, mystical experience for both of you, shoveling in a jar of strained beef is rather likely to lead to temper tantrums, which set a bad example for the child.

It may be well to remember that no sensible baby likes strained food. He would much rather eat dust balls. Realizing that dust balls won't give him the energy to cry for six straight hours, most babies will tolerate a moderate amount of food if it is presented with imagination.

Be a little creative. Don't just say, "This is a spoonful of spinach. Open your yap." Rather approach him with, "This is a giant green vulture. Eat him before he eats you."

Some babies seem to have no opening in their throats; the food dribbles back out immediately. Let me assure you that there is an opening. If you wish to test this, give him a nickel and see how fast it disappears. Beets and spinach, however, trigger a tiny red reject button at the base of his tongue, causing the food to be precipitated forward and out. If you will dip the nickels in the spinach, they will slip right down. This is rather expensive, however.

The generally accepted method is to scrape the rejected material up off the chin and reintroduce it seven or eight times until it is all consumed or has been absorbed by his bib, whichever occurs first.

The most thorough way to clean up is for both you and the baby to take a bath in sheep dip. This is not always practical. A fairly satisfactory job can be done with ammonia and a roll of paper towels, although you will have to have a professional repaint the ceiling.

It is usually permissible to disregard carrots in his hair, but do not ignore food under and between his chins. If left for any length of time, strained peas corrode and cause an angry scrofulous-looking welt to form which is very difficult to explain to your mother-in-law. If you do get caught in this unfortunate situation, pass it off as a hereditary fungus carried by the male gene. That should hold her.*

How do you avoid such perils? Necessity may or may not be the mother of invention, but mothers are inventive. Examples:

1. Buy a tarpaulin, drop cloth, piece of oil cloth, or sheet of plastic to cover the floor. Then feed. This will not, of course, protect the walls or you.

2. Cut a slit in the center of the new drop cloth—don't substitute a dry-cleaner's bag—just wide enough to admit baby's head; then drape it around him, high chair and all. This has the added advantage that a playful hand can't send an unwary spoon flying across the room. It has the disadvantage that most infants won't enter into the spirit of the arrangement; they scream mightily. This keeps their mouth open and prevents the food from staying in.

3. Buy slickers like the New England lobster-pot men wear. One for you, one for baby, one for daddy. Get suited up before each feeding.

4. Sit high chair in the middle of the bathtub—provided the tub is wide enough. Otherwise, use the shower stall. Let the food fly as it may, the cleaning up's easy. However, you may end up having all your meals in the bathroom.

None of these appeal to you? Then, do as many mothers do, but who won't volunteer the information unless you ask about it: they don't spoon-feed their babies.

Centuries ago women hit upon the idea of dipping clean cloths in milk for baby to suck when breast-feeding was an impossibility, such as with orphans. The next step, obviously, was adding cereal and letting the baby suck the pap off. This led the early settlers to making "pap cups," forerunners in some ways of the moustache

* Copyright, 1973, Universal Press Syndicate

cup, that allowed them to "pour in" semiliquids. The danger here lies in the "pouring." Then with the advent of rubber nipples and bottle-feeding, inventive mothers jumped with joy. They mixed a gruel, put it in a bottle, then made a big hole in the nipple. What was actually happening, of course, was that they were again *pouring* the solids down the baby. And this could be dangerous since the baby can't yell, "Stop!" But baby doctors could and would and did.

But there is a safe way to do it by bottle, you know. One in which the baby starts it, slows it down, speeds it up when he wants, and stops it any time he wishes. One using cross-cut nipples. But not the ones you buy for milk—the cuts are too small. Instead, use a single-edged razor blade to enlarge the cuts one-fourth to one-half inch longer to begin with, depending on how easily your gruel passes through. A slightly too large cut should be put aside for the older baby who can take gruel that's quite thick. The baby should be held just as you would hold him if bottle-feeding formula, in a more upright position than many women use for breast-feeding.

Endorse the bottle-feeding of solids idea, and you'll discover that meal time, even after the introduction of solids, can be a joy. One that doesn't take forever, nor deteriorate into a contest of wills, nor require expensive hot plates and food warmers, nor result in the cleaning up of all participants.

Are there positive reasons for such a regimen, besides saving the mother time?

Yes. Sucking strengthens the muscles needed for talking. As such it should be encouraged. Spoon-feeding does nothing in this regard; and some experts believe it may, in fact, increase the child's interest in thumb or pacifier.

Yes. The introduction of new foods is easier. When you spoon-feed, you are introducing two new things at once. The dislike of the spoon—a very natural, normal thing since it delays the satisfying of appetite, involves a cold, hard, metal object, not a soft, giving, warm nipple, and dumps a gob of food in the wrong place in the mouth—the dislike of the spoon may lead to dislike of the food. The mother, in an effort to overcome the dislike of food, begins to doctor it up—adding more and more sugar until the liking for sugar overcomes the dislike of the spoon. And sugar isn't good for a baby.

Yes. It makes the introduction of finger foods easier. From the time your junior is ready to sit up, bottle-feed him solids, then allow him to join you wherever you eat. As you eat your own dinner and talk and generally show that dinner time is a nice time of day, he can practice his small motor skills in peace on the high-chair tray. You'll notice that his early voluntary, as compared to reflex, grasping starts with a crude palming in which both finger tips and thumb remain inactive, with the index, fore, and ring fingers doing the work. But as days and weeks go by, the thumb comes into action and the grasping becomes more of a finger than whole-hand activity.

When that happens, Mother Nature says baby is ready for finger foods. He already has a tooth or two or even four, but not enough for chewing. At this stage put a piece† of easily digested food, which may or may not need mouthing, before him. I used puffed rice, my sister something else. She calls this the Cheeri-Os stage. Into his mouth it goes . . . then out again to reexamine it. The next time it goes in his mouth, he may move it around a bit to feel it. And before he knows it, it's dissolved. He swallows. He's learned to eat. Simple as that.

Yes. It makes the supplementation of breast-fed babies easier. A friend of mine calls it the "Magical Manna Method." Her baby refused anything but the breast. So she tried mixing up a gruel for the bottle. Success.

You may wish to try doing it in the blender to prevent lumps from blocking the nipple and to closer approximate a thick version of what he has already been eating.

Which brings up the question of do-it-yourself baby food.

DO-IT-YOURSELF BLENDER BABY FOODS

Five years ago, the topic wouldn't even have come up. Then came ecology, and a reevaluation of our environment, and of our foods. Food additives, such as monosodium glutamate, came under fire and were voluntarily removed from commercial baby foods even though the Food Protection Committee of the National Academy of Sciences-National Research Council reported, in July 1970,

---

† One piece to begin with. The child under the age of one should *never* be given more than two pieces at a time because one goes in his mouth, one stays in his hand, and the third teaches him the law of gravity.

that the MSG added to commercial baby food supplied "only a minor part of the total dietary intake of children of this age." In other words, since it is a naturally occurring amino acid and a constituent of all common food proteins, a baby will get it anyway from the proteins he receives from breast or bottle.

Other food additives, such as the nitrite that resists the growth of clostridium botulinum spores, have also come under fire. Most were never in commercial baby foods to begin with, but those that were, the baby-food people banned.

Then modified starch came under fire. First by the organic-foods people as being highly indigestible, and then by mothers, who complained that when the baby was spoon-fed directly from the jar, the unused portion thinned out. Dr. Richard Hein, General Manager, Research and Development, Heinz U.S.A., explains that this is why baby-food manufacturers recommend that only the portion needed be removed from the jar with a *clean spoon* and the rest refrigerated until later use. "It may be stated that the amylase thinning of baby foods is called to our attention by a number of consumers. The reaction results from transferring this starch-digesting enzyme from the baby's mouth to the food in the jar, and a rapid thinning does occur. . . At least, it is proof the starch is digestible."

Sodium levels were criticized, too, and the baby-food people who had never salted to adult tastes reduced their salting levels, even though no one knows just how much or how little salt a baby needs.

After that, the water levels of baby food were condemned, with consumer-oriented magazines at the fore. It should be pointed out that, and again I quote Dr. Hein,

> The solids level in baby foods are such as to provide the proper nutrients per serving . . . the proper consistency, mouthfeel, and texture.
>
> As another criteria for solids level, strained fruits and vegetables are normally at the solids levels of the straight pureed fruit or vegetable. This criteria is then carried over to reciped products, meats, and dessert items.
>
> For an additional thought on this subject, water is the most abundant constituent accounting for 50 to 75 percent of the baby's weight depending on age and baby fat. Deficits or excesses of more than a few percent are incompatible with health. Our internal regu-

latory system for the amount of water required on a daily basis is a superb mechanism. For infants the normal rate of turnover of water is about 15 percent per day in the young infant. For anyone who has ever diapered a baby boy and experienced the "fountain effect" it may appear the turnover ratio is 100 percent per day.

Please note, a reasonable allowance for water intake is 1.5 ml/ Kcal for infants according to the NRC-NAS Report ≯1694 published in 1968.

Using this figure of 1.5 ml. per Kcal and for the six-month infant with RDA of 900 Kcal, the infant should consume 1350 ml. of water per day, which, of course, includes the free water in the milk and solid foods. Milk at 24.8 ounces or 700 gms. and about 11 to 12 percent solids will contribute 616 ml. of this water. The baby-food intake of 19.6 ounces including fruit juice averages about 13 percent solids and thus contributes about 480 ml. of water. This totals to 1096 ml. of the 1350 recommended. Thus, the baby will require something over 8 ounces of additional water on a daily basis. Perhaps these comments are indicative that some thought has been given to the solids levels of prepared baby foods.

Thank you, Dr. Hein.

"Another danger of infant foods in jars is that it is difficult to tell whether or not the foods have been contaminated. . . . Jar caps that show whether the jar has been opened were invented in 1963. It's a rare baby food that has them even yet [1972]," says one critic of commercial foods.

I really don't see how it's fair to condemn commercial food makers for possible contamination when the contaminators are mothers like you and me who open baby-food jars, taste them, and return them to the shelf. As for the jar caps, in 1969, I didn't find a single jar without them.

As for chemical additives, ask yourself if you would give your child:

    (a) NaCl
    (b) $C_6H_{12}O_6 + H_2O$
    (c) $C_{12}H_{22}O_{11} + H_2O$
    (d) $C_6H_{10}O_5$
    (e) Ascorbic Acid

a = salt
b and c = two forms of sugar
d = flour
e = Vitamin C

Why do I go into such detail about what is "wrong" with commercial baby foods? Because these criticisms have led to the "great leap forward" in infant feeding and nutrition: the do-it-yourself baby-food cookbook.

Within one year more than eight such books on the subject came on the market. Each puts forth the desire to save American babies from the "poisoned, spoiled, adulterated products of the food industry," and to do so with little work and less money than canned baby foods cost.

Let's examine their premises.

PREMISE #1: Using leftovers is the way to save money. They forget to mention that in order to keep the saline level low, no salt should be added to foods during cooking. Thus in order to use food designed for you and your husband, you must put the adults of the family on a *salt-free diet*. Nor do they mention that *boiled* foods, which are the only ones soft enough to mash with a fork, have the big three of B vitamins (thiamine, riboflavin, and niacin), as well as vitamin A and vitamin C leached out of them.

The only way to rescue some of these vitamins is to use the cooking water in processing the food; i.e., using a blender.

Nor do they mention that in using a blender, the minimum amount of liquid to be used is one-half cup (or enough to cover the blender blades) *no matter how much food you have to blend*. Thus, that spoonful of peas, the last carrot stick, the one extra pork chop will make up into a surprising amount of pureed food, each of which will contain one-half cup or more of water.

PREMISE #2: They suggest that you make your own baby foods from scratch using their recipes. To do otherwise is "like feeding your husband a thawed-out TV dinner every night."

This is fine if you are prepared to do the cooking necessary. For example, you are already going to cook between 2,000 and 2,200 *meals* (not dishes, but meals) just for you and your husband in the first two years of your baby's life. In that same period of time, your child will need almost 2,000 meals, not including bottles, if you delay adding solids until six months.

Are you prepared to cook 4,000 or more different meals in the next two years, so your baby will eat a perfect diet? Or will you do as many do-it-yourself-baby-food-making mothers do and plan all the meals around the baby's needs?

Just how fond is your husband of Liver/Potato Loaf? Carrot-Cheese Souffle? Lamb Barley Stew? Meatball Soup?

And if you can get him to agree to such unusual foods, for whose taste buds are you going to season your foods? Your husband's, which have dulled with age, even if he is only in his early twenties, or your child's? How can you judge what will taste good to that child? Don't go by the baby-food cookbook people; one pair will tell you on page one of their book that commercial baby food "tastes flat and dull. It lacks variety." Ten pages later, they'll explain that the reason a two-year-old wants to stay on his old bland diet is that he doesn't like "strong tastes. He doesn't like spice or variety or strength in his food."

According to H. M. I. Kiley, M.D., whose book *Modern Motherhood* (Random House, 1966) deals with the baby from the point of view of fetology (the science of the unborn) and who also happens to be the mother of five, "babies do not seem to develop a noticeable sense of smell until they reach nine or ten months of age. A very young baby, for example, will eat almost anything—vegetables, eggs or bacon, it seems to make little difference—although that very same food may prove an anathema to him six months later and he will violently reject it. This is because the sense of taste depends, to a very great extent, upon the sense of smell—as any of us will realize when we have a head cold and 'everything tastes the same.'"

It was this very lack of sense of taste that caused six infants to die in 1962 when their hospital-made formula was inadvertently made with salt instead of sugar. They couldn't tell sweet from salty, and vice versa.

But that, of course, was the story of *newborns*. Dr. Kiley tells us that once a baby's sense of smell "becomes more acute, he is far more selective about what he will accept. Vegetables especially may offend him, and he may violently reject the peas or cabbage he happily accepted a few weeks before. . . . He is much more sensitive to strong tastes than adults are. He is not being bad tempered and un-co-operative when he violently rejects certain foods. The infant's taste is so fresh and keen that disagreeable flavors can actually be painful to him. . . . The main thing to realize is that children have tastes quite different from those of adults." Agreed. Now what?

Nowhere do I find a statement that the recipes in these cookbooks have been taste-tested by X number of children, ranging in age from X to X, something I should judge a necessity if we as adults are unable to judge how a recipe should taste to a child and must therefore rely totally on the cookbook as being accurate.

One author even says as much. "Stick to the recipes, even when you are tempted to season your baby's food to your taste." She's the one with the one-fourth cup instead of one-fourth teaspoon of salt in a recipe. She also says that all her recipes have been tested for taste and texture. But she doesn't say by whom.

Those same recipes, tested by others, came up with "very bland flavor" . . . "too salty," . . . "no lamb flavor" . . . "texture unacceptable, similar to a sandwich spread, unsuitable for three-month-old baby" . . . "texture unacceptable, stringy" . . . "too rough" . . . to mention only the negatives.

Speaking of which, what are the qualifications of the other authors of said cookbooks? One is a member of the La Leche League, which makes her a successful breast-feeder but not necessarily a cook. Another is a Madison Avenue copywriter. Another is an optometrist (presumably this lends insight), still another a housewife without children, and another a Ralph Nader-type lawyer—he's the one that the others quote on the dangers of additives. Just don't buy his book for the recipes. Besides the fact that there are only twenty-one of them in the book, the quantities are inaccurate: his baby's cheese soufflé calls for twice as much salt as one for an adult, and his fruit dessert calls for *one-third cup* of sugar to one-half cup of banana.

As for the likening of commercial baby food to the serving of TV dinners, there are some husbands I know who prefer TV dinners to the cooking they're already getting. And other husbands, who do not like TV dinners, will be living on a fairly consistent diet of them for the first couple of weeks after the baby is home. Don't turn your nose up at serving TV dinners, they can be a wife-saver.

PREMISE #3: If you feed your baby commercially packed jars of baby food, you are depriving him of the best available nutrition.

On whose authority is this made? A nutritionist's? No. A doctor's? No. Is the statement accurate? Not according to such world renowned people as Paul Gyorgy, M.D., discoverer of Riboflavin, Biotin, and vitamin B_6, who says, "Of course, you should feed canned baby food. No woman is so poor that she can't afford the few cents a day it costs to feed her baby right with jars of baby food." Would he make his own baby food? He would not. "Too much bother, besides Gerber and Heinz and the others, they're perfectly reliable. And compared to today's meat prices, cheaper."

And Dr. Gyorgy says about organically grown foods: "Nonsense, it makes no difference. Synthetics are chemical compounds and so are we. In fact, synthetics are actually cleaner and purer than some natural ones. For example, under no circumstances should you use cod liver oil. The vitamin A and D in it are very small; everything else can be harmful."

Is this man, whom Adelle Davis refers to for authoritative statements in her *Let's Have Healthy Children* (New American Library), out of step with the times?

Not according to Cortez F. Enloe, Jr., physician, nutritionist, editor, and publisher of *Nutrition Today,* the most widely read magazine on nutrition in the world, with a circulation of over 200,000, including such food experts as dieticians and physicians.

He agrees with the ex-president of the Association of American Pediatrics that such do-it-yourself baby-food making will put infant feeding back fifty years. Dr. Enloe and others say that the reason infant mortality rates have dropped in this country is due to the discovery of drugs, vaccines, and other antibacterial substances that protect infants from infection . . . and from improved child sanitation and feeding. But the reason that the life expectancy at birth that you and I enjoy has increased so greatly is "due largely to the fact that infant feeding has been taken out of the home."

However, Dr. Enloe looks upon these baby-food cookbooks with a biased eye. In a speech to the Food Editors Conference, October 3, 1972, he admitted as much. "So that there won't be any doubt as to what I think of these books, let me say that if these guides to nutritional health of babies were judged by the same standards by which food and drugs are measured, the FDA would have seized them on publication day and banned them from the market place as misbranded, adulterated and dangerous to health. And so they are."

How are they dangerous? Well, for one thing they advocate introducing various specific foods at specific times. As early as four to six weeks, in at least two cases. This is a matter which should be determined by your pediatrician, *not* by a cookbook.

For another, in order to be different, to be individualistic, they advocate their own specific feeding plans.

For example, one book recommends that you start your three-and-one-half-month-old bottle-fed baby (four-and-one-half-month breast-fed) with bananas and meat, each once a day, being sure to "concentrate on iron-rich meats such as liver." And cereal is not added until seven and one-half months.

Do you have any idea of how much "iron-rich" meat you will have to give a baby per day to reach his RDA (Recommended Daily Allowance) of mg. iron per day as compared to feeding one-half ounce of commercially prepared baby cereals? Let me show you.

To feed your baby the iron equivalent of one-half ounce of commercial baby cereal, you would have to feed him:

> 16 ounces (1 pound) of lean beef
> > or
> 10 ounces of beef brain
> > or
> 9 ounces of ham
> > or
> 14 ounces of beef heart
> > or
> 16 ounces (1 pound) of chicken
> > or
> 8 ounces of corned beef
> (don't do it—they use nitrites in preserving it)
> > or
> 80 ounces (5 pounds) of codfish
> > or
> 8 lamb chops

And those are not typographical errors. I said five pounds of codfish and eight lamb chops.

Besides being expensive, it is a physical impossibility to stuff that much food into a six-month-old child or younger. No wonder the incidence of iron deficiency in the Chicago Head Start program was 316 percent and that the incidence of nutritional anemia in hospitalized infants six to thirty-six months old was between seventeen and forty-five percent.

And do you know how much an adequate amount of cereal

would cost you for a whole year? The same author gives us the total cost for cereal for a year, "beginning at two weeks old, $3.15." Anyone know where you can get eight lamb chops for that little?

Oh, by the way, just to show that I was being fair, my equivalencies came from the tables in Adelle Davis's book *Let's Eat Right to Keep Fit* (New American Library, 1970).

Which does bring us to cost.

Let us assume that you have the equipment needed to prepare your own baby food—

blender	grater
small paring knife	vegetable brush
rubber spatula	double boiler
slotted spoon	enamel saucepan
measuring spoons	fruit juicer
measuring cups	heavy aluminum saucepan
food mill	stainless steel saucepan
meat grinder	cheesecloth
vegetable peeler	aluminum foil
tongs	plastic wrap
wire-mesh strainers	waxed paper

For the use of each, see *Feeding Your Baby: the Safe and Healthy Way* by Ruth Pearlman (Random House, 1971). (Note: some books also call for a pressure cooker.)

The only things you need are the raw materials and the recipes. Some recipes call for produce and products from health-food stores; let's discount those since it means extra shopping for you, and at higher prices. Besides, Adelle Davis does all her shopping in regular stores. If she can, so can you.

And while we're at it, let's assume that you elect to use an iron-fortified cereal, rather than a pound of lean beef per day.

Now, what will it cost you to feed your baby commercial foods versus homemade foods?

The Natural Baby Food Cookbook (Nash Publishing, 1972), which has received high praise from food writers for its illustrations of how much more expensive it is to rely solely on the commercial baby foods, gives us one example. It is, in the author's words, "a very unusual case, since this baby's parents were excessively concerned with sterility and did not present her with any food or drink from the table at all during her first year."

It is interesting to note that this is the one, the only example given to show how much more expensive is ready-made than homemade.

Anyway, this author's total is $216 a year for commercial baby foods ($3.15 for cereals, $21.60 for fruits, $36 for meats and vegetables, $36 for egg yolks, $70.50 for junior dinners and desserts, $12.75 for teething biscuits and baby finger food meat products, $36 for juices). This was in 1972, when food prices were low.

Even at optimum usage at peak 1973 prices, I find her strained-fruit costs 25 percent high, her vegetables and meats 20 percent high, her egg-yolk figures 50 percent high, etc. For example, she would have us believe that a child of six months was drinking eight ounces of orange juice a day. And continued to drink that much every day for the next six months. Ridiculous.

As compared to that she offers us a woman "who makes even her own cereal and breads and uses the freshest and least contaminated (and therefore most expensive produce in each dish)."‡ Granting that there is a corollary between cost and freshness and/or contamination, for which we have been offered no corroboration, we are again given no basis for her figures. However, they work out to $123.60, including $3.59 for cereal and $9 for egg yolks, according to her figures.

The trouble is that the mother involved is obviously not using the same quantities of food. Let me show you what I mean. For ready-made mother A to spend $36 on egg yolks in six months, she had to be spending 20¢ a day. Since a jar of egg yolks in April of 1973 cost 29¢ for three and one-fourth yolks, she must, as a rule of thumb, be using at least two egg yolks a day. Mother B, using the same two egg yolks, would spend, at 49¢ a dozen, $14.70; at 59¢, $17.70; at 69¢, $20.70; at 79¢, $23.70; at 89¢ $26.70, etc.

And in each case, she would have 360 egg whites to use up. At

‡ Presumably organic foods, since they are undoubtedly the most expensive. Gyorgy says, "I'm against the organic food fad. These people are using fear psychology against nutritionally sound food." He's the discoverer of those three B vitamins. The man the World Health Organization has sent around the world. He's the man who taught the more knowledgeable pediatricians their stuff.

an average of one and one-half cups of egg whites per angel-food cake, mother B will be able to make six angel-food cakes a month for six months for the cost of only thirty-six cups of cake flour and fifty-four cups of sugar.

But mother B didn't spend that much, she spent only $9. Which means, if she were using the same quantity as mother A, that mother B was getting her eggs for 29¢ a dozen. Let me at them! I'll take a case, and another for my mother!

Enough of that. At least the authors of the book didn't come out and say you could save 50 percent of your food bill, like another one did. Which is equally untrue.

Now, let's hear from the other side. In February 1973 the Gerber baby-food people fed the total diets of 377 infants over a four-day period into a computer. The diets were obtained from a sampling balanced for age, sex, income, education of parents, and geographic distribution. In other words, they included all the possible variables.

One of the things they looked for was do-it-yourself baby foods. Once all of those were identified, the Gerber Home Economics Department made all of them up using *both* fresh produce and adult canned goods. The cost per ounce was determined, for both fresh and canned. Of these, the least expensive cost was fed into the computer bank, and cost comparisons were made. However, no equipment costs, no time allotments for labor charges, no wasted-food allowances were included.

The results, which were offered to me without reservation of any kind by Dr. Robert A. Stewart, Director of Research, Gerber Products Company, showed that without a doubt the woman who makes her own baby food can save money. How much she saves depends to a degree on what she feeds. In one instance, a mother spent 34¢ less a day then she would have had she used commercial baby foods; in another, the home-prepared diet cost 7¢ a day more.

However, the average cost of all the food consumed in 1,508 infant days was 66¢ a day (with a low of 43¢ and a high of 89¢) of which 28¢ (10¢ to 46¢) was for commercial baby foods. If home prepared foods had been used to replace all of the commercial baby foods, the total cost would have been 57¢ a day (36¢ to 78¢).

THE ACTUAL DIFFERENCE IN COST WAS AS LITTLE

AS 6¢ A DAY AND AS MUCH AS 14¢ A DAY. THE AVER-
AGE WAS 8¢. And this did not include the cost of a blender, or
pressure cooker, or food grinder . . . and especially, it did not include your time.

While they were comparing those 377 babies' actual diets for
cost, they also compared recipes for baby food against their own
Gerber product. These are the results for a range of recipes covering fruits, vegetables, main dishes, desserts.

Recipe	Cost per ounce do-it-yourself	Cost per ounce of comparable canned food
⌗1	.02	.02
⌗2	.02	.02
⌗3	.01	.02
⌗4	.025	.045
⌗5	.075	.08
⌗6	.225	.08
⌗7	.02	.02
⌗8	.0025	.02
⌗9	.05	.04
⌗10	.06	.04
⌗11	.006 (not a mistake)	.02 (not a soup, as other is)
⌗12	.01	.02
⌗13	.01	.02

Of these recipes, it should be noted that in one case (Recipe
⌗8) the Gerber product was iron-enriched, and thus represented a
savings in terms of supplementary vitamins. Of the others, the
major differences were between do-it-yourself meats and commercial, and between a soup (that yielded 7 cups—imagine how long
that's going to take to feed to baby. I hope it freezes. Use ice-cube
trays, and when each cube is frozen remove and place in bag—
lots of work) and a meat-vegetable dish with nowhere near the
water content of the soup, which also contained salts and nitrites
the commercial product didn't.

It should be noted that baby-food prices seem to increase much
more slowly than do consumer-product prices.

How valid will this comparison be when you read it, months
from now? Very valid, since the cost differences, in my opinion,
will have closed. Food prices for meat, fresh fruits, and fresh pro-

duce are soaring as compared to canned items. And as compared to baby-food prices, they're out of sight.

I would say that compared to other foods, baby foods have been, are, and will be a bargain . . . economically!

The cereals, however, have increased. By about 10 percent total over three years. Still the cost of one-half ounce of such cereal, the amount that will supply *all,* 100 per cent, of a baby's RDA of iron, is less than 2¢. Compare that to the cost of sixteen ounces of beef or eight lamb chops.

PREMISE #4: It takes only a little time, a small effort, and routine equipment.

We've already covered the equipment (only don't buy a two-speed blender as one writer suggests, it's too limiting)—the effort depends on you. What about the time? Well, *professionally* prepared, by cooks who know what they're doing, seven sample recipes in one cookbook took between five minutes and four hours and fifteen minutes to prepare. . . . That five-minute one sound good? It was for applesauce, certainly not one of the world's most complicated recipes.

The dessert recipe took the second least amount of time: three-fourths of an hour: The main course dishes averaged between one and one-half and two and one-half hours of cooking.

Judge for yourself. Look through these cookbooks, check the recommended cooking times. You will find time and time again that it takes you longer to make a baby version of an adult-type dish than it does to make the same dish for you and your husband. This, of course, may be the fault of the cookbook. In fact, it *is* the fault of the cookbook.

For one thing, why a cookbook for babies? Is the one you use for yourself and your husband so unnutritional, so unappetizing, so undesirable? If so, how will preparing the baby-food cookbook dishes ready your child for the time when you serve him the same foods you and daddy are eating?

Regardless of what you choose to do in terms of ready-made or commercially made foods, may I save you some money?

DON'T BUY A BABY-FOOD COOKBOOK.

Your baby doesn't need stews and soups and other cooking conglomerations. He needs to learn the tastes of simple foods, and the simple combinations of these. Once you've gone past the ordinary in vegetables, choose and use recipes you already like. Look first for two- or three-ingredient recipes, preferably those which only use one more ingredient than the child already knows: Example: scrambled eggs grow into cheese souffle (addition of cheese) and that into macaroni and cheese (addition of pasta).

And whatever you do, *don't add salt!*

A PERSONAL NOTE: "Did you," you ask, "use commercially prepared foods or homemade?" The answer is yes. Yes, I used commercially prepared foods, and yes, I made homemade. But I must confess, my son was less happy and so was I with the latter.

I refused, for example, to make my uncomplaining, long-suffering husband, who took relief bottles at 2 A.M. and walked more than his share of floors, I refused to feed him foods planned for baby. In fact, if forced to choose between foisting TV dinners on Senior or three-month-old Junior, Senior would win hands down. He, at least, cleans up his plate and wipes his chin.

Reduced to either cooking separate meals, which wasn't practical to begin with (except with frozen vegetables in the reclosable bag that allows you to cook one ounce at a time), or using leftovers, my thrifty mind glommed onto the idea of using that extra little dab for J. R. This caused me to change one of my own precious preconceptions.

I do not believe in cooking leftovers. I believe in, if anything, undercooking. I cringe when I hear of home economists having "clean-out-the-refrigerator Sunday-night dinners," when one deviled egg and one-half peach and two tablespoons of tomato aspic, etc., are put forth for one and all to munch on. Can you think of a better way to punish your family for not cleaning their plates? But, in the interests of homemade baby food, I planned for leftovers. I planned wrong. Using leftover vegetables, steamed rather than parboiled, didn't work. Green beans were in truth "string beans." The semicrisp "young peas" taste we liked caused hulls in the blender. The carrots looked curdled. I had to recook the food before blending. Then the taste seemed cooked out. And when blending, I used much more water than I'd planned.

Wondering if I were an oddity, I checked with my friends. The mother of six said, "Do-it-yourself? You're crazy. Maybe for the first; after that who has time?"

The traveling mother said, "Feeding do-it-yourself means canning and freezing and headaches. It's so much easier to just pack

up what you need in the way of canned baby foods and open
when the mood strikes the baby."

The ex-dietician from one of the largest-area hospitals, a
woman who created special menus for special dietary needs, said,
"What? Who me? Why?"

The mother of twins who said, "Yes, have you seen what they
charge for one of those small jars of meat?" admits today that 88¢
a pound (5.5¢ an ounce) is pretty cheap for meat.

OTHER COSTS BESIDES THE FOOD COSTS

Heat Plate

Unnecessary. Feed your foods at room temperature; you won't
need to heat them. And in case of traveling, such foods will always
be at the right temperature. Remember, it's easy to get foods too
hot, almost impossible to get them too cold.

Spoons

Demitasse spoons have been recommended for years. However,
they are no more effective than other baby spoons. Which in turn
are not, at spoon-feeding time, any better than regular spoons.
When it comes to the child's wielding the spoon, the shorter the
handle the better. The heavier and firmer the handle the better.
Watch out for the extremely tapering narrow handle—no good.

Forks

The fork is a civilized utensil, one not known for years. In its
adult form it's not for babies. Its tines should not be sharp, and
should be close together. Their length should be no more than the
bowl of a spoon or less.

Part 3

Shelter

Experts predict that a child's share of basic housing costs (mortgage, taxes, utilities, and insurance, but not operation) will take an average 28¢ out of each dollar you spend on him, with the exact amounts fluctuating depending on the age of the child. In this instance, the first two years are the hardest, the preschool next, and the in-school years (when the drain on utilities is eased) the lowest—but the variation from year to year is never more than $100.

Not included in this calculation are the "start-up charges," which can be quite sizable, averaging between $380 and $550 for his baby-type furniture. If you elect to go into transitional furnishings at about two, when cribs, etc., have been outgrown, you can expect another outlay for "Junior" or "Youth" furniture. This can easily cost you another $100 for bed, mattress, and linens. Of this, approximately 25 percent may be recoverable because it will be usable with adult furnishings.

If you have added up the costs per year and come to an astronomical sum in the five figures, remember that built into these charges is the cost of a public school education, either through direct school taxes on your real estate or through your prorated share, via your rent, of your landlord's school taxes.

Chapter 6

Environment Is Everything —Part One: Necessities

In April 1973 I spent the good part of an afternoon in an office building outside Washington, D.C. There, I listened to tale after tale of how infants and children have been killed and maimed and injured. And these were not tales of the horrors of war in Southeast Asia, but tales from the United States and Canada.

A day later, I spent a good part of a day in the attic of my home. There, I found and inspected the weapons that kill and maim and injure children: a baby's crib, a playpen, a jumperwalker, a high chair, an infant seat, and more.

And every one of these was manufactured not by sadists or child-haters, but by men who analyzed what mothers wanted, and then supplied it. No, it was not some hidden, sadistic, or destructive urge within mothers that inspired those men. It was simply a mother's desire for time to herself. Her recognition that carrying a child around is heavy work. Her dislike of bending over. Her very real protective instinct to keep her child safe by keeping him under wraps and out from underfoot. Her need to get up and go, pack up and leave, fold up and put away. Her desire, my desire, your desire to be more than just a mother. To be a woman, a wife, a person as well as a mother.

Who can argue with these desires? In themselves they are understandable, realistic, natural. Unfortunately, they lead to less understandable, unrealistic, unnatural—totally undesirable results. They lead to hundreds of deaths, thousands of injuries—the hurting of the very babies you and I have spent nine months nurturing within ourselves. The whole thing's wrong, cruel, unfair. And the people in Washington, at the Consumer Product Safety Commission, are doing something about it.

You may already know of some of their work: The warnings about the dangers of plastic dry-cleaner bags, the changing of clear glass doors to ones with obvious designs, thus preventing people walking into and through them. But what are they doing about children specifically?

For one thing, they're warning mothers about potential hazards to children, just as mothers have always been warned against allowing their children to play with matches. Okay, you say, everybody knows that children shouldn't play with matches. It may be a mother's fault if her child gets hurt. I agree. But what about the thirty-five children who required emergency treatment during January 1973 in the few hospitals involved in a special National Electronic Surveillance System because of injuries caused by their cribs?

Be honest, if you had to name the one place in your house where you would think a child would be most safe, wouldn't you name his crib? Yet between 150 and 200 children are killed by strangulation each year by their cribs, and 50,000 more are injured.

How? Too many ways. Since interior dimensions of cribs are not standardized, it is difficult to get a mattress that fits properly. Therefore, a child may inadvertently wedge himself between mattress and crib and suffocate. More commonly, the child uses projections within the crib as a makeshift ladder. Up he goes, over he goes. If he lands on his head, concussions, fractures, maybe death could be the result.

The third and most common is also the most horrifying. The child wiggles his body through two slats of his crib—the body slides through easily, but not the head. Results? A fast death from a broken neck, a slow, agonizing death by hanging. If the mother is nearby, she may hear an unusual sound or gurgling and be in time to rescue her child. The mother who is too far away will enter the baby's room to see his lifeless body dangling from his "safe" crib eight or more inches above the floor.

Dr. John E. Summers, M.D., was one of the first to warn about the spacing of crib slats, back in the April 1966 *Consumers Bulletin*. His own daughter had a close call which caused him to investigate cribs on the market. He said then that slat spacing of three and one-half inches is too generous, too dangerous. He warned about the climb-out dangers, the ladder-effects designed into cribs, the hazards in the release mechanisms for crib sides.

But his warnings and recommendations must have fallen on deaf ears, for seven years later, Senator Charles Percy of Illinois was again warning the public that faulty crib design was killing our children. Yes, the industry had set up voluntary standards in 1970 to change slat spacing to make it safer, from three and one-half to three and one-fourth inches; but according to Senator Percy's office, as of February 21, 1973, a preliminary report of an investigation showed that more than 50 percent of cribs sold in the Washington, D.C., area exceeded the three and one-half-inch standard. They weren't sold by Montgomery Ward, however. From the beginning this firm has endorsed, supported, and followed the stringent proposed regulations.

Other statistics, based on 1972 nationwide measurements of 97 full-sized wood-slatted cribs (representing over 300 styles available on the retail market and nearly 100 percent of production), according to Charles C. Edwards, M.D., Commissioner of Food and Drugs, showed 85 percent were using the three and one-fourth-inch voluntary standard spacing, while only 15 percent had slat spacing of over three and one-fourth inches and none more than three and one-half inches.

The problem is that those three and one-fourth inches are too much. And so are three inches . . . and two and three-fourths . . . and two and one-half. In fact, more than 71 percent of infants up to six and one-half months old could, according to an FDA study, slip foot-first through those voluntary three and one-fourth-inch spaces. That's where the Food and Drug Administration's Bureau of Product Safety's Division of Children's Hazards comes in.

They have drafted mandatory regulations requiring manufacturers to keep those slats no more than two and three-eighths inches apart. And that could stop the hangings of hundreds of children in the future.

But they did more; they standardized interior width and length, and set minimum mattress sizes to fit that interior. That should stop children from being wedged between mattress and crib and suffocating.

And more. They set rail heights determined by the average size, strength, and agility of an eighteen-month-old. That should prevent children from toppling over the sides.

There's more. They are regulating the locking devices that secure the drop sides so they're inaccessible to a child from inside the crib. And that should prevent fractures of the arm whose hand reached out and unlocked the crib sides. They are also requiring that a minimum force of ten pounds will be needed to activate the release mechanism. That will prevent the family dog's brushing against the lever and releasing the side as he runs under the crib. That should save several trips to the emergency ward.

And there's still more. They are trying to stop the use of horizontal or other surfaces inside a crib that might be used as a toe hold for the adventuresome child eager to explore the outside world. However, after a certain age, and by a certain height (at least thirty-five inches), the determined child will be up and out without the use of toe holds, or even the use of his legs. Safely enclosed and supposedly immobile in a blanket sleeper, our child could and would get out of his crib at will. At that state, a regular bed is the only answer.

Hopefully, by the time you read this, you will be unable to go into a store and buy an unsafe crib. But what about the crib you can borrow from a friend? Or the one advertised for sale cheap in the local weekly, or the one the folks at the garage sale will let go for a fiver, or the one that's been sitting in the family attic waiting for another occupant, the one you slept in as a baby, the family heirloom?

Technically, those cribs will be illegal to sell—as to the friend's and family's, that's a tactical problem, which might be forestalled by buying a safe crib before you are offered the unsafe one.

How much will that crib cost you? More than the present unsafe ones, of course, but spokesmen for major crib manufacturers, such as Simmons, maintain that the costs will increase only slightly. However that may be, you can, if those regulations go through, feel perfectly safe and assured buying the cheapest crib on the market.

NECESSITY #1: A PLACE TO SLEEP

In shopping for that crib, there are many factors to consider. For example: If the crib's headboard and footboard are identical, only one drop-side is needed. The crib with one drop-side is cheaper than the crib with two drop-sides.

The crib that offers you the most mattress-height positions is the most convenient for you, and the one in which your child can remain the longest. For as he grows up, you drop the mattress. Check the mattress holders. Frequently, you can lower those fasteners yourself, turning a two-position crib into a three- or four-position one. And that's a saving, dollarwise.

Height is another factor to consider. The ends of the beds range from thirty-eight to forty-five inches high, but those are variations in design only. Almost all have about the same side rail height. It's a psychological thing. They know most mothers think the higher the sides the better—which is untrue, it's the distance from mattress top to top of side rail that's important. So don't go by overall height. Go by depth of the slatted side, the deeper the better . . . and by leg-length, which determines how convenient the bed is for you. The convenient height is the one at which you can lean over the drop-side and pick up the child. Which, if you are somewhat-inflated-in-the-front-pregnant, may be a little difficult for you to judge. However, perhaps you can work out your own rule of thumb from this: at five feet nine and one-half inches, I find most cribs to be perfect, with a few a bit on the high side. If you're not a tall one like me, better check the legs of your choice to make sure you can cut off the necessary inches. Or perhaps removing the casters will work for you.

Another way of determining optimum height is to stand sideways next to the crib—the rail height should be lower than the bottom of your rib cage to allow you the most comfort in bending.

One word of caution: Approach the cutting off of those legs with care; don't take the whole five inches, let's say, off at one time. Do it gradually, so you can change your mind.

Other factors that should influence your selection of a crib include:

Finish
Painted cribs cost less than "antiqued" cribs, which cost less than solid, naturally finished decorative woods such as walnut. An unfinished crib could be the cheapest of all, depending on the paint used, which must be LEAD-FREE. Beware of using your mother's crib, or any antique crib, if the paint on it (even under-

coats) predates 1950. It takes so little lead to poison a child that authorities have now discovered children can be poisoned by breathing minute particles of lead flaking off lead-painted walls.

Design

There are two basic designs: The crib with solid head- and footboards and slatted sides, and the crib that's slatted or spindled all around. Each has variations, advantages and disadvantages:

(1) *Solid fore and aft:* These are less expensive than the all-around slats. They can have built-in toys (which can be dangerous and which most children never use). They can have attractive, clever decals or scenes on them—some shops specializing in small people's things, for example, will even custom decorate such a crib for you with purple cows or Raggedy Anns, or butterflies, etc., inside or out. The outside scenes, of course, are for your amusement and pleasure, not your baby's because he can't see them. The advantage of having the design custom-done for you is that (*a*) it's uniquely yours, and (*b*) you can put the picture where it will do the most good: on the inside of the foot of the bed. That way your child can enoy it.

The cribs that have identical head- and footboards are slightly less expensive than those with different ends. Since you don't have to worry about which end is which, you can choose one with but one drop-side instead of two, another saving.

The disadvantage of these solid-ended cribs is that visibility is limited to looking out either side. This becomes a real disadvantage if the crib is placed lengthwise against the wall. In that case, the baby has only one way to look. Soon, his head will reflect that fact—it will flatten on one side. A simple matter to correct, but bothersome. Just reverse his position, putting his feet where his head was. When flattening occurs on that side, you go back to your original position. It's for this reason that many mothers put the headboard against the wall and let the crib jut out into the room. The baby will roll his head into shape.

I should mention that there is a gimmick crib out that has very interesting possibilities for those who can afford it—and it's not the most expensive crib price tag, by any means. What it does have is a solid, transparent, plastic end, increasing the visibility from that crib by 25 percent. In addition, there are colorful circles painted on it, which can be seen from either side, thus pleasing both parent and child.

With the cost of lumber soaring, there may be a day when we'll see all-plastic molded cribs. The baby could see and be seen . . . would be protected from drafts and wouldn't need bumpers . . . toys wouldn't fall out and feet couldn't dangle. It sounds like a dream, except for one thing. Babies use those slats for a purpose: to pull themselves up to a standing position—a much better way to achieve that than by using your living-room coffee table.

(2) *All-around slatted:* The most expensive of the cribs. It offers 100 percent visibility, enabling the crib to be placed anywhere. Toys can be fastened anywhere on it for easy access and the best view. But. There's always a but. Many babies like to sleep in a fetal position. This is the reason why the baby you put down in the middle of the bed ends up hours later with his head smack up against the end of the crib. With a spindle crib, he gets red marks from the bed and you get nasty looks from your mother-in-law. Therefore, an added expense is required: you need to buy a bumper to go around the inside of the crib. More on that later.

Speaking of fetal positions, baby's first bed could be his crib in a nice, quiet nursery somewhere. It might better be a closer approximation of the environment he's known for the past nine months. What was it like inside the placenta? It was constantly warm, it was buoyant, it was resilient—if he had to uncross and recross his legs, he gave you a good kick and the placenta gave.

It was crampy, too, forcing him to stay curled up with his bowlegs crossed at the ankle, his arms clutched tight to his chest, his head resting upon his legs. Floating on water, he knew no up or down, but always had the security of enveloping warmth around him. He was, if you will, swaddled with you.

To come from the perfect environment—except for the jouncing and bouncing the carrier commits—to come from that to the ups and downs and chills and hot waves of our imperfect temperatures . . . to come from total security to a cold, indifferent, foreign freedom . . . to come from a dark cozy world into one with many suns that brighten the hours even to the extent of hurting the eyes . . . to come from familiar everyday, rhythmic sounds to infinitely variable noise levels, coming from this perfection to imperfection, I, too, would have colic—and a darn good case of it.

To make the transition easier, for his first bed use something smaller than his crib, something more confining, more crampy, more closed in. A bassinet is nice, but expensive. A suspended rocking cradle is nicer, but more expensive. The old-fashioned, on-the-floor cradle infants have been entrusted to since A.D. 400 is even more expensive—and hard to find, except in antique shops.

But these are traditional answers, not the only ones. A dresser drawer placed on the floor—that will do just fine. A plastic laundry basket costs but a bit, yet makes everything seem special (a ribbon woven in and out through the web adds the touch it needs perhaps). I even know a mother who made use of a wicker dog bed for her baby, and then gave it to her doggy. The point is that you can spend hundreds of dollars for a cradle, tens of dollars for a suspended one, a handful of dollars for a bassinet (but then, after buying the furnishings of that bassinet, actually spend more than you would for a suspended cradle; more on furnishings later). Or you can spend nothing by making do.

NECESSITY ⚮2: SOMETHING TO SLEEP ON

Although you make do to begin with, eventually he will have to have a crib. The crib itself can be a cheap one but don't stint on the mattress. After all, your child will spend most of his time for his first two to two and one-half years flat on his back or tummy. There are three types to choose from: hair, foam, and innerspring. In choosing your mattress look for firmness, durability, weight, and cost.

The hair mattress is usually the most firm, but not terribly durable. However, if you do not choose to have a batch of children, and therefore can buy a new mattress per child, durability is less important here. What is important is that hair mattresses can be highly allergenic. If your child has allergic tendencies, you may have to replace his mattress. Since for health reasons mattresses are unreturnable, you face the additional cost of a new mattress: $20 and up.

The innerspring mattress is very durable—the one to choose for the large family to follow. It is also heavy. Very heavy. More than twice as heavy as a foam mattress, almost double the lightest hair mattress. With these you must make sure that you have a handle to use in turning and carrying. The cost of an innerspring mattress depends on the number of coils in it. The more coils, the more money. Thus you'll find some mattresses are $20 and others double that.

The third type, the cheapest of the three, by many, many dollars, is the foam mattress. These are the mattresses that will just outlast the child's crib life, for they are even less durable than the hair mattress. However, they are also the lightest weight. And the best foam mattresses are as firm as an inexpensive inner-spring.

Whatever mattress you buy, the ticking should be waterproof, with the seams as flat as possible. Handles and ventilators are desirable, too. Look for guarantees, for brand names like Simmons. These are your only protections, because stores legally need not accept the return of your mattress.

Because of the importance of buying a good mattress, you need to feel it and punch it and look it over. So don't buy by mail order, if you can help it. Especially don't buy by mail order if the description of the mattress is vague, like "matching mattress" or "complete with innerspring mattress."

And this applies to buying crib sets on sale, too. Frequently the store will have the headboard of the crib on view, with the mattress carefully stored in its box waiting to be taken home sight-unseen.

If you buy crib and mattress separately, make sure the two are the same size. And the way to do that is by measuring each, not by taking somebody's word for it. There should be as little play as possible between mattress and side—no more than the width of a finger or less. Once cribs are standardized by FDA regulations, this should not be of importance, except that manufacturers will be able to deviate from those standardizations so long as they supply a matching mattress. In this situation, if you fall in love with the crib, you're stuck with the mattress, and vice versa.

Frequently, buying a matching set will be cheaper than buying separately, but you may be paying for more accessories on the crib or more coils in the mattress than you deem necessary. Check into this.

NECESSITY #3: A PLAY PLACE

Some children live in a prison environment. When they are not in their slat-sided cribs, they're in their slat-sided playpens. Obviously, on those with bottom elevated above the floor, wide-slat spacing is a problem. But no more, we hope, since the proposed crib regulations will also cover wooden playpens, at least as far as the placing of the slats is concerned. But there are other factors to consider. The abacus arrangement of beads could be dangerous, and the floor collapsible, and the hinges protruding and sharp. These you'll have to check for yourself.

More popular—and dangerous—than the wooden playpen is the mesh one. The safest, a fine mesh one with a top, whose mesh looks more like veiling or mosquito netting, is castigated by psychologists who feel "a child might feel closed in in a box, segregated from people, uninvolved in the world around him." For these experts, the psychological drawbacks to the physically safest playpen available to us makes it mentally and emotionally unsafe.

The Product Safety Commission recognizes the validity of this kind of hazard in what looks like the ideal answer to playpenning. Therefore, playpen regulations will not be proposed in the near future. Thus, it's up to you to recognize the dangers and overcome them.

Playpen mesh comes in three kinds: the very fine, already discussed; one-half inch, which is a medium grade; and one inch or more, sometimes known as ladder net. Most playpens come in the medium grades, whose dangers are less obvious than the bigger mesh. For example, a finger could be caught and twisted in this mesh, a button caught and held, resulting, if it were a button on the back of the neck, in strangulation. Why do I say if? There are no ifs about it. It has happened. And children can use this net to climb—especially if they are not wearing shoes, which they shouldn't be.

The wide "ladder" mesh could possibly catch a button and cause a similar problem but its major hazard is its climbability.

In addition to basic materials, there are differences in overall design. For example, the wooden-slatted playpen comes in a square that folds up. The mesh designs can be oblong or circular. The oblong is designed specifically to fold up with the toys inside even, that is, if they're small. The circular folds, but clumsily and not with toys inside.

Speaking of toys, the slatted pen allows for the loss of them through the slats, with resulting wailing. A mother can spend a good part of her time retrieving the toys that are supposedly amusing her child so that she can get something done. The mesh rectangle keeps the toys in, but packs both toys and the young child into a corner. And its collapsible sides create a safety hazard, as well.

The circular playpen is not designed, like its oblong cousin, for packing up and going. It's a stationary type of playpen. The one you put in a room and leave there. It has no dead ends or corners to stifle a child, it has no slats through which to lose toys, and it has no easily accessible place to purchase it here in the U.S.A. It can be purchased, however—in a medium-to-fine net—in Canada, or from Mothercare, Cherry Tree Road, Watford WDS 5SH, England.

The round and the mesh rectangle cost approximately the same, although the round offers more square inches of actual playroom, while the square wooden ones cost about the same as an *extra*-large squarish mesh one, both of which cost more than any others.

NECESSITY ⅜4: A FORM OF TRANSPORTATION

An active child using the playpen is a ready candidate for a jumper-walker, or walker-bouncer, or whatever a particular manufacturer chooses to call his thing. These are so important to a child in today's physical fitness oriented society that your pediatrician, noting a child's physical development, may actually prescribe the purchase of one. Whether or not it would be considered tax deductible I don't know. But if wheelchairs are, why not rollingchairs?

The problem with walker-jumpers is that (a) they walk, and (b) they jump. Last things first. The jumping mechanism involves a spring—a coiled spring—that, in expanding, could allow a finger between its coils; in contracting, could pinch, destroy, or amputate a finger between its coils. Therefore, the springs should be enclosed in some form of tubing, or even a piece of discarded garden hose.

There's another hazard created as the coil expands and the metal frame of the seat is forced down. A finger caught between the seat frame and where it connects with the jumper base, a finger caught there can easily be amputated. So look for a one-half-inch or wider metal spacer that prevents the seat frame and base from making contact. It's good finger insurance.

In the four-legged walker, those with bumper guards around their legs to protect your furniture from the walker, there are no means of protecting the walker from the furniture. The child who goes one way, hooks a leg under a table, and then decides to go another way, can easily upset himself. Maybe even flip the table over.

Therefore, I do suggest you look into a walker that has its four legs connected by metal rods or tubing. In addition, it should be noted that the wider the base, the more stable the walker. The major problems with it are involved in the speeds these less-than-year-olds can build up: four to five miles per hour. When they are going full-tilt and hit a doorjamb or carpet, the result is instant disaster.

When buying any walker, check to see that the plastic seat is heavy, heavy plastic, securely fastened to the metal frame. If possible, the frame should be padded in front and in back. Spacers should be used to prevent any two pieces of metal from coming together and catching a finger. The tray in front should either be fixed in place or difficult to remove. Any gimmicks, such as bead strings, should be securely fastened. The bigger the casters on the bottom, the more stable the walker and the easier it will roll.

Now, I should like to speak my piece. Say it and get it over with. I can see the advantages of a child's having a walker. I see no advantages to having the walker bounce or jump or whatever else they want to call it. Between 90 and 100 percent of the built-in hazards involved with walker-jumpers come from the fact that they jump. What's wrong with a child's amusing himself by walking? Why does he have to jump or rock or bounce? Is he interested in mobility—which a walker gives him—or a rhythmic up and down motion his own legs can supply him? Add to the fact that the walker jumps, the fact that the walker jumps and folds, and you've empirically doubled the hazards involved . . . and the finger tips cut off and the fingers amputated. Enough said.

NECESSITY #5: SEATING UP HIGH

At a certain age a child needs, for the *mother's* sake, to be elevated to table height. This calls for a high chair. This calls for another piece of furniture designed not for the child's safety but for the mother's convenience: with nonprotruding, easily tipping legs, with vinyl-covered, washable though slippery cushions, with quick, flick-of-the-hand, easily fastened and unfastened trays, with lightweight, metal frames that, hurray!, even fold up.

Well, let me tell you that if *you* were forced to sit in that swaying Eiffel Tower of a chair, you'd quickly force the change of design in high chairs.

To say that today's high chairs are unbelievably unstable is to say that your child is incomparable to any other—both are absolute truths. Nothing is easier to tip over than a high chair, either backwards or to the side. With the tray in place, it is more difficult to tip it over forwards, but the family German shepherd can.

That nice sterile, easily cleanable metal tubing of which it's made fascinates children, especially when the tubing isn't capped. The child sticks his finger into the tubing that forms the arm of his chair. It fits, he's pleased, his mother doesn't notice. She reaches for him and lifts him out of the chair, ripping off the end or more of his finger. Oh, that nice sterile, easily cleanable metal tubing.

But don't blame it all on the tubing. After all, the child was the one interested in the hole, any hole, like the long slot on the arms of the chair where the tray gets enmeshed, also with a finger.

Let me put it this way, the way Elaine Besson of the Product Safety Commission does, "If there's a hole of any kind within the reach of little fingers, you have trouble for those little fingers."

Remember the wooden high chairs with the wooden trays that were hinged to the chair at the top of the rear of the seat? Clumsy they were when putting the tray over the child's head; and the tray didn't fasten into four positions, nor was the chair guaranteed machine washable, nor was it sterile. But it was one thing, one thing the others aren't. It was *safe!*

There wasn't any narrow, ready-to-be-outgrown seat. The seat on the old-fashioned chair was wide, with room for a toy or two. There weren't any slippery, easily washable plastic cushions to help your child slip down in front. The old-fashioned high chair was carved to fit a derriere. Let the child slump down on the seat and he was fixed in place, not ready to be impelled forward. The old wooden tray? Sure, you had to carry a sponge or dishcloth or paper towel to it, but it held a child's dinner and a plaything or three unlike any of these other trays do.

And you know, the funny thing of it all is that those nice, shiny, modern, hazard-filled high chairs are selling for real money (as much as a crib), while those old fuddy-duddy high chairs can be seen sitting sadly in secondhand shops and priced at less than one-half their more modern cousins.

When shopping for a highchair, stand back—way back—and take a look at it. You don't want a Washington Monument—a narrow pillar reaching for the sky—you want an Empire State Building with a broad base that may trip you once or twice but without overturning the chair. You need, your child needs, stability, and that comes from a big, broad base.

There's another type of high chair available. It's known by various names. What it is is a chair that uses physics to stay in place. It has two arms that clamp down on the table top and two legs that are wedged up against the table bottom. The combination keeps the chair in place, allowing the child to eat at a kitchen table just like everyone else.

There's no tray, no protruding chair feet (also no footrest), nothing but a chair. Great, isn't it? Except for one thing. The child that wiggles and fidgets and moves around? He can walk that chair right off the table and into disaster. Think about it.

Again, amidst all of the devices into which we strap our children to feed them, there's a gimmick one that bears investigating. It's an infant-seat that fastens onto a base to become a high chair. The cost is high, much more than standard high chairs. Yet the idea is stable as is the chair, and certainly worth looking into. And looking *for,* since the chair is new and not in wide distribution.

NECESSITY #6: A MOBILE SEAT

Before a child graduates to a high chair, he's bound to be placed in the newest, "most convenient thing ever" as one mother put it —the infant-seat. This is a molded plastic seat that today's mothers swear by. They put it in the tray area of a shopping cart. They use it as a miniature high chair for feeding baby. They strap it in the car with seat belts as a baby's car seat. (Not safe!) The baby who can't hold his head up likes it, too. He gets to see more of the world than he ordinarily could.

Before I go any further, I must admit that to me the infant-seat is the world's greatest invention, compared to which a jolly jumper or a walker-jumper or a rocking chair are mere piddlings of ideas.

But infant-seats are only as safe as the surface they're on. The problem stems from the fact that the child is not held immobile within the seat. He can jump and kick and knock it over for example, off the dryer and into the washing machine. He can kick and kick and "walk" it from the nice safe formica counter into the water-filled sink. The infant-seat on the floor is extremely safe. The trouble is that mothers don't put it on the floor. They put it up where height becomes a danger, and the active child a menace to himself.

Another problem is that manufacturers string beads or balls or other playthings across the front of the seat in an effort to—take your choice—amuse the children or busy the children. They mislead mothers into believing that a restraint is present. Not true. Only fastening the seat belt will keep the child securely in the seat.

Since I truly believe that the infant-seat has become a necessity, not a luxury, I am also pleased to know that the manufacturers of infant-seats are working on formulating standards themselves that will do away with the tip-slide-collapse-walkaway problems presently inherent in infant-seats. The only flaw in the ointment is that the standards will be voluntary. And you and I have been burned by that flame before. In clothing. In shoes. In cribs, etc. I hope that this time we're wrong.

If not, baby-proof the infant-seat yourself. Fasten the seat belt every time. Get rubber tubing, as close to the same size of the metal base as possible. Cut lengths of it, several short pieces are better than one long one, and slit them lengthwise so they'll fit over the wire back support and keep it from slipping. Also, there are rubber bases available for outdoor furniture that would be ideal for this.

NECESSITY ✕7: A PLACE FOR TOILETING

Sooner or later—and the later the easier for you, the child, and the actual doing—you will begin toilet-training your baby. For this you will need but two things for girls, a seat and a receptacle; for boys you will need to add a deflector if he is going to urinate sitting down. However, manufacturers offer you many, many variations on that pair. Basically, they boil down to three concepts: the potty chair, the training seat, and a combination of the two.

The potty chair. It has certain inherent advantages and disadvantages. To begin with, it is the right height. As many child-psychiatrists have pointed out, there is a definite physiological need for some children to have their feet planted firmly on the floor in order to "push" when having a bowel movement. The mothers of these children must either invest in a potty chair or delay toilet-training for a ridiculously long time. The major disadvantage of such a chair is the receptacle that comes with it: someone has to empty the pot and clean it.

The most expensive of these chairs is the all wood chair/potty chair: a dual-function chair (no pun intended). The seat lifts up to reveal a second seat with a hole in the middle. The idea here is that the child will use the chair for just plain sitting as well as necessary sitting. Aesthetics aside (I, for one, frown on potty chairs of any kind in the living room), the problem is that the child may get confused as to which seat is for which function. Or, he may refuse to use the chair for either purpose, which means you need to buy a second chair for that use. And, for boys, it means you have to be present each time he toilets so that you can attach the deflector; otherwise you have a floor to clean.

Almost as expensive is the folding wood potty chair, which has the obvious great advantage over its more solid, more expensive cousin—it is easy to lug around when you go visiting. It is not as rugged, though, and has been known to fold up at the wrong time.

The least expensive is the molded plastic chair with the receptacle molded in as part of the body. The only problem is you have to wash the whole thing, not just the receptacle.

The training seat. It's a seat that fits atop the toilet seat. But not all training seats fit all toilet seats, so check. Many mothers think it makes training easier since the child may have already made the connection, thanks to his mother and daddy's forethought, that adults use the toilet for their bodily functions.

But what about the child who's rendered incapable because of dangling feet? For him, there are training seats with footrests, and even training seats made to look like saddles complete with stirrups. (Saddling a toilet is almost as difficult as saddling a horse, so why not avoid the problem.)

The major advantage is that there's no pot to clean. The major disadvantage is that you have to be there to put the child on and take him off, otherwise nasty spills can occur, especially dismounting.

Things to look for when buying such a seat: no fancy deflectors (would you believe they come in such impaling shapes as swans, upturned beak and all?) that could injure a child when he's trying to get off; no deflectors that extend only above the seat—they should extend down into the toilet below the level of the regular toilet seat; and try to avoid plastic that isn't colorfast to urine. Yes, you heard me. Some of the cheaper plastic seats change color and turn mottled when exposed to urine. I suggest you check, but the method is strictly up to you.

The potty-chair/training-seat combination. If there can be said to be an "in" fashion in toilet-training, this is it. With such a chair, you can go either way. You can even find one that helps condition your child to toileting. It plays music whenever something lands within it. Which makes it almost something of a toy, doesn't it? You know it. And you may find it being used as such. What happens then when you try to make the switch from chair to toilet and the music stops?

Chapter 7

Environment Is Everything —Part Two: Options

The title of this chapter could well be "One Woman's Necessity Is Another's Luxury." For although some things, such as the crib, might be considered absolute necessities, others, such as the youth chair, are not. Here's one example:

The Changing Table
Nine out of ten purchased changing tables in the U.S.A. look the same. They have padded tops, swivel-out clothes trays, a "wicker look," compactibility, and just as many disadvantages:

(*a*) They are not inexpensive. A basic model costs close to $25. If the manufacturer adds a clip-on tray or a clothes rod, the price escalates. Depending on the durability of the pad, it may need replacing within a year or so—long before the next child needs one.

(*b*) They are not safe enough from the design standpoint. At least not the way so many are sold, with "security straps" that depend on mother's remembering to use them. And mothers don't, and mothers won't, and mothers shouldn't be forced to. Recognizing this, most of the makers of these tables do offer a guard rail attachment that will prevent roll-offs of young infants. The guard rails are something of a nuisance for the very reason that they are effective; they form a barrier between you and your infant. Many mothers don't like this, and the stores know it. Therefore, some don't even bother to mention the matching guard rail to the mother.

For example, the dressing table featured in the adorable "Lambs and Daisies" coordinated baby furniture in a typical Sears catalog is shown without guard rail, nor is one even offered. A further search of the catalog turns up two more changing tables, both of which have roll-off protection, but that fact isn't deemed worthy of mention in the description of one.

The catalog of Montgomery Ward, which has been active in supporting furniture-design changes for increased infant protection, offers two changing tables. One, shown in full color, has built-up sides to prevent roll-off. The one shown in black and white does not, nor is a guard rail offered for it. Interestingly enough, the difference in price between the one without and the one with guard rail plus a removable caddy tray is only $3. Aren't those three dollars a better investment than a trip to an emergency ward ($8 to $10) or a doctor ($5 to $10) or dentist or undertaker?

A search in local children's furniture shops will turn up more tables without roll-off protection than with. Plus a surprise—those *with* are often exactly the same price as those without.

(*c*) They are not safe from the point of view of use. The idea behind the swivel-out drawers is to bring the clothes within mother's easy reach. This is certainly true of the top one, but to use each lower drawer forces mother or baby-sitter to move farther and farther away from baby—and that's dangerous, as anyone who's handled a squirming baby knows.

(*d*) They are not convenient. All the stuff you need is either on the attachable, optional caddy or stacked on another piece of furniture somewhere. Where, for example, do you put the seven-dozen-high stack of diapers? Or how about the diaper pins? Oh, no, not into the vinyl pad—you're ruining its waterproofing.

Why, then, do mothers buy them? Because their other choices are limited. More expensive. Less convenient. Unsafe. In lieu of a changing table, stores will offer you a changing-table-topped chest of drawers. Sears and Ward's each has one or two in its catalog. Because the chest of drawers is a major, permanent furniture purchase, its price reflects it.

Unfortunately, pulling out drawers to get at clothes is as inconvenient as reaching into swivel drawers, but with a difference. It normally takes two hands to open a drawer. What happens to your ever-present, protective one-hand-on-junior-at-all-times policy then? It takes quite a reach, since you also have to step back to allow the drawer to open. Of course, this has the advantage that if junior rolls off he lands in the drawer.

And of all the padded-top changing-table-like chests of drawers I've seen, not one has had roll-off protection, just that quote security unquote strap. Understandably so. When you remove the pad to convert it back to a chest of drawers, who needs the roll-off protection?

Alternatives to Changing Tables

All you need is a padded surface, approximately 18"×36", which can be placed at the best height for you. With this you have the equivalent of the majority of ready-made changing areas. A safer bet of course is a padded area surrounded by a guard rail or a wooden fence. You can make it yourself or have it made. Baby furniture specialty stores can make them. Complete with guard rail and pad, and sized to fit a standard piece of furniture. The cost? Less than a sawbuck.

To use as a base? A sturdy card table, maybe. Stack baby's things between his pad and the wall, which keeps them within easy reach. When you lean over to get his clean gown, your body becomes his roll-off protection.

A secondhand buffet would let you put the baby in the middle, diapers at one end, supplies at the other. Everything is within easy reach of your hand without your bending over. You will find the various compartments and drawers in a buffet most handy for baby's things. When you are done with it, which might be as long as three years later, convert it back to its original purpose or sell it. Secondhand buffets don't depreciate very much. Or, you might buy a dry sink to use for changing. Unfinished is cheapest. The recessed area in the top has built-in, roll-off protection. The shelves above are ideal for baby's everyday needs. Underneath can go the big items like vaporizer and blankets. Years later, it makes a good-looking bar.

Consider building shelves, a wide one for changing baby, others up above. Having clothes stacked up where you can see them and reach them easily is most convenient of all.

For an unorthodox but perfectly good alternative to the fenced-in vinyl pad, use a soft, vinyl, portable baby bathtub. It's deep enough to be protective, it's soft enough to be safe, it's a handy thing to have around for bathing. This way, you amortize the cost by day-to-day use. Which brings up another subject.

Bathinettes/Bathtubs

The bathinette is a relic of fifty years ago. It's clumsy to fill and difficult to drain. It presents the problem of lifting baby out and putting this wet, slippery child somewhere else that's safe to dry and change. It is also too small to pay for itself before it's outgrown.

Skip the bathinette. Instead, consider one of the soft, soft vinyl bathtubs. Remember as you do that in the hospital nursery your son never received a real bath, only a sponge bath. If you feel leery about giving your baby a tub bath, don't bother to do so at least for the first six months. After all, you're washing his bottom every time he eliminates. You're washing his clothes every time they get damp. You're washing his face every time he drools or spits up.

What's left of this baby to get dirty? "His head!" some mothers will say, spouting dire warnings of cradle cap. Cradle cap has nothing to do with whether you wash your baby's head every day or once a week or once a month. It's a dermatological problem caused by seborrhea. It is treated—not cured—by applications of oil that loosen the crust. Soap and water won't do that.

Actually, the best place to bathe a baby is the kitchen sink. It's the easiest to fill and to empty. It does not require a separate investment the way other strictly-baby things do. It does have however, the same problems that the baby-tubs have—the problem of safety. Beware of turning on the wrong faucet. And hot water drips. Line the bottom with a diaper to prevent slipping.

The child's head must be supported by, if you're right-handed, having the child face you with his feet nearest your right hand. You reach under his head with your left hand and grab either the left shoulder or arm of the baby. In the process, you create a bridge behind his head that supports it.

You will notice that over and over again, I refer to your baby as he or him. I'm not a chauvinistic anything. I'm just a victim of convention. But the "he" business does remind me that any male child lowered into a pan or sink or tray of warm water should have a diaper draped over his penis. Otherwise the walls may receive a urine bath. Girls also have this tendency to eliminate when placed in water, but nowhere near as explosively.

Until now we've dealt with those items that could or could not be considered necessities. Now come the genuinely optional ones.

Portable Whatevers

This is the fold-it-up-take-it-with-you choice you must consider in light of your social and business obligations. In other words, if you must take your child with you to many places, you should invest in something to put him in when you get where you're going.

The rectangular mesh playpens will fold up easily and with the toys left inside. Unfortunately, most children do not associate a playpen with going to sleep. The result? A cranky child who wants to go to sleep but is told by his surroundings that he should play.

The portable crib-playpen-car-bed has many advocates. Including me, as long as there is money available for this extravagance. In a two-story house, the crib-playpen-car-bed can be used downstairs as an alternate crib, it can be used outdoors for an extra playpen, it can be used as crib or playpen or car-bed with proper adaptations on all those long turnpike trips in a station wagon.

Alternatives to portable beds. Place baby in center of a double bed, surround with bolsters and pillows. Then double-check frequently, the younger the child, the more frequent your checks. Or, spread a sheet on a carpeted, draft-free floor, let the child sleep there. It's not as comfortable as the bed, but 100 percent safer.

Alternatives to portable playpens. Place baby in a corner of the room where there are no electric outlets, create a barricade with folding chairs placed on their sides. Not fancy, not the best choice, but it works.

Alternative to the alternatives. Rent. Most of the rental places have cribs, portable cribs, baby carriages, play pens, strollers, etc. Their charges are minimal, and for an extended stay they become extremely inexpensive. And you will find renting infinitely more convenient than lugging a big crib around. Double-check such cribs for safety.

With all or none of those things, you are set for the first two years, or approximately thirty-five inches. By that time, the crib is outgrown and you face another choice.

Junior or Youth Furniture

A youth bed is a cot with removable sides, but only at the head of
the bed. It has two main advantages. First, it sits closer to the
floor so that a fall out of bed isn't too bad (and all children fall
out, partial sides or no sides). Second, if space is at a premium,
the bed takes less space in the room.

Disadvantages. The youth bed, too, is outgrown and will have to
be replaced, so a large element of optional expense is involved.
Especially since once the bed is outgrown it has no other use. It's
too low for a comfortable seating area, too short to be used as a
guest bed. If you use fitted sheets, they will have to be discarded,
along with mattress covers and protectors. As one man who
makes his living selling children's furniture said, "When it comes
to buying junior beds, don't."

Alternatives to youth beds. A standard bed without side guards is
the most practical, but falls will occur—you have to expect them.
(Side guards are a temporary help in preventing falls at the head
of the bed, not the foot; but once off, the falls begin.) The point is
that your child has to learn to stay on the bed, and learn it so well
that even in sleep when he rolls to one edge, he'll reverse himself
and roll back to the center.

Some doctors advocate putting babies into adult beds as early
as possible—at least by the time they can stand. The reasoning is
that cribs are unsafe. A fall from mattress height, they know, is
not as far nor as bad as a fall from the top of the crib rail.

Junior chair, or youth chair. This is the other typical junior piece
of furniture. It is a first cousin to the barstool with a low back. In
comparison to a high chair, it's shorter in height as the result of
lowering the back to eliminate unnecessary head support, and
dropping the seat closer to the floor. Its seat is wider, the footrest
lower in order to be in better proportion to the child's own measurements. And, of course, the youth chair has no tray.

Some high chairs convert to youth chairs—but not very successfully. That's because in attempting to design something to fit both
a baby and a child, with their different trunk/leg-length propor-
tions, you get mishmash. If you're determined to have a youth

chair, may I suggest you look into the one offered by IKEA of Sweden (address: S343 00 Aimhult, Sweden). They'll send you their catalog on request, which is in Swedish. However, ask for a translation of the description of the youth chair.

What purpose does the youth chair serve? They're too high to use in place of a dining-room chair, they're too uncomfortable to use as a sit-and-play type of chair. But children know they're good for using to climb up to the candy cupboard. And they are just the right height to allow a child to see what's happening in the sink or on the range. And curiosity combined with convenience spells trouble.

Alternatives to youth chairs. A bar stool, a kitchen stool, a step stool. If they're going to use it as a ladder, why not you? Look for these at secondhand stores, etc. Remember though that without rungs or steps, the child can't safely climb up into it himself . . . and that a swivel seat, which might seem fun, might just fling him into trouble.

Toddler Chair

This is a chair so low that the child can sit with his feet resting on the ground. The traditional one is the wooden rocking chair. These have inherent dangers because of the rockers. Too violent rocking will tip them over.

If I were asked to name the most useful, most inexpensive, optional item I own, it would be a toss-up between the walker (because of the delight it gives its user in terms of freedom of movement) and a *wicker* toddler chair—it's lightweight and movable, it's versatile, it's washable. At our house it has even been hooked on to the back of a tricycle and used as a pedi-cab. It has also gone outside next to the sand tire, and it has gone upstairs to sit on when mother types. And it's done all of these things with junior-manpower, not mother-power. Its cost? About $4 in 1973.

Besides the child-size chair for baby, you'll need an adult-size chair for you.

Mother Chair

Whether breast- or bottle-feeding, you'll need a comfortable chair to do it in. There should be good support for your back, arms at the right height to comfortably rest your elbow as you support the weight of your baby. The height from seat to floor should be such that you don't find yourself sitting tippy-toed to keep your lap at the right height to support your baby. If breast-feeding, the back should be more upright than is necessary for bottle-feeding.

Traditionally, the answer to this situation is a rocking chair. Rocking chairs, however, can come dear—as costly as your crib. Therefore, unless you are already a confirmed rocker enthusiast or can find an old one secondhand, investigate other possibilities. A captain's chair, a dining-room chair, a chaise longue even. Whatever your choice, look upon it as a possible addition to your whole household, not just a nursery item. And comfort plus utility for two people is your new criterion.

One more thing. Some babies do not like to be rocked. At least, not in rocking chairs. Although the motion of the rocking chair is supposed to be duplicating the motion he has known in the womb, it isn't. Instead of being rocked back and forth as he was in utero, you're holding him sideways. Which is why pacing the floor with him held to your shoulder may seem much more comforting. When your feet give out, try sitting down cradling him in your arms, and then swaying from side to side. It works. And you don't need a rocking chair to do it. Just a plain, old, ordinary, everyday kind of chair. Alongside that chair you will need something on which to keep feeding needs.

Table

If you happen to have an end table at the same height or higher than the arm of your chair, fine. Otherwise, consider a card table . . . use a chest of drawers as a table . . . put up a shelf . . . utilize your changing table . . . employ a desk. A bookcase or toy chest used as a table now will be of use later for storing stuff. Look around, see what you already have that can be pressed into service. A plant stand, perhaps.

The size of your table will limit what you can put on it. Here are some possibilities:

Radio

A two-o'clock feeding seems shorter and less tiring when you have a radio keeping you company. And a radio can keep your child company. We kept one going twenty-four hours a day on low volume, and the baby loved it. He was constantly bathed in sound as he had been in the womb. The music was relaxing, the voices reassuring, and other household sounds seemed muted and less alarming. The cost? Only pennies a day for an electric radio. A transistor-battery-operated one might cost more, depending on the size and cost of its batteries.

Tissues
To clean up spitups. A cloth diaper will do fine; disposable diapers will not, they're too awkward to use.

Lamp
If a musical lamp is chosen, find one that can be wound up with one hand—that's all you'll have free for the first nine months. Turning it on must be easy, too. Groping for a pull chain can be a nuisance. Easy cleanability is a factor, also—especially in an allergic child's room. The lamp should be bright enough for you to be able to read medicine labels by, for example. Which means it's too bright to use as a night light.

Night Light
I consider one of these an absolute necessity, but for me—not the baby. We kept one going all night so that I could see how the baby was doing without turning on lights or stumbling over my own feet. You can buy one that fits in an outlet—or make one by using a porcelain receptacle, available at all hardware stores, and wiring it. No switch is needed, although one is nice. Try a cool, soothing 25-watt blue light. It's not as bright as the clear, nor as eerie as other colors. If you have a hangup on pink for a girl, try a pink bulb.

There are two other advantages to using a night light. One, the child does not become as sensitized to exterior contrasts of light, i.e., he doesn't wake up at the first crack of dawn, therefore, you don't wake up. Two, he doesn't object as much to going to bed when it's light outside.

As far as fear of the dark is concerned, I consider it a legitimate one; that is to say, a normal one. And one that is easily cured by leaving the light on. I only wish other problems were so easily solved at the cost of about one penny a night.

Solutions to Outgrowing the Growing-Up Furniture

There is nothing anyone can do about that except design furniture that grows. Montgomery Ward, for example, offers a "Grow-Up Crib." For under $100, not including sales tax or shipping charges, you can get a crib, toddler bed with open-up gate, junior bed, and adult-type Hollywood bed—all in one. The problem is that if your child is destined to be more than a five-footer, you will still have to replace the bed.

ADULT FURNITURE

At one time or another (it could be as early as eighteen months— or as late as five years), your child will outgrow his crib and need a new place to sleep. If you have gone the youth-bed route, you can postpone your decisions on adult furniture for several years. Eventually, however, his or her feet will hang over the ends of the bed; and, Li'l Abner not withstanding, that's uncomfortable.

If you prefer not to make an investment in substantial furniture before the child is into puberty and expressing ideas of his or her own, you can make do.

Make-do Bed

Don't stint on the mattress and box spring, they are important healthwise. Do invest the less than $10 needed to get a frame that will keep the mattress and box spring off the floor and allow you to move the bed when cleaning. Do forgo the unnecessary expense of the spiffy-looking headboard with matching night tables. Do consider painting a "headboard" on the wall or mounting a long cushion at head-height for your child when he is reading in bed.

Make-do Dresser

Any three- or four-drawer chest will do, even a steamer trunk could be the answer. The thing is to look for one that can be used elsewhere in your house later. If you decide to buy a *good* dresser (not necessarily a bedroom type), protect the top with a piece of linoleum, plywood, or carpeting. That chest will be putting in some rough years, and the top is where that wear and tear will show.

Make-do Desk
Buy two filing cabinets and mount a piece of plywood on top of them. A shelf that folds down from the wall is another solution.

Make-do Not for You?
Then, try the secondhand and Salvation Army stores. The pickings are usually pretty slim. And those great "finds" you see pictured in magazines aren't as easy to find as you might believe; that's because most secondhand stores deal in schlock "modern" furniture. But it's worth a try.

Used Not for You?
Then go for unfinished furniture with plain lines. If you can afford it, buy two beds in preparation for the days when your child has overnight guests.

Chapter 8
Cuphooks and Barricades

This will not be a long chapter. Its purpose is contained in these statistics for a recent year: 26,500 deaths, 4 million injuries, $1.9 billion in losses. All these the result of home injuries.

Your child is going to fall, and fall, and fall some more. It happens, it's part of growing up, it cannot be completely circumvented. It *can* be made as safe as possible. Example: learning to ride a tricycle will result inevitably in falls because the trikes are designed wrong; but such falls are less injurious if they occur on a carpeted floor and not on a concrete patio.

The worst common falls occur on steps. Thus, an investment in some sort of barricade at the top of the stairs is wise. Then, after a fall knocks a tooth loose, you will discover, as I did, that a barricade at the bottom of the stairs is equally wise.

What kind of barricades? You could rig up your own, but you probably won't. Instead, you'll invest, and wisely, in a ready-made gate. Either the traditional folding one that is hooked to the door frame in a semipermanent installation. Or a portable one that locks into place with a pressure bar.

Consumers Report, in January 1973, did a complete rating of twenty-six different safety gates. They found all twenty-six to be acceptable, some more so than others. They found great variations not only in style, but in price. Even variations in price for the same gate at different stores. I suggest you take a look at the ratings before buying a gate. I have used both kinds and found that neither did a 100 percent effective job.

The portable sliding gate (the mesh type that Consumers Union recommends for first consideration) was viewed not as something to look through, nor as a barricade to keep one from going through, but as a short wall. One to be climbed over.

And the child who could climb out of a crib with his feet enclosed in a sleeping blanket had no difficulty going over the top of the gate. Fortunately, that gate was at the bottom of the stairs at the time.

Our experience was that the portable gates were a nuisance to open and close because it took two hands to do so. Thus, a trip to another floor meant putting things down, opening the gate, moving our burdens, closing the gate. Then repeating the whole business at the other end of the stairs. Well, you know as well as I do how long that lasted. Over the top we went, too. And that could easily have meant a serious fall for one of us.

The permanent folding gate which needs but one hand to work, and looks like a picket fence, did not encourage climbing over by either generation of Bennings. But it's not perfect either. For one thing it makes a terrible racket at 6 A.M. when shaken by a determined toddler. For another, its openness encourages the throwing of toys through it for mother to retrieve, over and over again. Worse than that, the same openness when combined with its pliability can result in the painful pinching of little hands and fingers.

Then, there's the installation of it. In plaster walls, the screws make large, unsightly holes; with dry walls, special molly bolts have to be used to secure the screws. Combine either with a rental home, and this may rule out the possibility of using a permanent folding gate.

Windows

Less common but more serious falls occur from heights: from trees and countertops and second-floor windows, to name a few. A child is much like a cat—he can go up almost anything. It's the coming down that's a problem.

Now, obviously you can't cut down all the trees on your property, nor board up your countertops—those call for a wary eye on the child. But you can do something about windows. During the winter, storm windows should be securely fastened, the windows themselves locked. In warm weather, when a breeze is desired, open your window from the top.

Other potential dangers can only be spotted from a child's point of view. And I mean that literally. Crawling around on all fours is undignified, uncomfortable, and enormously effective. Things to look for:

Electrical Outlets

Children love to put things in holes. Putting things in outlets is even more fun since not everything will fit. That's a challenge, and one few children will refuse, even three- and four-year-olds. What to do? You can buy little covers that will fit over the outlets and keep them inaccessible to your little one. You can teach him that outlets are no-no's by telling him they're HOT. (Did you know that the first word after *ma-ma* and *da-da* is usually *hot?*) And you learn to come running when things are quiet.

Electrical Cords

A dangling cord calls for immediate action on your child's part: a tug. And down comes your favorite lamp. What to do? Well, if your favorite lamp has a breakable base, exile it to safer territories. Otherwise, eliminate all unnecessary lamp cords, radio cords, stereo cords. The necessary ones must be hidden to some degree behind more solid pieces of furniture.

Rugs

As you are crawling around, do you feel anything giving underneath? The throw rug that moves under you will give under your child. It should be anchored down by means of undermats or tackings or special sprays.

Ashtrays

Everything at your eye level is game for your child. Ashtrays particularly since they offer the opportunity to mess. The best solution is the hard one: quit smoking, something that if done before the fifth month of pregnancy can prevent premature birth as well as increase the baby's birth weight.

Can't give up smoking? Then give up convenient ashtrays. Find an unbreakable ashtray of some sort and carry it about with you.

Decorations

Ornaments, statues, whatever. If you value the item, you won't put it down within the reach of your child for the first four years of his life. Then do it with trepidation. I suggest this for the sake of: first, the safety of your belongings—having a child should not be a material punishment; second, your temper—having prized possessions broken does not make for sweetness and light; third, your child's personality—at this stage in his life, covering the first four years, he doesn't know what break means. He breaks not out of orneriness or carelessness but out of a desire to learn and to create; these qualities are to be cultivated, not discouraged.

THE KITCHEN IS NO-MAN'S-LAND . . . . NOR CHILD'S

The kitchen is one great big booby trap for youngsters. There are a few changes you can make that will do a bit, just a bit, to protect your child. Only constant surveillance plus the ESP every mother develops will be 99 percent effective—the other 1 percent will escape you.

Range

Teach "hot" by letting the child touch the normally poorly insulated oven door (after testing for too hot yourself). Buy a range with controls on the same level as the cooking surfaces or behind them, never down on the front of the range where curious hands might find them.

Teach yourself, condition yourself, talk yourself into always turning skillet, pan, or pot handles back away from the front of the range. Thus, a curious, growing hand can't grab disaster.

Keep the child away from the range when frying or broiling for fear of splattering grease or when opening the oven door, which could allow scalding steam to escape.

Refrigerator

The refrigerator is the safest of the appliances in the kitchen—when operating. When disconnected, it's a killer unless the door is padlocked or roped shut. Your working refrigerator is quite safe—because a blast of cold air will hit the child when the door is open, and closing the door against such a push of air from within takes more muscle than one arm of a toddler can provide. So, few if any fingers can get caught with both hands pushing the door, especially since it has its own rubberlike edging.

Freezer

With the freezer the same is true, but less danger is involved than with the refrigerator since there is less incentive to go into it. Fortunately, the upright freezer and refrigerator do not have doors that swing shut automatically. Not true of the chest freezer. A child in search of ice cream may not be able to open the door high enough to lock it upright and prevent it from falling back down upon him. This could topple the child into the freezer or inflict a serious injury, even a broken back.

Sink

The sink is hazardous primarily because of what's in it—like knives or dishwater. Even empty, it still affords easy access to a good scalding with hot water. Problems like this can only be noted —and solved by vigilance.

Dishwasher

The dishwasher is frequently a source of great pleasure to children; the cycle dial of ours has been played with by several children, who feel important working the control of an adult machine. But from the point of view of the child's safety, the advantage of a dishwasher is that the door on the front-loading models would have to be pulled shut from inside, and most models do not offer the right handholds. On top-loading models, however, you have the same problem that you do with chest freezers.

THE MAJOR PROBLEM WITH ALL OF THESE APPLIANCES IS NOT IN THE FACT THAT THEY ARE PER SE DANGEROUS EITHER BY ACCIDENT OR UNKNOWING DESIGN. THE PROBLEM IS THAT YOU USE THESE APPLIANCES DAY AFTER DAY, TIME AFTER TIME. THE CHILD WHO LEARNS BY IMITATION—IS THERE ANOTHER WAY?—IS AUTOMATICALLY EXPOSED TO APPLIANCE HAZARDS, BEWARE! BE VIGILANT!

Cabinets and Counters

In themselves cabinets and counters are harmless. Their dangers lie, literally, in what is within them: the drawer of knives . . . the medicine cabinet that is also being used as a candy cupboard . . . the household cleaners under the sink. These are the common causes of problems with young children in the kitchen. Rearranging your kitchen materials is one answer; the other is to remove all sharp, pointed, caustic, and poisonous substances from within reach of the child on the floor or up on a chair or step stool.

Do as much of this as you possibly can. Otherwise resort to some sort of locks. Special baby-proof cupboard locks are on the market, but they're expensive. Combination-type padlocks are another answer. The cheapest uses a key, a key hung on a cup-hook-way, way up in a cabinet—and seldom if ever put in place while the child is watching.

Speaking of cuphooks, these are the cheapest hangers in the world. They put things up high—and with children, UP is the keyword.

Cuphooks to the Rescue
Keys. House keys, car keys, tractor keys, jewelry-box, any ring of keys needs to be hung from cuphooks. Scissors—kitchen, yours, baby's—they all can be hung safely out of the way on cuphooks. Diaper pins are never lost completely when you hang some spares from a convenient cuphook. That extra pacifier, in case you have a sucking addict, hangs conveniently from a cuphook.

Use your imagination. Mother is the necessity of invention, or something like that.

ACCIDENT PREVENTION FOR CHILDREN*
(*Chart does not read across*)

• Typical Accidents (in order of frequency)	Behavioral Pitfalls	Precautions
FIRST YEAR		
Inhalation of food or foreign objects.	After several months of age, can squirm and roll.	Do not leave alone on tables, sofas, etc., from which falls can occur.
Motor vehicles	Later creeps and can pull self erect.	Keep small objects,
Burns		harmful substances,
Falls	Puts anything in	and all "hard" food
Drowning	mouth.	—peanuts, carrots—
Poisoning	Helpless in water.	out of reach.
		Do not leave alone in

• *Typical Accidents (in order of frequency)*	*Behavioral Pitfalls*	*Precautions*
		a tub of water; check water temperature before bathing. Provide with proven adequate restraint in automobiles.
	SECOND YEAR	
Motor vehicles Burns Drowning Inhalation of food or Poisoning Falls	Able to roam about in erect posture. Goes up and down stairs. Has great curiosity. Puts almost everything in mouth. Helpless in water.	Use gates to block off stairs and unsafe areas such as workshops, kitchen. Put caps on unused electrical outlets, keep electrical cords out of reach. Keep screens in windows. Keep medicines and household poisons under lock; all sharp or small ingestible objects out of reach. Keep handles of pots and pans on stove out of reach, and containers of hot food away from table edge. Provide with proven adequate restraint in automobiles.
	TWO TO FOUR YEARS	
Motor vehicles Burns Drowning Poisoning Falls	Able to open doors. Runs and climbs. Can ride tricycle. Investigates closets and drawers. Plays with mechanical gadgets. Can throw ball and other objects.	Begin firm safety teaching at home, out walking and in the car; be a good example and be tough; don't let up until they're grown. Keep screens or guards in windows.

• *Typical Accidents* (*in order of frequency*)	*Behavioral Pitfalls*	*Precautions*
		Keep knives, electrical equipment out of reach.
		Prohibit firearms in house.
		Teach dangers of fire —keep matches out of reach, prohibit lighting stove burners unless done in parent's presence only.
		Teach risks of throwing objects, slamming doors, tieing things around neck, running into street after ball or pet, running with glass or metal objects in hand.
		Teach traffic safety; be firm about remaining in restricted areas and never crossing streets.
		Provide with proven adequate restraint in automobiles; refuse to start car until all in it are belted and have doors locked.

FIVE TO NINE YEARS		
Motor vehicles Drowning Burns Firearm missile Falls Poisoning	Daring and adventurous. Control over large muscles more advanced than control over small muscles. Has increasing interest in group play;	Teach techniques and safety rules for bicycling—restrict riding to safe areas. Encourage skills in swimming; prohibit swimming without adult supervision.

• *Typical Accidents* (*in order of frequency*)	*Behavioral Pitfalls*	*Precautions*
	often follows suggestions of playmates without making safety judgment.	Prohibit firearms in house; teach dangers. Provide with proven adequate restraint in automobiles; refuse to start car until all in it are belted and have doors locked.

TEN TO FOURTEEN YEARS

Motor vehicles Drowning Firearm missiles Industrial-type Burns Falls Poisoning	Need for strenuous physical activity. Plays in hazardous places until facilities for supervised, adequate recreation are provided. Need for approval of age-mates, leading to daring feats.	Have firm rules regarding where child can play, swim, or bicycle. Provide with proven adequate restraint in automobiles; refuse to start car until all in it are belted and have doors locked. Provide safe and acceptable facilities for play and social activities. If you cannot prohibit firearms in the house or their use, at least instruct in safety.

* By Thomas E. Shaffer, M.D., Professor of Pediatrics, Ohio State University. From Nelson-Vaughan-McKay: *Textbook of Pediatrics,* 9th Ed. [that's the big, fat book your baby doctor is always consulting]. Adapted from Thomas E. Shaffer, *Pediatric Clin. N. Amer.,* W. B. Saunders Company, Philadelphia, 1969.

Part 4

Medical

Medical costs vary wildly, depending on whether you have an accident-prone daredevil or a super-cautious watchful one . . . on whether you have an allergic baby or an impervious-to-everything one . . . on whether the normal germs are making the rounds, or if imported flus are on the scene.

However, you can figure that as a national average, $35 is spent per year per person for prescription and nonprescription drugs. Semiannual checkups will cost you around $15 per year. An only child's share of your health insurance will be $50 per year. In addition, during the first two years there will be more frequent visits and special inoculations and vaccinations to be given. Figure another $100 for that. Your medical total should be about 5 percent of the cost of raising a child.

What is not included, however, is the cost of bringing that child into the world. This can be substantial and does not include prenatal and postnatal charges (X-rays, routine tests, prescriptions, etc.). The costs of merely delivering a typical 1973 baby were:

Obstetrician . . . $225 and up (for routine delivery, no com-
plications).
Delivery room . . . $75 and up (includes use of labor room
and anesthesia).

Nursery charges . . . $15 and up (daily charge, for routine,
                              not premie care).

Hospital room . . . $65 and up (national average per day
                              charge, multiply by num-
                              ber of days in hospital).

Pediatrician . . . $25 and up (usually a flat fee for daily
                              visits, but could be a per-
                              day charge).

Circumcision . . . $15 and up (includes doctor and operat-
                              ing room charges).

Or $740 *minimum* for a five-day stay. If everything goes all
right, of course. For nonroutine delivery, the costs are much
higher. For example, in 1970, Blue Cross/Blue Shield in their
magazine *Perspective* detailed a $1,541 charge for a Caesarian de-
livery of a girl (no circumcision fees included). And they
predicted bills of as much as $2,500 for the care of a premie. And
the sky's the limit for either C-section or premie care in hospitals
in New York and California, where hospital charges are already
over $100 a day for the mother alone. Hopefully, your health-in-
surance carrier will be picking up those bills, either in full, or a
substantial part of them.

But what about the child whose delivery is normal but nothing
else is? If you do not have major medical insurance and expect a
baby or already have a young child, get some. It could be the only
thing between you and financial disaster in terms of raising the
child in need of either immediate or years of extensive medical
care.

Chapter 9

Wanted:
One Mommy Doctor,
One Baby Doctor

The mommy doctor and the baby doctor usually are not the same.

THE MOMMY DOCTOR

He or she is either an obstetrician-gynecologist who may specialize in either obstetrics or gynecology but can do both, or a general practitioner, who may be harder to find than the OBGYN.

Does it make any difference what kind of doctor you choose? Not for the normal woman who goes through a normal pregnancy and normal delivery—and has a normal baby—but for everybody else, it could.

The *obstetrician-gynecologist* who specializes in obstetrics (prenatal, birth, and postnatal care) is the most experienced of the doctors in this field because he does but one thing: delivers babies. He's seen everything, he's done everything, and so he sometimes may seem somewhat blasé. You'll walk into his waiting room and find a dozen women in a dozen different degrees of pregnancy. If he's one of the top OB's at a large hospital, you might see as many as three dozen women—again every one pregnant. And it's not at all unusual on your part to wonder if you're just a name and a chart and a bulging tummy to this man rather than a real, live person going through something new and exciting.

Let's face it, that can be traumatic. However, as your time nears, he becomes more approachable. You may even wake the night after delivery to find him checking in on you just in case.

So what do you get in return for joining what seems at first like a mass-production line of baby producers? Experience. A man (or woman, of course) who really knows his business and yours. A man who isn't going to have to stop and check a textbook when faced with whatever rare problem you decide to come up with. A man who is not apt to decide you are a high-risk patient and shuttle you off to another, more experienced man.

With the *obstetrician-gynecologist* who specializes in gynecology, the difference is evident when you walk into the waiting room. You will probably see a dozen women, many of whom are not even a wee bit pregnant. It rather boosts your ego a bit to note their knowing glances and smiling looks. They are there for birth-control devices, menstrual problems, Pap tests, and so on, not for prenatal care. Actually this man has the same training as his obstetrical friend, but may not have as much experience in actual delivery.

On the other hand, long after this baby is born, you'll be needing a gynecologist, so when you choose the dual-purpose man, you may solve two problems at once: You get your baby delivered and your future feminine needs taken care of all by the same doctor.

The great advantage of *the general practitioner* may also be his greatest disadvantage. He takes care of you before the baby's born, delivers the baby, then takes care of both you and the baby as the baby grows up. And he'll treat your husband's poison ivy at the same time. That's fine. But remember, because he is so versatile, he probably has less experience in any given area than a specialist in that area.

If you have a difficult pregnancy, chances are your GP will call in an OB-GYN for consultation. The chances are also good that at some hospitals, the GP may not be permitted to deliver babies —surgically or at all—that privilege being reserved for OB-GYN's. In which case, he may not actually deliver your baby himself.

The choice is yours. Just as nobody will know your baby as well as you do, so nobody knows what you will need from a doctor. Is it important to you, mentally and even spiritually, to put your trust in an all-knowing expert? Or is it more important that your doctor be able to call you by your first name without having to look at a chart? Then again, are you one of those people who want to visit a doctor and be treated for every little thing from dandruff to a plantar wart at one time?

On the other hand, does it make you feel more confident to know that your dandruff is being treated by a dermatologist while your own personal podiatrist (not to be confused with a pediatrician, or baby doctor) is whittling away at your warts? The better you know yourself, the better the choice you'll make. Go back and read those last few questions again. And answer them. Whatever your choice, it will prove the most economical for *you* in the long run if the doctor gives you confidence.

By the way, I have spoken to dozens and dozens of obstetricians. In each case, I have inquired about fees. How they're set, what factors influence them, etc. In not one case have I heard of an OB who wasn't willing to adjust his fees downward to fit the economics of the patient. Nor have any of the OB's I've talked to been able to give me the name of a doctor who wouldn't. So don't think you can't afford the doctor you want. You may very well be able to.

Once you've made your choice, what do you do? Look up "Babies" in the Yellow Pages? Well, that certainly is a starting point, but it doesn't work, nor does looking under Obstetrician-Gynecologist and expecting to find a $2'' \times 3''$ ad listing your man's qualifications. Doctors don't advertise—at least not that blatantly.

Turn to "Hospitals" instead. Take down the names of all hospitals within a thirty- to forty-five-minute driving time of your home. Call each and ask for the doctor-expert: the head maternity nurse or the nurse in charge of the delivery room. Ask her for the names of *three* obstetricians—do not ask for one name, nor for the "best" doctor! That she won't do, but the names she gives you will be those of the best doctors she knows. If you're interested in a specific type of doctor, one who supports natural childbirth or "conscious childbirth," say so.

If you really want the one who you can assume ought to be the very best—if the hospital is a teaching hospital—ask who is in charge of the obstetric service. This man should, by all odds, be the best available because he is supervising the interns and residents, as well as commenting on the capabilities of his peers. But again, if upon meeting this man, you don't like him, he may not be the *best* for you.

Another effective way to find a doctor is to ask your family doctor. If he simply reaches for a medical directory and jots down a few names from it, you have just as much chance of getting a good doctor by starting with the Yellow Pages. If he names names and gives reasons why, the odds are he knows the *right* doctor for you.

Now, if you want the very best, there's one more question to ask of the family M.D. (particularly if he's fairly young and has pictures of his family on his desk). Ask him if he would mind telling you who delivered his own children. If he entrusted his own wife to one particular man—and money wasn't the reason why (remember, doctors don't usually charge each other fees, they have what's known as "professional courtesy," or you-scratch-my-back-I'll-scratch-your-back)—then it must have been because that man was the best around.

Still a third way to find a good doctor is to check your local phone book for the Childbirth Education Association. If your town has a chapter, you're in luck. Among its members are experts on doctors, men and women in a position to evaluate the men and women who are delivering the babies where you live. Not only will they be able to give you a list of three or more names, but they will also have the time to talk to you and tailor the list to fit your needs and desires. Then, as a last resort, I'd ask my dentist, the pharmacist,* anybody but my best friend for a doctor's name.

Why not the latter? Because you can lose more best friends that way. Suppose your friend had an easy delivery, and you'll have to have a Caesarean section. Is she really in any position to judge the merits of her doctor as a surgeon? Of course not. And it may just be that as a surgeon her doctor is far from the best—then your abdomen's going to carry the scars of one lost friendship.

Besides, there are fad doctors. A woman who has real leadership ability can make one particular doctor *the* doctor of the year just by championing him to enough people. And if there's one thing you don't want, it's a doctor whose business comes from the puffery of nonexperts, even if they all are officers in the local gardening club.

---

* Actually, pharmacists can be very knowledgeable in this area. You could do worse than consult one—informally, of course—on such a matter.

Factors to Consider When Choosing a Mommy Doctor

Special likes/dislikes. If you have your own ideas about the birth of your baby, you may have to shop around until you find a doctor able or willing to go along with you. For example, if you want your baby in your room with you after birth, you will need to find a doctor who has operating privileges at a hospital with rooming-in facilities. That's a fairly easy one since you begin by finding the hospital with such facilities, then call their "doctor-expert," as has already been described. Other likes/dislikes present other problems.

Caesarean section. Caesarean section is the society way of having a baby, complete with bikini-cut (horizontal incision just above the pubic area). This is major surgery, surgery most doctors do not perform unless medically necessary. A preplanned, deliberate C-section is frowned upon—and so doctors charge more, much more for it.

Home delivery. Although it happens accidentally all the time, most doctors are unwilling to deliberately assist in home delivery because of potential dangers. Example, suppose you need a C-section and no operating facilities are available. Suppose the baby had difficulty breathing and no resuscitating facilities are available. Etcetera. Although this is the fad of the moment, home delivery takes real planning and the financial wherewithal to arrange to have doctor, nurse, pediatrician, emergency equipment and supplies on hand when the baby chooses to be delivered, say, at 3 A.M.

Natural childbirth. The term natural childbirth is used here to mean childbirth without the use of pain-killing drugs, as advocated by such best-selling books on pregnancy as Marjorie Karmel's *Thank You, Dr. Lamaze* (Doubleday, Dolphin) and Grantly Dick-Read's *Childbirth Without Fear* (Harper and Row, 1970). The reliance here is on exercises, techniques, and mental and physical conditioned reflexes that enable practitioners of this form of obstetrical delivery to give birth relatively, or even completely, painlessly. To experience natural childbirth, you need several things: determination and persistence on your part, especially when it comes to exercising; the support of your husband, who plays an important role before and during delivery; a willing doctor who is able to spend the time educating and working with you; the money to pay the higher fee such a doctor charges for a natural-childbirth patient as compared to his other patients, because the former take more of his time during pregnancy and delivery. PLUS: the physical ability to give birth naturally. The woman with a small pelvis may not be able to, nor the woman whose pelvis is normal, but whose baby's head is even larger. (It also helps to have a high pain threshold.) So, before you decide on this form of childbirth, get an evaluation of your body. Above all, do not look upon natural childbirth as some sort of trial, or as proof of your womanhood.

It is worth noting that the Drs. K. Jean Lennane and R. John Lennane, of England—the birthplace of natural childbirth—believe the natural-childbirth concept to be illogical and ineffective; instead, they recommend conscious childbirth.

Conscious childbirth. Conscious childbirth differs from natural childbirth in the sense that the use of pain-killers is not banned. For example, the Drs. Lennane suggest epidural analgesia. In other words, they knock your bottom out, not your head. The advocates of this form of delivery agree with the natural childbirth followers in that every woman, they feel, should be educated and prepared as to what will happen to her during delivery. They feel she should have at her disposal the means to deaden pain if she wishes it, and she should be awake to see the fulfillment of her nine-month pregnancy. Again, this educating takes time on the part of doctors and they charge accordingly. But more and more often, conscious childbirth is coupled with the use of nurse-midwives to reduce those fees. However, this is not a requirement of conscious childbirth; any doctor can do it in any hospital if he chooses.†

---

† If you cannot find such a doctor through normal channels, write to the International Childbirth Education Association, P.O. Box 5852, Milwaukee, Wisconsin 53220, or see if there is a local chapter near you.

Unconscious childbirth. Also known as knocked-out childbirth. This is still the overwhelming favorite method of childbirth—among cowards and noncowards alike! You won't have any trouble finding a doctor who will agree to this, but you may have trouble finding one who will keep his word (and when you find out that he won't, it's too late—the delivery's under way). Don't get me wrong. In 99 percent of those cases, the doctor is acting to your advantage or your baby's. That's because the anesthesia given to you to knock you out also can knock out the baby. That is dangerous. Thus the doctor who cares will put off giving you unconsciousness for as long as possible. That doesn't mean that he won't give drugs and medications to lessen the pain, including the epidural analgesia used for conscious childbirth. For unconscious childbirth, you will not be charged extra by the doctor, but rather by the hospital for medications, anesthesia, and the services of the anesthesiologist.

Induced childbirth, or delivery on schedule. This is a form of childbirth done usually for the convenience of the doctor, not the mother, except for movie stars and others with contracts or pressing engagements necessitating their knowing for sure the latest possible day the baby will come. Labor is initiated through drugs and can then take the form of conscious or unconscious childbirth; natural childbirth is usually ineffective here. If the doctor schedules your baby at his convenience, he does not charge extra for it. If at your convenience, he probably will, on whatever basis you are able to pay. In either case, you will have to pay extra for hospital charges.

What all this comes down to is: when you start dictating likes and dislikes to a doctor, you have the problem of finding one who will acquiesce, and you face the prospect of paying extra to have those desires catered to. See the next chapter for suggestions on avoiding or compensating for those extra charges.

Team Practice
A trend in obstetrics. It has great economical advantages to a doctor since his expenses are split with another doctor. Paying only 50 percent of a nurse's salary, for example, gives him the

latitude to adjust his fees down to some degree to meet your income, which is a financial advantage for you.

However, in other ways team practice is a mixed blessing. Take those special likes/dislikes we've just discussed. If you have one of those, you must find a *team* of doctors who will agree. You also face the prospect that the doctor who has worked with you and educated you in, say, natural childbirth—which demands empathy and trust between doctor and patient—will not be present at your delivery since it is his turn to hold office hours and his partner's to deliver babies.

Sometimes what you find is not a team of childbirthers, but a surgeon/baby-deliverer combination. Explanation: all obstetricians must, by training, be gynecologists, and all gynecologists must be obstetricians. Yet the functions are different. Some OB-GYN's prefer to do hysterectomies, terminate ectopic or tubal pregnancies, excise ovarian cysts, and perform tubal ligations, for example. Others prefer to deliver babies. Teamed up, the combination offers a complete service that will care for all your female-type conditions for the rest of your life. However, sometimes there are excellent reasons for a doctor having a preference for the gynecological or the obstetrical service. One might, for example, delight in operating—he could be quick to resort to Caesareans, and major surgery is always dangerous. Another may feel the opposite—he might delay doing a C-section until too late.

THE BABY DOCTOR

Of much greater importance to you than your choice of an obstetrician is your choice of pediatrician. For one thing, you deal with the former for less than a year, whereas you and your pediatrician will be working together for years and years. For another thing, the pediatrician begins with a handicap not faced by his obstetrical brother: new pediatric patients can't talk. Thus, the baby doctor needs to be a top-notch diagnostician and a detective to boot. He must work from clues, not facts. He must be cognizant of every possible thing that could go wrong anywhere in the child's body. He is the only medical specialist who specializes in everything.

The good pediatrician knows when a telephone diagnosis is as good as an office visit. He knows when the child should come to him, or he to the child, or the child to a hospital now, not tomorrow, and vice versa. These are major decisions that will be made over and over again in the years to come, major in terms of the health, even the life, of your child, not to mention your pocketbook. Speaking of which, remember that the most expensive office visit could be the one you didn't make when you should have.

How do you go about finding this paragon of the pediatric world? Frequently, your obstetrician will suggest one or more baby doctors for you. Other times, friends will do so. If I had to choose between the doctor recommended by doctors and the doctor recommended by friends, I'd choose the latter—just the opposite of how I'd choose my "mommy doctor."

Although your obstetrician is able to evaluate the pediatrician from a medical point of view, that's not enough. You need to know how a doctor acts under near-crisis, and supposedly-emergency-but-not-really conditions. Only the mother who has dealt with him will know this for sure.

And the greater your confidence in your friend, the better. Besides, friends can let you in on the best way to handle your doctor. For example, some doctors freeze if there's the slightest note of hysteria in a mother's voice when she calls. Other doctors feel that if a mother is calm and exhibiting no emotion, the situation does not deserve any emotion, i.e., it's almost under control.

The problem is that the pediatrician, unlike the obstetrician who has just delivered you, does not know *you*. He doesn't know whether you're habitually hysterical or preternaturally calm. And his job is complicated for him by the books you read. They tell you to remain calm, to not jump the gun and call your doctor at the slightest excuse. They tell you you may be the cause of the problem. As one doctor-author says, "When I meet the mother of a newborn baby, usually in the hospital nursery, I write down on my chart whether or not I expect the baby to develop colic. In other words, I make a prediction. I am correct many times." He would be even more correct if he wrote down colic on all charts, since it is estimated that 40 to 60 percent of *all* babies develop colic, even those with calm mothers.

Now you're hearing from this source and that that colic is the result of: overhandling, nervousness on the part of the mother, indecisiveness in handling, gingerliness in handling, improper feeding (breast or bottle), the mother, the mother, the mother. You can understand why a new mother will attempt to control her normal anxieties or fears when conversing with this strange man, her pediatrician. She's wrong to do so. One hundred percent wrong. If you're nervous, say so. If you're concerned, say so. If you're afraid, say so. Don't be afraid of acting like the typical new mother—nervous. If you feel something is worth calling the doctor about, it's worth explaining *why* it seems like a problem to you.

Let's get back to choosing this guru for your first mothering years. Perhaps you can't find a doctor through recommendations. (Be leery of "he's the one all of us go to," in other words, a fad pediatrician, which is even worse than a fad obstetrician, since the latter lasts only nine months, the former lasts up to twelve years.) Call your local medical society. They'll give you three or four names of doctors in your area.

Or, do what you did when you were looking for an obstetrician: call the doctor-experts at the hospital where you will be delivered. Speak to the nurse in charge of the Newborn nursery, ask for a list of pediatricians. You'll get three or four. If you want more, call the hospital again after the nurses have changed shifts. Again ask for the nurse in charge of the Newborn nursery and ask her for a list of pediatricians. If one doctor's name appears on both lists, you can be sure he's truly top-notch; if two doctors' names appear, they're probably very good; if all three names are the same, something's wrong. No two nurses agree completely on anything, especially doctors.

Gather together all the names you've been given, rate them for their physical proximity to you, and begin investigating them long *before* the baby is born.

And the way to do this is by interviewing them.

Stage One, Over the Telephone:

With what hospital(s) is he associated? If he is not associated with the hospital at which you will be delivered, a staff or consulting pediatrician will be called in to care for the baby to begin with. Thus, your carefully chosen pediatrician will not be there to perform hospital tests for such things as PKU, or phenylketonuria, the inability to properly dispose of a substance present naturally in some foods, which leads to mental retardation. Now, please, don't let me frighten you unnecessarily. In some states this test and others are done automatically, regardless of the pediatrician.

However, there are other problems with the newborn—and let's be realistic, the doctor who expects to care for a baby for three, five, ten, or more years is more apt to be genuinely, selfishly interested in your child than the man who knows that five days later another man will be in charge.

Thus, the consulting pediatrician will not spend the time with you explaining, discussing, advising you on problems you will face. This is especially true of breast-feeding. To breast-feed successfully you need the help not of your obstetrician, although he should be informed of your decision, but of your pediatrician. He is the one you will turn to for medical and even psychological help.

What are his office hours? His telephone hour? Obviously the man who keeps the most office hours is the most accessible after your baby is born. The man who takes a two-day (or worse, three-day weekend) is not as effective as the one who is available five and a half or six days a week regularly, and as many as seven days a week on occasion.

Does he have a telephone hour, that time each morning when any and every mother can call and be sure of reaching the doctor and getting advice? When is it? A 6:00 to 7:00 A.M. telephone hour can be great for the mother with an early-bird baby. But for the mother who is trying to indoctrinate her child into civilized habits, such as sleeping until 7:00 or 8:00, an early telephone hour is useless. I would say, as a rule of thumb, the later the telephone hour, the better for you. If there is a *real* emergency, you can always wake the doctor up. But if the child slept through the night successfully, he can last another hour or two until the doctor is available.

Would he welcome a visit from you to discuss your baby-to-be prior to delivery? If he would, make an appointment. If he wouldn't, scratch him from your list.

Note that of fourteen doctors I have talked to about this aspect of choosing a pediatrician, only one said he would charge for the visit. The others welcomed the chance to learn about the mother and have the mother learn about him.

Stage Two, In Person:

The first thing to do is assess the doctor's office. Is it close to the hospital at which you plan to be delivered? The closer it is, the more apt the doctor is to be available in case of hospital emergency, and to make use of hospital laboratory studies.

Where is the office located? In some cold, stark, sterile building where he pays high rent, or in his home, with the resulting built-in income-tax deductions? The patients pay the difference in higher fees and greater inconvenience. The pediatrician with an office in his home can be reached all hours by banging on his door and tossing pebbles at his windows. The pediatrician who operates like a business disappears after office hours. Yes, he may be more rested than the other; but a rested, unavailable doctor is totally useless while an unrested, available doctor at least gives you a fighting chance.

What does the office look like? Is it modern, plastic-furniture-filled, with a mere scattering of magazines for mothers? Then you can bet your bottom dollar that your treatment by this pediatrician or pediatricians—this type of office is typical of group practice—will also be modern, sterile, and no more explanatory and elucidating than he can manage. If the atmosphere at your pediatrician's office is that of a factory, then you can be assured that unless you protest loudly, vehemently, and often, you will be treated like a product of an assembly line. But the automation does not usually result in lower fees for you. Instead, the doctor is able to squeeze in more high-paying patients per day.

On the other hand, see if the office is designed with children in mind. There should be small, child-size chairs, a toy chest filled with toys for all ages, including those a child might use individually, and those several children might manage. And do not be concerned if the toys do not look sterilizable. Few diseases, if any, are transmitted purely by touch. Those that are will be transmitted regardless of the toys.

Assess his examination room. If he has strictly examination rooms, rather than a combination office-examination room, it may be that he is guessing at things, because he does not have a set of his medical books in every room. The doctor who operates such a setup is frequently a man who works by rote: at such and such an age such and such a shot should be given, such and such food should be eaten.

I have a confession to make. I questioned whether my good-natured, easygoing, relaxed pediatrician was really the one for me; so I made an appointment with another one, one who had been highly recommended by a doctor. Here's what happened: I walked in and a receptionist greeted me by filling out in triplicate a form that had as many spaces as an income-tax return and asked many of the same questions. One form was used for billing purposes, another for diagnostic comments for the doctor's records, and another for the mother to take home. Terrifically efficient, you must admit. Then after filling out this form, we were admitted to the examination room. The doctor arrived, examined the baby, and listened to my comments, which were concerned with allergies. He immediately changed the formula to another, non-cow's milk, one and then said that by such and such an age, my son should have been on such and such foods. On the way out, I had to pass the receptionist with her sign that said "MAKE CHECKS OUT TO ——— IF CASH IS NOT AVAILABLE." I felt like part of an automobile assembly line, and obviously I did not go back there. Watch out for these characters. Their chief concern is making money. If you feel as if you're part of a factory, forget the number of women in the waiting room and bail out. Pediatricians are not in that short supply.

Ask him some questions:

1. What is his attitude toward drugs and medications? If he's for them *"if necessary,"* rather than being for them or anti-them regardless, you can bet that what he does prescribe he believes is necessary.

2. What is his attitude toward antibiotics? Nurses will tell you that they themselves are against doctors who are quick to prescribe antibiotics, primarily because such medications can cause allergic reactions, destroy helpful, necessary bacteria, and can be resisted by bacteria after repeated use.

3. Ask him what he believes is the cause of colic? If he won't or can't say (which is how he should react), ask what will prevent colic? *Tip:* If the doctor tells you that breast-feeding prevents colic, you have a problem, since many a mother will tell you that

she breast-fed her baby and he developed colic, which didn't abate until she discontinued breast-feeding. No one knows why colic happens. We even see it among our litters of puppies. It is an interesting commentary on the research done to save babies that children live through colic today, whereas puppies seldom do; their deaths are known as the "fading-puppy syndrome."

4. Ask him whether he recommends breast- or bottle-feeding. After all, no matter which you do, you will need his help. I do not believe a doctor should show a *strong* bias either way, but if he does, it should be on the side of breast-feeding, since this will make him less money and take more of his time.

5. What is his belief about demand- versus schedule-feeding. Some doctors are more radical or more conservative than others. It's up to you to find one who fits your own radical or conservative beliefs. By the way, "radical" changes from day to day— fifty years ago a radical was one who demand-fed; today a radical is one who schedule-feeds. Obviously the weak baby cannot be allowed to exist on self-demand, nor can the big, fat, demanding baby be allowed to overfeed.

6. When does he believe in supplementing or adding solid food? The age at which children are introduced to solid food differs from as early as two weeks to as late as one year, depending on whom you ask. Unfortunately, too many doctors work by the calendar and say that by such and such an age, Junior should be eating such and such. Obviously this is untrue. The baby born two months premature is not the same three-month-old baby as the one born two weeks late. Yet the doctor, in terms of food supplementation, is classifying them as the same. Wise doctors will tell you to let the baby tell you when he's ready for solid food. This is good, this is right, but this is not, for the novice, 100 percent helpful since I don't know (and you probably don't know) how to tell when the baby is telling you he's ready for solid food. So ask for clues.

7. Ask what he thinks about weighing the baby daily. One of the signs of growth is obviously a weight gain. And as such it must not be ignored. And your doctor will, as a normal part of a physical, weigh your child. As he should. But you shouldn't be weighing the baby any more frequently than that. Don't buy the "fat baby is the healthy baby" idea. The child whose ribs are evident,

not obvious, is better off than the child who shows fat creases all over. If you have a choice, your doctor should lead you to a skinny baby rather than a fat baby. Your child will be better off later.

8. Ask your doctor how he treats diaper rash. He can prescribe special medications; he can tell you what to do diaperwise (which will always be switching from whatever you're doing to something else). Or he may suggest the open-air, complete-nudity treatment. Many doctors like it. Many mothers don't—especially indoors. Those mothers will tell you that the undiapered child, whether boy or girl, can saturate a room with urine without even trying.

9. How does he feel toward allergies? There are those doctors who are overaware of allergies, and those who pooh-pooh the whole thing. His attitude toward formula changing can give you a hint. Years ago the formula was changed at the first sign of an upset. Now, the pendulum has swung to the other extreme, and doctors will avoid changing the formula until absolutely necessary. Look for the happy medium.

10. What is his schedule for office visits and immunizations? See "An Ounce of Prevention," Chapter 12, for a typical schedule. If your doctor deviates from that schedule by any great degree, find out why. It is possible, of course, that a new vaccine may have been discovered. It is also possible that three visits over a two-month period instead of two will make him an extra X number of bucks.

Team Practice

Although team practice can be desirable with a mommy doctor, many mothers prefer the solo-practicing baby doctor. They figure he'll grow to know the baby and his mother better. Unfortunately, the tendency among doctors is for group practice.

The advantages of practicing in groups include shared expenses, personnel, and equipment along with more free time. In 1966, the solo practitioner put in 62 hours and saw 118 patients a week; a doctor in group practice put in 63 hours and saw 144 patients. Multiply those visits by the $7 average national fee and you'll see another advantage to group practices *to the doctor*. But not to the patients, since these doctors had 20 percent less time with the groupee.

Cost Factor

Although team-practicing produces more patients in fewer hours, you will not find the fees to be correspondingly lower.

To best handle the cost situation, note whether your doctor posts his fees. If he does so, copy them. You may find that his charges vary depending on the time of day he's called upon, or, if he makes house calls, how far away they are. Does he have a basic fee plus varying charges for shots, tests, etc.? Does he charge for telephone calls? All or just long ones?

If the fees aren't out in the open to be seen, ask for them.

Always check your bill, and if you have a question, speak up.

At what stage should you consider switching from your pediatrician to a family doctor? From a financial point of view, that depends on whether your family doctor is an internist or general practitioner. If he's a GP, he *might,* but only might be cheaper than the pediatrician. If he's an internist, you can bet your bottom dollar he'll cost you more than your pediatrician will. (Of all the medical specialties, pediatrics is the lowest paying.)

Except for the financial angle, there really is no great advantage to switching to a family doctor before your child has outgrown the chairs in the doctor's office. Most tall teen-agers feel uncomfortable going to a "baby" doctor, and that should be your cue to make the switch.

There are great advantages in sticking with a pediatrician through your son's or daughter's childhood. For one thing, he has a complete history of your child and his inoculations (many doctors will send out reminders that boosters are needed that particular year). For another, he'll be more cooperative about making out those medical forms you'll need for school.

Chapter 10

Oh, Those Doctor Bills!

And those hospital bills are doozies, too. But they're worth every cent if they save your life . . . or your baby's life . . . or prevent future pain for you . . . or prevent the 25-percent chance of a serious birth defect due to prolonged labor and oxygen starvation. Some experts say one birth in ten shows complications, and 3 percent of all births are so complicated that without *expert* medical care, death may occur to mother, child, or both.

And the woman who is in the greatest danger is the woman who has shown absolutely no signs of risk, the woman who is the prime candidate for less than expert medical care or even home delivery, the woman who is in her first pregnancy, since nothing is known about the type of baby she produces. And that is probably *YOU*.

However, you can benefit from some wise shopping for medical care for you and your baby.

DOCTOR BILLS FOR YOU

Your OB-GYN or GP

The most advantageous to you financially is the obstetrician who charges a flat fee that will cover all prenatal visits, your delivery regardless of method, and postpartum care of your reproductive system (including family-planning) for one year after delivery. With him you know just what you are going to spend, and can act accordingly.

Your next best choice is the obstetrician who charges a flat fee for all prenatal visits, your delivery if non-Caesarean, and specified postpartum care. The latter usually includes one or more visits at specified intervals after you have been discharged. With him, there is only one chance of a budget jolt—the cost of the C-section, for which he usually charges extra because medical-insurance carriers will pay extra for it. Be sure, if you do not have such insurance, that you inform him of this fact. He may forgo the extra fee.

Your third choice is the general practitioner who, although able to set a flat fee, may have to send you on to an obstetrician if your condition so warrants it. Nor will he be able to predict the costs of any surgery that might be necessary.

Your worst choice is the doctor, of any sort, who charges on a per-visit basis. This means it is to his advantage for you to come more frequently than you might have to, and to your economic but not medical benefit to go as few times as possible.

Alternative to the OB-GYN or GP: The Nurse-Midwife

I'm not talking about those old grannies that show up in horror films, I am talking about a new trend in medical care which involves specially trained, registered nurses working under the direct supervision of an obstetrician. These women can work for a hospital or a maternity center. After your initial visit with an obstetrician, the nurse-midwife supervises your follow-up visits. This has great advantages for you. For one thing, she can spend much, much more time with you than the normal doctor can. She will, in many cases, have gone through labor and delivery herself, experienced the discomforts of pregnancy, the frustrations of first motherhood. She can empathize, she can sympathize, she can advise from both a medical and a woman's point of view.

During labor, she will be with you for every second—and this is an enormous advantage over the cold labor rooms in some hospitals where you lie timing your contractions and listening to the sounds down the hall. The swearing and cursing is unbelievably virtuoso. The screaming is harrowing, the moaning frightening. It all makes you wonder about what is going to happen to you. But having someone with you helps. And not just a husband, who is, of course, great comfort, but not always allowed in hospitals. The nurse-midwife is prepared to handle all emergencies involved in a vaginal delivery and is an authority figure you can rely on and lean on. That's worth a lot.

And, for the time being at least, there is a great economic advantage to having the nurse-midwife in attendance. She, even when combined with the services of a staff obstetrician, costs much, much less than a doctor in private practice. It's a form of discrimination, but it works to your advantage. However, with the nurse-midwife you have to go to the hospital that offers her, and you have no choice of doctors.

Alternative to any Medical Supervision: Do-It-Yourself

Don't do it if you're very young, in your teens, or ancient by medical standards—in your thirties or over. Don't do it if you're poor or poorly educated. Don't do it if your mother had trouble bearing you or another sibling. Don't do it if you're addicted to any drugs. Don't do it if there's a chance you have syphilis or gonorrhea—these can affect the baby. Don't do it if there's a family history of diabetes or high blood pressure. Don't do it if you've ever miscarried or had a still birth. Don't do it because you're broke; if that is the case, call your local health department and ask for suggestions.

Alternative to Do-It-Yourself: Clinics

At a teaching hospital. Much of your care and even your delivery, if routine, will be handled by residents and interns under the supervision of instructors—the same men whom private patients are paying hundreds of dollars. If your delivery is not routine, you may be delivered by the most expensive man in the city—but your fee isn't the same as his private patients'. However, you will probably not see the same assistant twice—it makes care rather impersonal, and hard on you psychologically.

At a community or proprietary hospital. Either staff or private physicians will handle every aspect of your care, including delivery, and family planning.

Others. Sometimes using an out-patient clinic will result in your receiving a package deal, say, $300 for everything; prenatal care, delivery, postnatal, hospital costs, lab fees, etc. And by calling hospitals in your area, you may find some federally sponsored programs, handled cooperatively with your state health department. They will offer you all prenatal and postnatal care free (including baby-sitting, dental care, transportation to and from the clinic, the help of a social worker) as well as the services of an obstetrician free. All you pay are the hospital costs, which may be nominal.

HOSPITAL COSTS

Labor, Delivery, and Anesthesia

This is usually a flat charge and what you don't use, you still pay for. Example: The baby comes so fast that you are immediately wheeled into the delivery room upon entering the hospital—you still pay for the labor room since it's included in the flat charge.

However, in hospitals that do not charge such a flat fee, you can sometimes save by having your baby delivered in the labor room instead of the operating room. However, the charge for the labor room is so small, it is not to your advantage to try to time your arrival so that you go right into the delivery room. Babies just don't cooperate—they sometimes arrive too soon.

As for avoiding the anesthesia charge by electing natural childbirth, don't bother. Most hospitals insist on having an anesthesiologist on a standby basis for *all* deliveries. Frequently his standby fee is as high as the most expensive form of anesthesia he might provide. He is there not just for you, but for the one-in-four chance that a baby may need resuscitation of some sort.

An alternative to anesthesia is analgesias. Some, the minor ones, may be included in the hospital's flat fee. However, most hospitals charge for every pill they push and every medication they give. In this instance, avoiding an analgesia in favor of an anesthesia is a savings, but avoiding an anesthesia in favor of an analgesia will cost you money since you still pay for the standby anesthesiologist.

However, at some hospitals, your doctor can elect to do without the standby man, but you risk the chance that he may be caring for you at the time when your baby needs his attention, or vice versa. Talk this over with him on your first visit, and again near full-term, when he is in a better position to evaluate your condition.

Room Charges

The private room is the most expensive, and its cost is rarely covered in full by the health-insurance carriers. And requesting such a room is often a green light to the doctor who adjusts his fees to meet the patient's means—whether that's up or down. It also has certain disadvantages to the woman who might have a postdelivery hemorrhage, etc. There's no one else there to yell "Fire!" I, for one, owe my life to a roommate who went for help when I needed it and was unable to do so.

A private room is required if you choose to do rooming-in. However, at some hospitals this means that you will not pay a nursery charge. The savings (the difference between the rate for a private room as compared to a semiprivate plus nursery charge) could be as little as $6 a day or as much as $15 a day. In return for this savings you are totally in charge of your baby for twenty-four hours a day. An ex-nurse and a volunteer with our local Childbirth Education Association calls this "Dump rooming-in— They dump the child on you and you're on your own. If you don't know how to diaper a baby, there's no one there to show you. If the baby isn't nursing properly, you have no one to turn to. And you don't get your sleep." Is a savings of $6 a day worth it?

To rub salt in the wound, at some hospitals where "dump rooming-in" is the rule, there's no adjustment made in nursery charges. The hospital explains this by pointing out that they must maintain a nursery for those mothers who don't want or can't use rooming-in facilities. The patient who's had a Caesarean, for example, has undergone major surgery—she's in no position to oversee her baby twenty-four hours a day.

And for every woman who can't use such facilities, there are ten that don't want to use them. As one nurse put it, "The second time around it's not a thrill, it's work. Most mothers are more interested in a rest before getting back into the rat race."

At other hospitals, rooming-in is more flexible. The mother has the baby as much or as little of the day as she wishes, and she can use the central nursery as an alternative. Here, rooming-in can be a pleasure. But it is no less expensive than the old all-babies-in-the-nursery policy. This is, in a sense, unfair, since the hospital is getting some free labor from its patients, labor that needn't be paid union wages. However, it should also be pointed out that the obstetrical service of a hospital is not usually a money maker. It deliberately does not operate at 100-percent efficiency just in case a mother decides to deliver when the maternity ward is full. A margin for emergencies must be maintained. This usually means operating at about 70-percent capacity while being staffed for 100-percent capacity, which is expensive but for your benefit.

There's nothing like having your doctor decide you need to have a C-section, for example, when there's no operating room available. Maybe women can go through labor in hallways and deliver in labor rooms, but the place for operations is in the operating room, and the place for healthy mothers is in the maternity ward, not in a high-infection area elsewhere within the hospital.

Check-in, Check-out Times

Although you are not charged for the use of your labor room, delivery room, etc., by the *hour* (which would save money for the mother who pops her babies out and penalize the slow worker) you are charged by the *day*. It works like a hotel. If you check in before a certain arbitrary time, you will be charged for the previous day and the forthcoming day. If you check in ten minutes later, you would only be charged for the one day.

Explanation: Say your hospital's check-in time is noon. At 12:10, you get twenty-three hours and fifty minutes of attention for your first day's money. But the woman who checks in at 11:50 will be charged for those ten minutes before noon as if she'd been in the hospital for a full day. So, if your labor pains aren't close together, you can save $65 to $100 by delaying your entry to the hospital until after check-in time. In the same way, you should leave that hospital before noon to avoid being charged for an additional day.

Before you decide to check in later or check out early, be sure your hospital does things this way. Many are changing or adjusting their rates to avoid overcharging in a situation like this.

One way to save on room costs is to leave the hospital earlier. In the 1930s a hospital stay of seven to ten days, flat on your back, was the rule. Today the mean stay (including surgical deliveries) is four days, with more and more women going home on the third day. Some women would just as soon go home half an hour after delivering, but such an early departure does entail risk.

Another way to save is by checking your bill—CAREFULLY! Hospitals make mistakes, like everyone, and when questioned will either explain or adjust bills accordingly.

PEDIATRIC CARE

Once the baby is born and breathing, he becomes a patient in his own right. He may, in the case of a Caesarean delivery, which requires more attention for the mother from her obstetrician, even have his own doctor standing by awaiting his arrival into the world. In any event, he will have drops put in his eyes to eliminate any chance of infection of the eye due to gonorrheal infection of the birth canal.

He is then given an Apgar rating, in which his heart rate, respiratory effort, muscle tone, response to stimulation and color are rated 0, 1, or 2. If he was a Caesarean baby, he may be given a second Apgar rating within the next thirty minutes. All babies receiving a low score are given extra attention by the nursery staff.

In case of suspected Rh incompatibility, blood tests for that will be made from cord blood. If Rh incompatibility is found, the mother can be given a special medication that prevents development of sensitization within her for the Rh factor and eliminates the risk of potential brain damage for future babies. The medication is expensive, but worth it. In some states, on the third day, he will be tested for PKU (phenylketonuria) a disease associated with mental retardation, caused by impaired metabolism of the amino acid phyenylalanine. The PKU-baby's diet is carefully supervised to prevent mental retardation and/or seizures.

And then the baby is weighed and washed and his temperature taken. He will be seen every day by your pediatrician. Or a staff pediatrician if you don't have your own or haven't specified one or don't use one connected with this hospital. And each day the pediatrician will report to you and answer questions.

What will all this cost you?

First, you will be charged for every test made on your baby and for all medications administered.

Second, you will be charged either a per-day nursery charge (which can range from 20 percent to 50 percent or more of your own room rate) or a per-patient charge (that's in case you have "dump rooming-in").

Third, your pediatrician will charge you either a flat fee for in-hospital care or a per-day charge.

Fourth, if you elect in the case of a boy to have a circumcision done, you will have to pay for that (it's performed by your obstetrician, not your pediatrician).

EXTRAS

Lab Tests

Certain pregnancy lab studies are always done: blood-typing, hemoglobin count (either too much or too little as determined by a hematocrit) and Rh determination. In addition, the Pap test may be done, as well as serology and cultures. It is to your advantage to have all the tests done at one time and to pay one lump fee if possible.

You should also be aware that some of these, if not all, may have to be done again. In this case, if only the hemoglobin count is needed, there's no point in going through the whole blood study. Ask your doctor if a partial test might be done.

X-rays

X-rays may be necessary—TB testing, for example—that can be done less expensively through your local tuberculosis association, or similar group. Find out.

Ambulance

Ambulance, or stork service, as it's sometimes called, will bring with it another charge for you. If you use a local, volunteer ambulance service (which you join for a token fee), you may not have to pay for it if you're a member. If you're not, you should double-check to see if your insurance will pay for it. Sometimes they'll only pay for a hospital's own ambulance.

Financially speaking, in relation to transportation, you're better off to head for the hospital early, calling upon your local police department for an escort if necessary. But if you have to cross township or county lines, you may need to change police escorts. That gets a bit tricky. But it can be done. And you'll usually get good cooperation.

A WORD ABOUT CHOOSING A HOSPITAL

The safe hospital is the hospital that's always chock full of new mothers, the one that faces your special, one-of-a-kind, rare-with-a-capital-R crisis practically every day, and so knows what to do.

The most comfortable hospital is the hospital that is patient-oriented, that does things the way the mother and father want them, not the way the hospital staff wants them.

This is the hospital that believes a father is part of the birth process, and where he is allowed in the labor room as a matter of course, not special privilege. Where he is encouraged to be in the delivery room and, in the days that follow delivery, to help take care of his child.

Also, the good hospital treats mother as the intelligent being that she is. They know she wants to be educated as to what is going to happen to her, and they tell her what is happening to her in intelligent terms. She is encouraged to remain conscious during childbirth, but not to suffer in silence. Pain-killers should and would be given, but only so much, the latter in an effort to prevent fetal distress or depression. Rooming-in is made a flexible matter, a compromise between twenty-four-hour-a-day total care and only seeing the child at specified hours.

Almost all hospitals offer some of this. Others are more rigid, drawing the line, for example, at having the husband in the delivery room when things are not going smoothly. At the first sign of danger, he has to vamoose.

If I were you, I'd certainly at least investigate the family-centered hospital or maternity center.

One near me, for example, The Booth Maternity Center, has in its list of directions the following:

> 5. Enemas and shaving of pubic hair are not usually needed and are not routinely done.
> 6. Ambulation in early labor is encouraged unless contraindicated.
> 7. The expectant father will be provided with the appropriate clothing for labor. Once he has changed into his scrub suit he is restricted to the 2nd floor of the hospital. He must change to street clothes before leaving the 2nd floor.
> 8. Coffee and toast or crackers are available in the small kitchen

adjacent to the solarium. The nurse will help you prepare some refreshment when desired. Meals may be ordered from the nursing staff at a nominal cost.

Here's another service they offer:

After the first day post partum you may eat meals together with other patients in the solarium. Your husband may eat meals with you in your room or in the solarium at a nominal cost. Also at nominal cost, you may eat lunch or dinner with your husband and other children in the hospital dining room. Arrangements for the latter two plans should be made several hours in advance with the nursing staff. We regret that we do not have facilities to offer an invitation to other family members and friends.

And ask your husband if he'd be in favor of this:

Fathers are not visitors and may be with you and baby at any time from 9:00 A.M. to 9:00 P.M.

And do you know what their *total* bill is for all prenatal care, normal delivery (as opposed to Caesarean), postnatal care, three to five days of hospitalization, all pediatric care, laboratory tests, medications, including the services of a nurse-midwife—for all that, in 1973, you would pay $650.

Chapter 11

Stocking the Medicine Cabinet

In this day and age of fewer and fewer physicians for more and more patients, the mother of a newborn has to be part detective, part physician, part pioneer in order to guard the welfare of her child. She must be able to notice symptoms, record them accurately, relay them to her doctor. She must be able to take his instructions, record them completely, and follow them accurately. She must be able to improvise, jerry-rig, and make do when the drugstore is closed, her doctor out on a call, and her baby sick.

To do any and all of these, she needs the proper instruments. And that begins with a telephone, a friendly druggist, and a well-stocked medicine cabinet.

The telephone (or telephones). Next to each should be posted the pediatrician's number, the druggist's number, the nearest ambulance service and/or emergency ward, the poison-control center, a backup doctor, either the family doctor or even the obstetrician, or a pediatrician recommended by your own baby doctor. When emergencies happen, you should not have to thumb through phone books or rely on Information.

The druggist. Maybe you've been using the nearest cut-rate drugstore in the area. Now is the time to think of switching all your prescriptions over to the drugstore in the area which (*a*) delivers, (*b*) accepts charge accounts, (*c*) has an emergency night number. The last item is not as important as it may seem, however, since your pediatrician will normally have on hand all really necessary drugs that he might prescribe late at night. Or, you can call the local police department, explain your situation and they may be able to send you to an open drugstore or roust a nearby druggist out of bed.

The medicine cabinet. It could be your own, it could be a tray up on a shelf. Whatever you choose (and there are special babyproof medicine cabinets on the market), it must not be readily accessible to a child. Nor should you take any chances that accidents won't happen. If your child's medications are going to share your medicine cabinet, babyproof the contents of that medicine cabinet. See "An Ounce of Prevention," Chapter 12, for that; what we are interested in here is the contents of that cabinet—figuratively speaking—since, for example, a vaporizer obviously won't fit within the usual medicine cabinet.

INVENTORY OF A WELL-STOCKED
MEDICINE CABINET

These are the things to have on hand in case your doctor asks for them. If you live next door to a drugstore, you need not stock up on them. If you live two miles from a drugstore, have no car, and the baby's sick, you might be very happy to have spent the money on these items. Your pediatrician might disagree on certain of these items, so check the list with him. Items marked *** are ones for which you *must* get clearance from your doctor. The time to do all this could be while you are in the hospital and he's visiting you daily to report on your baby.

Cold-air vaporizer. The hot-water ones can make the room too uncomfortable for baby to sleep in. The cold-air one that you buy should be *big*. Big enough so that you do not need to keep refilling it every four, eight, or twelve hours. It should be big enough to run at least twenty-four hours without refilling.

The vaporizer should have some sort of safety feature that will enable it to go dry without burning up or out. You may even be able to find one that turns itself off automatically. You should be able to not only direct the vapor up and down and around, but you should be able to adjust the amount of vapor.

This is no place to stint. I know. I am on my second cold-air one, after having tried to save money by utilizing my hot-water one first, then buying a cheap one. A friend of mine who has given me generously of her own experiences as a mother of five has said that of all the many things made for children, the cold-air vaporizer is tops on her list.

Convertible ice bag, which can see double duty as a hot-water bottle. You may already have one. Just be sure it doesn't leak. Excellent for accidents. Use it cold to reduce swellings, warm for aches and pains.

Heating pad. Never use one with a baby, the cord is too dangerous; the controls may be set too high and child is unable to escape the pad; and there is always the chance that your child's urine will somehow penetrate the waterproof lining, with electrocution a distinct possibility. If you own a heating pad, put it somewhere out of sight and hopefully thus out of mind, so you'll never be tempted to use it with a child under the age of three. In fact, it is unwise to use it with a young child of any age.

Thermometers, oral and rectal. Don't buy; in this age of disposables, hospitals find it cheaper to use a new thermometer for every patient. When you check out, your oral thermometer is thrown out. So is your baby's rectal one. You can have them for the asking. Study the two so you know which is which—using an oral thermometer rectally can be dangerous. The reverse, although offensive to the fastidious, can be done. The oral thermometer has a long slender bulb designed so that it will register more quickly than the rectal one, which has a short, round bulb so designed to prevent possible puncturing of the rectal wall.

The rectal thermometer will do its work within a minute, coming within one degree of accuracy. Actually it takes less than half a minute to register 101° of a 102° fever, for example. Thus, with a squirmer, you will get a fairly good indication within seconds, and you need not fight your heir.

Be sure when reporting a temperature to your doctor that you tell him whether it's rectal (which will be higher than the others), oral (which is the lowest), or axillary (which is in between).

The oral thermometer should not be used on a child much younger than three. That's because (*a*) he's apt to bite the end off, which is dangerous, and (*b*) you have to make him sit too long (about three minutes) with his mouth closed. That's a fight. Better to use the oral thermometer in the armpit, closing the bulb between arm and chest, and get an axillary temperature.

In Case of Constipation: Call Your Doctor

Having one or more bowel movements a day is the rule for one baby. The next baby may have one every other day, another only one or two a week. Do not impose your own bowel habits on your child. Constipation is never the problem that it seems.

Infant enema syringe. This is a luxury. You may have need of it once or twice a year. There are other ways to accomplish the same thing more cheaply. DO NOT USE EXCEPT ON EXPRESS ORDERS OF A DOCTOR.

Infant enemas. They are prepackaged in four-ounce size for infants, larger for one-year-olds. They have a soft tip (some come prelubricated), the enema solution, everything. All you do is insert within the baby's rectum. They cost one-third to one-half as much as the syringe. Having one on hand could be convenient. I heartily recommend them if the doctor prescribes an enema, since you needn't worry about sterilizing anything, getting the temperature right, working with long cords to provide proper elevation, etc. If an enema is a necessity, this is the nicest way I know to give one. DO NOT USE EXCEPT ON EXPRESS ORDERS OF A DOCTOR.

Suppositories. Used in cases of constipation. You keep them in the refrigerator. Make more than a mental note of that because otherwise you may find yourself buying another jar six months later. Write yourself a big note and post it in your medicine cabinet. DO NOT USE EXCEPT ON EXPRESS ORDERS OF A DOCTOR.

Prune juice. Nature's laxative, so be wary of feeding it on a daily basis.

In Case of Diarrhea: Call Your Doctor

Diarrhea, once the leading cause of infant mortality, is an all too frequent problem of all babies since it may be caused by infection or allergy. Although doctors disagree, most mothers will tell you that teething and diarrhea go together. Me, too.

***Antidiarrhea medications.** Kaopectate has been the traditional one for years. Your doctor, however, may prefer another one. This is the type of thing you will find you really need for the medicine cabinet.

Ointments. To help clear up resulting diaper rash or diarrhea rash. A & D, Desitin, Diaparene, Zinc Oxide Ointment (especially if your child is zinc-deficient, because it will help heal wounds faster; however, few if any babies are zinc-deficient), Melynor Pediatric Ointment, among others. I've used them all. I have found little difference among the ointments, except that I suspected an allergic reaction to two of them. All ointments, I found, were better than petroleum jelly, which was far too soluble in the presence of urine.

***Electrolyte powders.** In the case of severe diarrhea, your doctor may recommend that you alternate diluted milk-feedings with a feeding of electrolyte formulas to try to restore the fluid balance in the body, along with replacing necessary chemicals such as sodium and potassium, thus preventing dehydration. Dehydration is the greatest threat to the life of a child with diarrhea.

Kool-Aid. May be suggested by doctor in an effort to make the electrolyte solution palatable to baby. Do not use any flavors that contain possible allergens, such as citric acid.

In Case of Nausea and/or Vomiting: Call Your Doctor

Nausea can accompany sore throats, respiratory infections that cause drainage of mucus into the stomach, or allergic reactions. When nausea changes to vomiting, or vomiting comes on suddenly, it could mean nothing more than a slight stomach upset, or it could be the first symptom of appendicitis or the aftermath of a head injury. Projectile vomiting (the food pours out or is shot out of the mouth, sometimes all the way across the room) is a positive symptom of food allergy.

***Anti-nausea medications.** Milk of magnesia in small quantities does the job, but your doctor may be concerned about its laxative qualities. It's a good thing to have on hand for the latter.

Coco-Cola syrup. This may be used with the older child for the relief of simple nausea. Beware of giving it to the chocolate-allergic child. It also acts as a stimulant for some.

In Case of Colds: Call Your Doctor

Believe it or not, there are people who welcome colds as a source of antibodies against future colds. Anyone who has seen a young infant suffer with a cold would wish the cold vaccine would be discovered tomorrow. Unfortunately it has not. Nor has vitamin C been shown to be the answer. In fact, a large vitamin-C intake can lead to diarrhea in children.

Syringes, nasal and otherwise. These were used decades ago to remove by gentle suction the mucus from the nose. They are dangerous in inexperienced hands. I own one, I must admit, but have been too afraid (sensible me!) to use it. There it sits, in all its pristine $2.50 (in 1969) glory.

***Decongestant.** Some are available without a prescription. Sudafed, for example, is one that your doctor may recommend. Taken by mouth, these alleviate the need for nose drops and nasal sprays—both of which are difficult to administer to a child and offer only temporary relief.

***Cough medicine.** Frequently your doctor will recommend a patent medicine, such as Romilar, because it does not contain habit-forming drugs. If the cough continues, he may *prescribe* one that is stronger. When he suggests a cough medicine, check to see how long you should wait before seeing positive results. You are then able to call him back before the cough becomes critical.

***Antihistamines.** Many a "cold" has turned out to be an allergic reaction to inhalants. For this reason, your doctor may prescribe an antihistamine. If you do have an allergic child, keep this particular prescription refilled. It may prevent a cough from turning into bronchitis, the sniffles into asthma.

In Case of Fever: Call Your Doctor

Children run fevers easily. But a fever of 101° is definitely a reason to call your doctor. You will find that temperatures soaring up to heights that might cause convulsions and brain damage in an adult will only make the child querulous. However, a high fever can cause convulsions, especially if accompanied by trembling and teeth chattering as if the body were chilled.

***Aspirin.** The infant cannot take baby aspirin in tablet form without its being mashed up and turned into solution. Rather than doing that, most mothers prefer to buy a liquid aspirin that is administered with an eyedropper. However, as the child gets older, a switch to flavored baby aspirin will usually occur because it's cheaper. Before you have an emergency, ask your doctor for recommended dosages—and overdoses. (A rule of thumb for the latter is a dosage over one-quarter-grain tablet per pound of child.) For the child allergic to aspirin, doctors can recommend equally effective non-aspirin products.

Rubbing alcohol. Rubbing alcohol is used in conjunction with cold baths to bring temperatures down. Not needed, and in fact, in a closed room the fumes may be dangerous. Use cold-water compresses instead at all locations where a pulse is visible: on the inside of wrists, ankles, and at the temples. A cold bath may be too chilling.

In Case of Accidents (You Call Your Doctor . . . and You Don't)

Usually the only reason for calling a doctor is to determine whether or not your child should be taken to a nearby emergency-treatment room. Unfortunately, accidents occur so frequently that you may find yourself working a shuttle service to and from the emergency ward. Thus, the mother of the beginning walker (or bike-rider or jungle-gym climber, and so on) learns to differentiate between Accidents with a capital *A* and accidents. The latter you treat yourself.

For accidents with a lower case *a:* do it yourself.

A first-aid book. Available through your local Red Cross chapter. A bargain at $1 plus any local sales tax. You might want to invest in two: one for your home, one for your car. This tells you whether the accident in question is really an accident or an Accident. If you can afford only the one copy, once it is no longer needed in the house don't consign it to a bookcase somewhere. Tuck it into the glove compartment of your car. It might save someone's life.

Antiseptic. I particularly like the ones that contain local painkillers. How well I remember having tinctures of iodine poured on a cut—I would have rather had the pain of the cut. I find children like the spray ones best; they make the treating more of a game.

Bandages, plastic. The bandage is the child's version of the Congressional Medal, Purple Heart, etc. Wearing a bandage can be very important to your child, and so, even though bandages come off sooner than you might desire, they should be used. The promise of one can take a child's mind off his hurt.

Pop-Ice, or whatever else they're called. These are plastic bags which contain a good-tasting solution that can be frozen for use as a Popsicle. They come in handy in cases of bitten tongues, cut lips, bloody noses. Keep in the freezer for emergency use. And you can even use them as is, without opening them, for teething rings. The child mouths the plastic bag and brings relief to his sore gums.

For Accidents with a capital *A:* CALL YOUR DOCTOR
Animal bites, other than family pet . . . Animal bite, severe . . . Bleeding, severe . . . Burns, big . . . Falls, followed by strange behavior . . . Fractures . . . Nosebleeds, over ten minutes long . . . Poisoning, even if only suspected . . . Sunburn, severe.

P.S. ADMINISTERING MEDICATIONS

1. A bottle-fed baby can have his medications mixed with a small amount of formula (except an electrolyte solution) and given that way.

2. An eyedropper, large-size, is useful for thin fluids; however, most are not calibrated into teaspoons. So you must calibrate it yourself for one-half teaspoon, one teaspoon, one tablespoon. The easiest way to do this is to measure out the quantities in water, actually suck them up into the dropper, and mark with nail polish or indelible marker. Thick, viscous liquids cannot be administered this way.

3. Spoons of various kinds can be used. The strange-looking baby spoon you may get as a gift, of sterling silver with a lip on one side, is very handy since you are practically pouring the liquid into baby. Check; most measure one teaspoon very accurately.

4. Special spoons available at the drugstore (sometimes for free!) have high sides to prevent spills. Then there's the combination spoon-test tube, which prevents all spilling and gets medications farther back into the child's throat. There's even a lighted medical spoon that operates on battery power. The light is sufficient to read labels and measurements, but is not bright enough to alarm or arouse the baby. Tots are fascinated with it. The spoon has a clear, plastic bowl, graduated to show one-half teaspoon and one teaspoon. It is available through File, Inc., Box 3006, 2622 San Mateo Boulevard, N.E., Albuquerque, New Mexico 87110. Cost: $1.99 plus postage. Write them for more information.

MAKING THE CHANGE FROM BABY MEDICINES TO ADULT ONES

About the only change that you make on your own—that is, without checking with the doctor—is from baby to adult aspirin. Four baby aspirin are the equivalent of one adult aspirin. And adult aspirin tablets are much less expensive than the strictly-for-baby kind. However, you will have to find ways to make that grownup aspirin palatable to your child. Mashing it up and mixing it with honey is the age-old way to do it. (Have you checked out the cost of honey recently?) Or you can try the prepared, fruit-flavored syrups marketed for mixing drinks or as ice-cream toppings.

Chapter 12

An Ounce of Prevention

MEDICINES AND POISONS, SOMETIMES THE SAME

Let's face it, certain medical expenses pay for themselves many times over, such as those incurred for vaccinations or dental checkups. Others, like fees for emergency room treatment, can be avoided in direct proportion to the number of precautions you take, the vigilance you show whenever your child is exceptionally, wonderfully quiet, and the use of those legendary eyes in the back of your head that all new mothers seem to develop. First, the precautions:

1. Request that all prescription medicines given you before and after the baby's birth be put into child-proof bottles or pill containers. Either ask your doctor to so specify, or paper-clip such a note to the prescription yourself, or tell your druggist when you call to get a prescription refilled.

2. Request that all directions for prescriptions be spelled out (do not let your doctor say, "Use as directed," because you might forget), that the container be labeled with the generic name of the substance, and that the purpose of the prescription be given. If your druggist won't do this or forgets, you do it. Thus, when your doctor says, "Give him a decongestant," you aren't likely to give cough medicine or antihistamines instead.

3. Keep all medications of any kind out of reach. And I mean out of reach. Even by the child standing on a chair. The best place is in a locked cabinet. Do not get in the habit of keeping medicines in the child's room. That's asking for trouble.

4. Do not rely solely on child-proof containers. By law, all medicines containing aspirin must be put in such a container. A check with our local emergency ward turned up four cases of aspirin overdoses in which the aspirin had been removed by a child

AMERICAN DRUGGIST COUNTERDOSES FOR THE HOME

POISONS

Acids · 18
Bichloride of Mercury · 14
Camphor · 1
Carbon Monoxide · 12
Chlorine Bleach · 17
Detergents · 17
Disinfectant
 with chlorine · 17
 with carbolic acid · 4
Food Poisoning · 7
Furniture Polish · 16
Gasoline, Kerosene · 16
Household Ammonia · 15
Insect & Rat Poisons
 with arsenic · 2
 with sodium fluoride · 11
 with phosphorus · 13
 with DDT · 7
 with strychnine · 6
Iodine Tincture · 3
Lye · 15
Wild Mushrooms · 7
Oil of Wintergreen · 9
Pine Oil · 16

DO THIS FIRST

- Call a physician—immediately.
- Keep the patient warm.
- Determine if the patient has taken
 (1) A POISON
 (2) AN OVERDOSE
- While waiting for physician, give appropriate counterdose below.
- But do not force any liquids on the patient— if he is unconscious.
- And do not induce vomiting if patient is having convulsions, or if patient is unconscious.

To Find The Correct Counterdose

- In one of the lists printed at left, find substance causing the trouble.
- Next to that substance is a number. This refers to counterdose bearing same number in the section below.

Keep all poisons and medicines out of reach of children

1
Induce vomiting with
- Finger in throat, or
- 1 tablespoon of syrup of ipecac, followed by a glass of water, or
- Teaspoonful of mustard in half glass of water.

2
- Give glass of milk, or
- Give 1 tablespoonful of activated charcoal, mixed, with a little water.
- Finally, induce vomiting—but not with syrup of ipecac. (See #1)

3
- Give 4 tablespoons of thick starch paste. Mix cornstarch (or flour) with water.
- Induce vomiting (see #1)
- Finally give glass of milk.

4
- Induce vomiting. (See #1)
- Then give 4 tablespoons of castor oil.
- Next give glass of milk or the white of 2 raw eggs.

5
- Induce vomiting (see #1) if patient is conscious.
- Give glass of milk, or activated charcoal in water.
- Give 2 tablespoons of epsom salt in 2 glasses of water.
- Keep patient awake.

6
- Give glass of milk, or activated charcoal in water.
- Induce vomiting (#1) if not in convulsions. Do not use ipecac if charcoal was given.
- Keep patient quiet.

7
- Induce vomiting. (See #1)
- Next give 2 tablespoons of epsom salt in 2 glasses of water—except in cases where diarrhea is severe.

8
- Induce vomiting. (See #1)
- Give 2 teaspoons of bicarbonate of soda in a glass of warm water.
- Finally give glass of milk.

9
- Give a glass of milk.
- Next induce vomiting. (#1)
- Give tablespoon of bicarbonate of soda in a quart of warm water.

10
- Give activated charcoal in water.
- Induce vomiting (See #1) but not with ipecac.
- Give 2 tablespoons of epsom salt in 2 glasses of water.

11
- Give glass of milk or lime water.
- Then induce vomiting. (See #1)

12
- Carry victim into fresh air.
- Make patient lie down.
- Give artificial respiration if necessary.

13
- Induce vomiting. (See #1)
- Then give 4 oz. mineral oil. Positively do NOT give vegetable or animal oil.
- Also give 1 tablespoon of bicarbonate of soda in a quart of warm water.

14
- Give glass of milk, or
- Give one tablespoon of activated charcoal, mixed with a little water.
- Next induce vomiting (#1) but not with ipecac.
- Give 2 tablespoons of epsom salt in 2 glasses of water.

15
- Give 2 tablespoons of vinegar in 2 glasses of water.
- Now give the white of 2 raw eggs . . . or 2 ounces of vegetable oil.
- Do NOT induce vomiting!

16
- Give water or milk.
- Then give 4 tablespoons of vegetable oil.
- Do NOT induce vomiting!

17
- Give patient one or two glasses of milk.

18
- Give large quantity of water.
- Give 2 tablespoons of milk of magnesia, or a similar antacid.
- Do NOT induce vomiting!

Rubbing Alcohol · 9
Turpentine · 16

OVERDOSES

Alcohol · 9
Aspirin · 9
Barbiturates · 10
Belladonna · 6
Bromides · 7
Codeine · 5
Headache & Cold Compounds · 9
Iron Compounds · 8
Morphine, Opium · 5
Paregoric · 5
'Pep' Medicines · 2
Sleeping Medicines · 10
Tranquilizers · 10

EMERGENCY PHONE NUMBERS

PHYSICIAN

POISON CONTROL CENTER

PHARMACIST

POLICE

HOSPITAL

AMBULANCE

FIRE

from a child-proof container. One of those container-openers was mine, so I know whereof I speak.

5. Do not administer any medicines without checking with your doctor first. This especially applies to homemade remedies, such as mineral oil being used as a laxative. Mineral oil is dangerous for children, as it can be absorbed into the lungs and cause a chronic form of pneumonia.

6. Never describe medicine to a child as being "candy."

7. Administer the medicine properly. WHATEVER YOU DO TAKE THE TIME TO DO IT RIGHT.

(*A*) Be sure you have the right bottle or container. If administering two or more medications at one time, use some memory device to keep yourself from giving the same medication twice. For example, remove caps from all medications to be given. After one is given, replace cap on bottle, if only loosely, to signify this has been used.

(*B*) Be sure you have the right dosage. Check each time to make sure.

(*C*) Don't *pour* medicine down a baby's throat. Give it a couple of drops at a time—or about ¼ teaspoon at a time. The older child will be able to take twice that at a time. But not until age three or more will he be able to clean up the spoon with one swallow.

(*D*) Don't give medicines in the dark.

8. In case of accidental overdoses, have syrup of ipecac on hand; know your poison-control center number; call your doctor.

The Counterdose Chart on pages 174–75, copies of which I have posted in both my kitchen and bathroom, was supplied to me by *American Druggist* and its editor, Daniel Kushner. The chart is revised annually to reflect the consensus of latest medical thinking, and has been revised thusly since it was first created in 1955.

I can vouch for its effectiveness since I have had, unfortunately, two cases of accidental overdose—you see, it happens to everyone —and in both cases, the chart told me what to do and what not to do while waiting for my doctor to return my call.

To get your own copies, suitable for posting in your medicine chest or within a kitchen cabinet, contact local pharmacist, the Junior Chamber of Commerce, or your poison-control center.

9. Lock up all items mentioned on the poison chart and put them up high. At one local hospital, half of the poisoning cases were caused by household products such as bleach, kerosene, lighter fluid, furniture polish, Drano, Liquid Plumber, and the like.

10. CLEAN OUT ALL THE DRUGS IN YOUR HAND-BAG. One well-baby clinic checked the contents of the handbags of all mothers visiting the clinic that day. More than half the mothers carried something—tranquilizers, birth-control pills, thyroid medications, aspirin—that could poison a child.

11. Adopt this attitude toward substances: If you wouldn't serve it to your family for dinner, it shouldn't be left where a child can get at it. Just because the smell or taste or appearance is repugnant to you, don't count on the same holding true for your child. Just remember the child who swallowed half a live snake; the other half was dangling out of his mouth when his mother found him.

INOCULATIONS AND VACCINATIONS

There is nothing more frightening to me in the way of news stories than the report that parents have become complacent about polio vaccinations. It frightens me that parents might forgo them because of the expense or effort. As of May 1973, the U.S. Public Health Service's National Center for Disease Control was warning that less than two-thirds of all children between the ages of one and four are adequately protected. Do yourself and your child a favor, have him immunized against polio. The disease is a crippler. Most public health departments will give the necessary doses free if the parent can prove a financial need.

In 1954 more than 18,000 cases of paralytic polio were reported in the United States. In 1970 there were none. In 1973 there were more than 30.

A Schedule of Immunizations Must Start After the Age of Three Months

Up to the time the child is three months old, the antibodies you have developed will protect your baby since they will have passed via your blood through the placenta. After that the child is on his own. Below is a recommended schedule that will, of course, be deviated from in case the child is ill. Note that it doesn't wait until antibodies are exhausted.

Diphtheria, Pertussis (whooping cough), and Tetanus (D-P-T). Four doses, the first at six weeks of age and booster 1 at ten weeks, booster 2 at fourteen weeks, booster 3 at forty weeks or at age nine months.

Polio "Sabin". Three oral doses, the first being given the date of the first D-P-T booster. The rest (2) given at the next two successive D-P-T boosters. Then a booster a year later. Remember it.

Smallpox. Opinions differ about the need for smallpox vaccination. It is not normally required these days except by certain school districts. In case it is given, the earliest should be at one year if there is no eczema on the child's body. Revaccination may be required on school entrance.

Measles inoculation. One injection at age twelve months.

Typhoid. Not given unless epidemic underway.

Tuberculin test (TB). Given at twelve to fourteen months.

QUESTIONS AND ANSWERS ABOUT DENTAL CARE

The questions are mine, the answers come from many sources, but especially from John K. Reimer, D.D.S., who has saved many a Benning tooth for lo these many years.

Q. When should I start caring for my future child's teeth?

A. While he's a fetus. You ensure that his teeth are healthy and strong by making sure you have an adequate diet during pregnancy. One that stresses the dairy foods, which are high in calcium. You also ensure that his teeth are *healthy-looking* by not taking drugs and medicines without your doctor's consent. For example, suppose you get the sniffles and know from past experience that a couple of tetracyclin will knock them out fast. Did you also know that too much tetracyclin can affect the appearance of your baby's teeth by turning them gray and dead-looking?

Q. I understand fluorides really fight tooth decay. Shouldn't I start using them as early as possible to protect my baby's teeth, such as, when I'm pregnant?

A. No. Doctors and dentists alike will tell you there's always the danger of fluorosis, a mottling of the enamel, even a pitting of the teeth of the baby. And there is some thought that excess fluoride can make the bones brittle and affect the kidneys. The earliest time to start supplementation of fluorides is when the baby is six months old, and even then, only if your water supply is not already fluoridated. Check with your local public health department to find out if it is, and what the concentration is. Then discuss fluorides with your doctor.

Q. Since children are going to lose their first set of baby teeth, why should I even bother with them or worry about them?

A. Many parents feel the same way, and it's a fallacy. Those baby teeth are extremely important. Many parents, in an effort to economize, keep telling themselves, "The tooth is going to fall out anyway, let's save the money for his real teeth." If you agree, you'd better save that money because you're going to need it. For one thing, if a back baby tooth is lost, the other teeth will move forward to fill the space. Then there will be no room for the permanent tooth to erupt or come out without dental assistance. In addition, the opposing tooth (the one either below or above the lost tooth) will move, too, either dropping down or rising up from the gum, and lock the occlusion.

Moreover, the loss of a tooth takes away a point of stimulation. What happens is that each tooth stimulates the tooth opposite it. This is necessary for bone growth and the continued eruption of the permanent tooth underneath.

Finally, those temporary baby teeth will have to serve your child for five to seven years in the case of the front teeth, and eleven to twelve years in the case of the molars.

Q. At what point should I begin brushing and flossing my child's teeth?

A. At the age of two. Prior to that there is a cuticle or protective covering on the teeth that Mother Nature puts there. That gradually wears away, and by the age of two the child should be brushing with a small, soft brush. By the age of three or four most children can brush properly and use dental floss with great accuracy. Like anything else you teach your child, imitation is the easiest way to do it. Perhaps you can let him sit on top of the clothes hamper next to the basin, with the mirror low enough so that he can see that he's doing what mommy does. He will enjoy it.

Q. At what age should the child first see a dentist?

A. That depends. If the child's gums are healthy, if there is no evident decay, if there is no malocclusion (abnormal bite, with lower teeth protruding or upper teeth protruding excessively), the first visit need not be until the age of three. However, if any of the aforementioned are present, the first visit could be as early as age two.

Q. How do you find a dentist that will take children for patients and be good with them?

A. Most dentists will care for children's teeth, but there are children's dentists, called pedodontists, who have special training in the handling of children. Many, for example, outfit their offices with child-size furnishings, etc., so that the office does not look so strange and forbidding.

Q. Aren't those special children's dentists expensive?

A. Yes, compared to what you've been paying for your dental care. But you will find that many regular dentists charge more for doing work on a child—primarily because such work is more difficult in terms of size and cooperation.

Q. Is there a right way to introduce a child to dentistry?

A. Although some dentists feel that it is better to bring a child in cold and let the dentist handle him, I disagree. One of the best ways is to take your child with you when you go for routine care such as cleaning of the teeth. Describe the tickling of the brush; he may want to feel it. With your child sitting in your lap, the dental hygienist can easily demonstrate the tickling.

Whatever you do, be sure not to make the dentist out to be an ogre. If you do make him out to be the modern equivalent of the bogeyman, your child may have serious problems dealing with the dentist for the rest of his life. The child should be made aware that going to the dentist is an experience, not necessarily pleasant, not necessarily unpleasant—just something we all do.

Q. Every parent worries about the possible need and cost of braces. Is there anything we can to do to avoid the need for braces?

A. You can marry a person who has good teeth; that's the best way, for most malocclusions are caused by heredity. And you can discourage thumb sucking after the age of four, especially daytime sucking. Nightime sucking is not as dangerous as it may seem, for although the thumb remains in the mouth, the jaw relaxes and the breathing is natural, thus preventing internal pressure on the jaw.

Remember, however, that any damage that thumb sucking might cause can be corrected physically. The damage you might cause mentally in trying to prevent or discourage it is not so easily corrected.

Q. If braces must be worn, when should they be done to be most effective and least expensive?

A. The earlier the better. In fact, if there is any question that a child might need braces, call in an orthodontist at age seven or eight. The best age for braces is that time when they will do the most good the most easily and quickly—or at a time when growth is still occurring. This is the period between eight and eleven, with nine and ten optimum. By age twelve and thirteen (this is especially true of girls, who are earlier maturers), bone structures will have matured and consolidated; and braces are less effective, more expensive, and unbelievably painful. It is better to be too early than too late. The more set the teeth become, the harder the job, the longer the wearing of braces, and the more expensive the cost to you.

Q. Teeth seem to be the casualty of many accidents. What should I do if a tooth is knocked loose, but not knocked out?

A. Use a little ice outside to control the swelling; homemade popsicles do a good job inside to control the bleeding. And wait. Teeth hit so hard they've been driven up out of sight have been known after a few days to drop down and tighten up. In fact, 90 percent of all teeth that have been loosened or moved will return to their original position and tighten up. A year later you might find that the tooth has changed color, which means the nerve has died. In a temporary or baby tooth, that might be unsightly but it does not mean the tooth should be removed. It is the best space-maintainer possible. It will not interfere with the growth or eruption of the permanent tooth underneath it. And a child can live with such a dead tooth for years. A permanent tooth can be splinted (with wire or plastic) to adjacent teeth and held in place.

The child's own resistance prevents infections, and before you know it the tooth will be as tight as ever. If the nerve does die, the tooth eventually may need nerve-canal work to prevent infection. But not immediately, not even soon. Just eventually. Such a death of the nerve does not, in itself, justify extraction.

Q. Suppose the tooth is not knocked loose, but knocked out?

A. In the case of baby teeth, there isn't too much you can do. The child will have to go two or three years without such a tooth. Since it's a front tooth, the space will not be usurped quickly by other teeth. The attempts to reimplant the tooth can cause more damage than just leaving it alone.

If the tooth is a permanent one and it's knocked out whole and the tooth can be found, it should be picked up, put in a little gauze moistened with water and taken to the dentist as quickly as possible (putting a little more gauze in the mouth to stop the bleeding and to keep the socket moist). The dentist is often able to do root-canal work and sterilize the tooth outside the mouth, replace it in the mouth, and wire it to the adjacent teeth. Although the tooth may discolor, it's a very fine basis for a porcelain jacket crown later on.

Q. But suppose the tooth is not knocked out, but is broken off?

A. It should be repaired. Even if all that means is putting a band around the tooth and filling it with cement. The point is that a baby tooth serves a purpose other than just being a means of biting and chewing. It paves the way for the next tooth. A permanent tooth is the only one your child will have, it must last him a lifetime. Even half a real tooth is better than an old fake synthetic.

THE OLDER CHILD AND SELF-MEDICATION

Don't. If you don't want your child taking the wrong kind of pills (that is, illegal and/or dangerous to health), then don't let him self-medicate. You keep control of the aspirin, the cough medicine, the nose drops, etc. Dole them out when and if you believe he needs them, and if you think he doesn't, don't dispense them.

Don't teach your child that medicine is candy, or that it tastes like candy, and you won't have to worry as much about pills given out by sick adults as Halloween candy. Do teach your child that only doctors, nurses, and Mother and Father are allowed to give out medicines, and he'll be that much safer from unthinking adults who are too quick to allow self-medication.

Do teach your child that medicines don't cure, they only help. Then, hopefully, you won't find him looking for cures in pill bottles or hypodermic needles at age sixteen, seventeen, eighteen.

Part 5

Education/ Recreation

On a national average, statisticians believe the direct out-of-pocket costs of educating a child do not begin until age six. You may, however, find yourself purchasing crayons, pencils, and "squeakies" (my son's name for ink markers), much earlier than that. If so, your education costs will be more than the $725.70 average total for the period six to eighteen.

If you elect to add a preschool education to your costs of raising a child, you may add on as little as $80 a school year, or as much as $1,000 per school year, for tuition charges alone.

Whether the cost of toys should be charged against education or made into a separate category depends on whether you belong to the "play-teaches" or the "play is child's work" schools of thinking. Whichever, you can assume you will spend an average of $80 per year for toys. (Approximately 50 million toy-age children equals a 4-billion-per-year industry.)

To the cost of education/recreation might be added the cost of baby-sitting. One writer estimated it to be $40 for the first year alone (five hours a month beginning at age four months)—this may be compensated for by the income a girl or boy can bring in when of baby-sitting age, which would lower another aspect of your costs accordingly.

Another cost sometimes included here is the cost of photographs. This could be as much as $100 the first year or as little as $5 for the nursery shot some hospitals take. It seems to me that said cost is a feature of the parents' recreation and not accountable to the cost of child-rearing.

Chapter 13

Toys That Teach

One of the most interesting aspects of the toy situation is that of all the research file folders that I have, each covering one chapter in this book, the biggest, the fattest is on toys. It is at least twice as thick as any other.

And that, I think, is the nucleus of the whole toy situation. Too much, not too little. There are more than 500,000 different *types* of toys on the market, more than 5 million different toys available. And each year more than 5,000 new kinds of toys go on the market. You can understand why the toy business is a *multi-billion*-dollar industry.

Why are we buying toys at such a rate? Everybody has his own theory, but it boils down to three different desires on the part of the parent. Not the child, the parent.

First: the age-old desire each generation of parents has to give their young what they themselves didn't have when they were young.

Second: the attempt to improve the child's lot in life, to help him develop to his full potential. In this respect we have bought the idea that a child's work is his play literally. If you're a typical mother, you'll look for the "toys that teach," and you'll feel guilty if you do not offer toys that offer your child different experiences, either physical, sensorial, mental, emotional or social. You're not at all like adults about whom one toy manufacturer complained, "Unfortunately, many adults don't regard the price of a toy as they regard the price of things for themselves. They may spend money easily for two hours of pleasure at a movie, for a new tie, for a good meal, for many other things, but hesitate to spend the same amount for a toy which may give lasting pleasure to a child."

Now you know and I know that's not you. Convinced that your

child needs toys to mature, you'd take in laundry to get the money to buy him the toys he needs.

And yet, the best toy, the safest toy, the most educational toy, the one toy that won't be outgrown and will continually adapt to his needs, the one toy that can literally increase you child's IQ . . . this miracle toy is you!

If you had to choose between buying your child an "educational" toy or buying yourself some play time with him in the form of convenience foods or diaper service or domestic help, the wise mother would choose the latter.

Out in Wisconsin there's a special school attended only by children whose mothers are poor and mentally retarded. They are part of a group of forty children born to mothers with below-average IQ's of 75 or under (100 is average). Half the babies were left at home with their mothers, the other half were picked up five days a week and taken to a special school, where for seven hours each day they were "loved, fussed over, and talked to." No experimental devices, no electronic gadgets, no new educational gimmicks were used there. Instead they were given exceptionally good mothering. The results? All those receiving the mothering tested out at an average IQ of 123. Of those who weren't, only three had IQ's of 100 or over. The rest were at 75 to 85.

Not convinced yet? Then take into consideration that the American Academy of Pediatrics Committee on the Infant and Pre-school Child states that parents may be wasting their money if they buy developmental toys in hopes of increasing their child's intellectual potential. There is no scientific proof of claims that certain books, toys, learning environments, programs, or systems will specifically contribute to an infant's or child's intellectual development.

Why, then, if mothers make such good playthings, have mothers turned to toys as substitutes? It may be an attempt to get around the teaching of doctors who twenty-five years ago or more raised the gruesome spectre of spoiling the child by playing with him too much. And some doctors are keeping it alive today.

In his book *Baby and Child Care* (Pocket Books, 1968), Benjamin Spock, M.D. is concerned about the parent who is "too eager to amuse . . . who is regularly playing with him most of the time he's awake—carrying him around or dancing with him or jouncing him on her knees or playing pat-a-cake or making him laugh." Why? Because "gradually he forgets to amuse himself." Yet a child first has to learn to amuse himself. Anyway, millions of mothers took him at his word, stopped playing with their children, and turned to toys instead.

Fortunately, we have the word of many, many psychiatrists and psychologists that YOU CANNOT SPOIL AN INFANT.

Toys do, of course, have a place in your child's life. There are times when you cannot play with him, and there are some games that can be more fun when played with toys. I know, for example, of no way to play ball without a ball or a substitute object. On the other hand, never have I seen such a chuckle of pure joy as my son gave whenever I combined diaper changing and saying, with a wide grin, "Yeah, yeah, yeah, said the little red fox." I know it's meaningless, but he loved it.

There are many books and pamphlets and articles and catalogs that give wise-shopping tips for buying and selecting toys. I mention in particular Creative Playthings' "Guide to Good Toys" (25¢), the U.S. Government's Bureau of Product Safety's "Toy Safety" (45¢), and a booklet/catalog for free from Childcraft Education Corporation. (See Appendix for addresses.)

The first and last are crammed with items for sale plus good advice, the other is just full of good advice. But the two disagree to some extent, with Creative Playthings saying, "Regulations to avoid any severe accidents or other health hazards are necessary, while exaggerated rules to protect children from the slightest scratch are unreasonable and can lessen play possibilities." The government says, "The need for increased safety for children is shown by the fact that more than 6,000,000 injuries a year are related to children's products—700,000 of them toy injuries." And this figure does not, I might add, include tricycle-bicycle injuries, which are over the million mark annually.

Obviously, we are all for safety—some more than others. Equally obviously, the new mother is not in a position to judge how easily a toy will be broken—otherwise she'd never buy it. If it will break into dangerous pieces, she'd never buy it. And if it will knock out a child's eye, she'd never buy it. If it will strangle a child, she'd never buy it. If it will electrocute a child, she'd never buy it.

If a mother knew how to tell whether or not a toy was dangerous before she bought it, she would put forth such an effective boycott that the government would not have had to ban more than 1,000 new toys most years.

However, you should *avoid* such things as:

- toys with sharp edges and protrusions—a bird with a pointed beak or a rocket with a pointed peak.
- toys made of hard wood that are not sanded on all edges. Look also for nails.
- no glass anywhere around a child, please.
- squeaker toys unless you remove the metal squeakers—which plays havoc with bath-squeaker toys; once the squeaker's out, the toy won't float right side up; your child looks as if he's surrounded by dead ducks.
- watch out for detachable parts, such as button eyes that your child might detach and swallow and choke upon.
- look out for toys that are filled with allergenic materials, or that are unwashable.
- don't put that big, adorable teddy bear, as big as himself, in his crib—the bear might become a stepping stone to up and out and hurts.
- flexible plastic is normally better than rigid plastic, which has a tendency to break into sharp-edged pieces.
- noose-shaped toys that might be suspended in the crib. I think of two in particular: one a teething necklace that I hung from a rod fastened across the crib. Our son caught his chin in it and could have choked to death if I had not made it a policy to check every time he was quiet. The other, a miniature trapeze developed by a Ph.D. from Harvard. It's supposed to strengthen the baby's arm muscles when he pulls on it; all I can see is the baby who hooks his chin over it (it's wide enough to easily accommodate the baby's head).

watch out for toys for the baby to hit that swing back and clobber him. One, a cradle gym-type toy, has miniature hammers hanging from it.

These are some pointers to use in selecting toys. But the best one I can give you is to try the toy yourself. If you use it as it is intended for your child to use and it doesn't break, nor come apart in your hands, nor injure you in any way—there's a good chance it won't injure your child.

Remember, the fewer the toys the fewer the chances of being

hurt. And the fewer you buy, the better the quality toy you can afford. So, look for homemade toy substitutes wherever possible.

From 0 to three months, or until eyes can focus. No toys are needed. Spend your time dolling up the nursery to make it more colorful. Suggestion: if you have 8½"×11" pictures of yourselves, mount them where he'll be able to see them. Or have them enlarged into posters, which can be done by mail order for less than it costs to buy circus or animal nursery decals. You can give your baby a great feeling of security by having pictures of you hanging about.

Around three months, or when eyes can focus. A mobile is worthwhile. Especially one *not* designed for mothers. Most mobiles are made to be looked at from the side—from where you view it—not from where he sees it, or from underneath. Don't waste your money on those. Make your own by suspending a wire coat hanger from the ceiling directly over the baby's head but out of his reach and tying spools of colorful thread, plastic cups, spray-painted jar lids, new jewelry, etc., from it.

When he starts to reach for things. It's time to suspend rattles and other objects from the sides of the crib. Use elastic thread to do so (you can buy it in any notions department for less than 50¢). Thus, if he pulls a toy, it snaps back into place, and more important, won't drop out of sight as it would if tied on with a long enough piece of string for the child to pull the toy toward him.

One of the best-loved toys from now until eighteen months is a group of brightly colored plastic discs on an oversize chain. (We called them "clackers," because of the noise they made.) No matter how they are manipulated, the effect and the sound are different. A homemade version could be spray-painted baby-food jar lids strung on a key chain. Make sure the holes in the lids are filed smooth.

At six months. Bath toys now come into vogue. If you buy them, remove the squeakers. Then stuff florist's clay or pieces of sponge rubber into the holes to get some semblance of stability. Better yet, use household objects, such as plastic cups, funnels, empty plastic bottles, and so on. Or cut sponges into bath-type shapes (fish, ducks, etc.).

A stack of rings is another favorite toy for most children. Not so much for stacking purposes as because the rings are easily handled and held onto. But then so are empty adhesive-tape rolls and cellophane-tape reels.

A good rattle toy is a plastic milk carton (one-quart size) with metal cap, complete with five clothespins (not the squeeze type) that rattle around inside. When the bottle is opened, it takes much shaking and work to get the clothespins out, much dexterity to get them back in.

At nine months. This is the put-things-into-things stage. Try a soft-drink six-pack paper carton into which go balls and rattles and anything else the youngster can find. Cut household sponges into 1½″ squares to use as blocks or perfect putter-inners. Cardboard juice containers in various sizes make an excellent nesting toy, and safe, too. Few tin cans have the rolled rims necessary to make them safe, but check and see.

At this stage, a child who is crawling is likely to enjoy balls. Balls of all sizes and kinds that he can chase or pretend to throw.

A little later, you will run into the push stage, when he crawls with one hand on the floor and the other on the toy. A favorite push-toy at this age is the "chatter-telephone," which gives him a flat surface on top to hold onto and really movable wheels. You may want to remove the receiver, which is just a hindrance at this stage. Later, in the pull stage, the receiver can go back on.

One year, give or take a few months. This is the push stage— walking. His walker-bouncer is an excellent toy for him to use. It's also very ego boosting. If you had been confined to a wheelchair for as long as you could remember, wouldn't you like to go pushing it up and down the halls to show the world you were perambulating? I would. So will your child.

Another toy you will find almost every child likes is the Playskool giraffe, a wheeled toy with a chairlike back and a handle on either side of the giraffe's head for him to hold onto. If you find your child rides it backward to begin with, holding onto the back and ignoring the giraffe head in front, congratulations! He's doing as most children do because the spoked back with its one long, curved top is more substantial, and thus more confidence-inspiring.

It is this same back that makes the toy excellent for pushing. Even at age three and one-half, you may find your child still using it. It can be hitched onto the back of a tricycle to take bears for rides, and it can be loaded with bricks and blocks to act as a wagon. It is proof positive that the most versatile toy is frequently the best buy.

After push comes the pull stage. Here, again, the giraffe with the cord through its nose can be used for pulling. Now the wagon-type pull-toys usually are preferred since they not only can be pulled, they can also carry things, which is important to little boys and girls.

Most push and/or pull toys are not properly designed—the handle at the end of the string is either not large enough or not comfortable enough for a small hand to grasp. Those with rigid handles instead of strings are push-pull toys and thus more versatile. Normally, when you get into toys designed either to be pushed or pulled and nothing else, how well they please is commensurate with the amount of noise they make. But the toy that isn't weighted at the bottom will not survive a determined trip. Make your own toy out of an oatmeal box filled with noise-making bells, bottle caps, etc., making sure none is small enough to swallow, just in case.

Other toys you will probably investigate, with possible alternates, are:

- *pounding benches* . . . get a piece of 2×4 and hammer roofing nails lightly into it to a depth of $\frac{1}{16}''$ or so. Invest in a cheap but well-balanced tack hammer for your child to use.
- *stringing objects* . . . emptied thread spools or pieces of macaroni strung on a shoelace.
- *shape sorters* . . . use a poker-chip holder and multiple-color chips; the child learns all one shape, but he also learns colors. A cardboard shoe box also makes a shape sorter. Cut slits into which baby-food jar lids will go, holes into which plastic practice golf balls will fit, squares into which small raisin boxes will go, and little holes for wooden dowel pieces you can cut and paint yourself.

- *lacing toy* . . . use an old shoe. A work shoe is excellent or a colorful sneaker (washed). Add a white shoelace, dyeing one half of it a contrasting color.
- *busy board* . . . attach workable hardware fixtures such as a hinge, bolt, door knocker, hook eye, cabinet knob, etc., to a piece of sanded plywood or soft pine board.
- *shovels* . . . use a kitchen spoon, or cut a half-gallon plastic milk carton off horizontally just below the handle. The bottom makes a pail, the top makes a great shovel for the sand box.
- *sand box* . . . in the center of the secondhand farm tractor tire put sand two or three inches deep. Give the tire a couple of coats of spray paint (green is nice) right over the clay and dirt stains to prevent any black substance coming off on your child. A bulldozer or grader tire may be better for the older child. Drill a hole near the tread on one sidewall, and use a saber saw to cut around the tire. The enlarged side goes up, giving more play room, but still providing a sturdy seat. Or your child, like mine, may prefer that deep, private spot to act out his aspirations in.

The bulldozer or grader tire is easier to come by in some parts of the country than the tractor tire. But I located over one hundred of the former and twenty-one of the latter in about forty minutes of telephoning. The cost ranged from free to $5 apiece. Call heavy-equipment dealers, farm-equipment dealers, and large tire companies. They're very cooperative.

If you have cats around, a cover might be in order. Use a round plastic tablecloth as much larger than the tire as you can find. Then either thread elastic through the edge or fringe, or sew weights on it at four equidistant points. You'll find that keeping the rain out is also a big advantage of the cover.

- *blocks* . . . make your own fabric ones out of squares of material filled with shredded polyurethane foam. For wooden blocks, make a trip to a local lumberyard and ask for the leftover pieces of wood near the saw where customers get lumber cut to size. Frequently these pieces are given away, or sold for peanuts. If you explain your need, they'll probably (*a*) give them to you, and (*b*) let you pick and choose from the pile. Although these may need some sanding, the same number of blocks purchased from a toy store could cost you $25 or more. Mail-order houses seem to be a bit less expensive.

For cardboard blocks, use cardboard shoe boxes taped together. However, don't expect them to be as sturdy as the ready-made. Comparison-shop. One mail-order toy company offers twelve for $9 or fourteen flatties ($20'' \times 8'' \times 2''$) and nineteen short-fatties ($5'' \times 8'' \times 1''$) for $12.

Also, save all sizes of milk cartons, preferably flat-top ones. By cutting them in half, and shoving one half into the other, you can make sturdy blocks. Covering with contact paper both strengthens them and makes them colorful and washable.

• *musical instruments* . . . use an oatmeal box to make a drum. Or cover the ends of a coffee can with pieces of inner tube and lace together with heavy cord or shoelace. Use pencils or small sticks to pound. Or, make a tambourine by piercing bottle caps and stringing them on a circular piece of wire. Another way is to tie bells on the edge of a paper or plastic plate. Make a delightfully noisy shaker by filling a milk carton or small plastic container with dried beans, peas, or macaroni.

• *puppets* . . . using a small paper bag, stuff one half with cotton or crumpled paper; tie the other half securely around a stick; paint a face on the "head" you've just made. For finger puppets, cut fingers off a glove and paint faces and bodies on them. (*Sesame Street* may spoil this by creating a desire for the real Oscar, Big Bird, etc.) Or make a potato puppet by cutting a hole for a finger or inserting a stick. Pin paper face on it or paint it. Another currently popular trick is to sew and attach material around the tops of Crazy Foam cans.

• *put-together toys* . . . use your discarded nurser bottles and caps. Better yet, invest in an old-fashioned percolator at an auction or junk store. Children like to have something to play with that looks like the things Mommy uses. A child will put the innards in and out, and take the top on and off a million times and never tire of it. Later, you can recoup the $2 or so you spent for it by using it as a watering can.

Which brings us to two things: practical life experiences and gender identification. The first is taught deliberately in nursery schools, the other is taught, without thinking, at home. First, a word of explanation. Practical life experiences involve learning how to scrub floors and use funnels and pour things from one container to another. They include stirring food and straining it, using a vacuum cleaner, dusting and polishing, and all the other aspects of Mother's work, as well as the carpenter/repairman aspects of Father's work. Most parents smile on this. But give a boy a doll or a girl a gun, and the smiles disappear.

Actually, playing with dolls does not make a girl feminine any more than playing with guns makes a boy masculine. Toys cannot teach your child his role in life. He learns that from watching the parent of his own gender. If the father, secure in the knowledge of his own masculinity, can cook dinner or care for a baby, his son can safely play with dolls and have dishes, etc. If the mother, secure in the knowledge of her own femininity, can do minor repair work around the house, her daughter can safely have her own tool kit.

It will not make one iota of difference what you give your child in the way of gender-identified toys, provided you and your husband know who you are. Nor should you even be too concerned about this. Too many times fears of homosexuality are ill-founded.

To be specific. Should boys be given dolls? YES! If it will calm your sensibilities, give him a boy-doll, which is, after all, the only kind of baby he is normally aware of up until the age of two. If the boy-dolls are too expensive (and besides, most only look like boys—they don't have the proper genitalia to prove they're boys), get a girl-doll—baby-type, not Barby-type.

What's the purpose of the doll? Well, to allow him to duplicate his father's actions—that's one reason. The other is to give him someone smaller than himself upon whom he can visit his aggressions (those punching clowns are too big—they look like they might fight back). He wants someone else to be in the same position he is, smaller than everybody and helpless in their hands.

What about cars for girls? The best push-toy invented by man, and you're going to keep it from her? That's bucking the trend. The trend to suburban living has made the woman driver the rule rather than the exception. Anywhere she goes, she must drive. She may actually spend more hours per week driving than her husband does. And years from now, her daughter can probably expect the same. So of course a girl should play with cars.

What about hammers and saws and other tools for girls? Why

not? In this day of the hard-to-find repairman, learning to use hammer and saw and screwdriver is a necessity for a woman. As is learning to cook, to some degree, a necessity for men.

Books

One type of toy normally bought rather than made is the book. If you're an egghead like me, you will probably be eager to introduce your child to the delights of reading. Just don't do what I did. I hied myself off to the biggest bookstore around and bought every book recommended for the beginning reader. And was I sold a bill of goods!

Most of the books sold today were designed to meet the needs of farm children of thirty years ago. Look at the ABC books, the most popular object-identification books. What does a cow mean to an inner-city resident, a duck to a child living in a development one hundred miles from a farm pond, an Indian to a child living on the second floor of a garden apartment? Another book says pat the bunny and feel how soft. Is anything softer than a child's skin or silkier than his hair? Or smell the flower, isn't it sweet? Put some perfume on one wrist and teach him fragrances that way.

The best object-identification book I have discovered is *I Spy with My Little Eye,* by Lucille Ogle and Tina Thoburn (American Heritage Press, 1970), with 356 pictures of familiar objects from a child's home environment. There's only one thing wrong with it —it has a tendency to put Mommy and Daddy to sleep because the objects are presented too blandly. Of greater value might be a Montgomery Ward or Sears catalog. At least they're free.

But that isn't the first book you need. Before you can begin identifying objects, you start with the two objects baby knows best: his mother's face, his father's face. From there you can progress to his body, etc.

There are no books like this on the market now, but you could make your own by clipping pictures out of magazines. I used our wedding album. I would go through the album identifying Mommy and Daddy, one by one, over and over. Then I'd ask him to show me Mommy or show me Daddy. If there were only two of us in a picture, he had a 50-percent chance of being right. And when he was, oh, was he praised and fussed over.

Later, when he had a greater grasp of language, I found that the books he preferred were always participating books. Not just books that he might hear passively, but that he could act out or imitate. Dr. Seuss's *Mister Brown Can Moo, Can You?* (Random House, 1970) although not written for this purpose, was one that could be readily adapted for child involvement. And so were the illustrated versions of *Teddy Bear, Teddy Bear* (Grosset & Dunlap) and Stanley and Janet Berenstain's *Inside, Outside, Upside Down* (Random House, 1968). Poetry that had a repeated refrain, such as some of those by Poe and Kipling, was as appreciated as some of the Mother Goose rhymes.

There is one type of book that you can make yourself, and that's the book that teaches a child how to handle the fastenings of his clothing. On one page there's a zipper and on another a buckle and on a third a set of eyelets and lacings. Go through your old clothes or the rag bag and look for similar items. If, instead of simply cutting out the zipper, you were to cut out a good size swath of fabric with it, you'd have one page of your book. The beauty of this is that you can look for larger, more easily managed notions than are in the books you buy.

As your child grows older, his preferences in books will change. Some children prefer environment-reinforcing books—books that reflect his own way of life. Others are learning the fun of pretending, and for them books that emphasize fantasy and unusual aspects of life are a good choice.

At some point during this period before your child goes off to school, you will, if you're at all a typical mother, purchase an ABC book. Watch out for the fantasy ones, those with weird objects rather than recognizable ones. The strangeness defeats the purpose of the book, which is to make a correlation between a letter and an object.

The cheapest way to beat the book-buying bug is to take out a library card. Many libraries have children's book librarians who are in a position to help you find the book your child will like. They can also supply you with all sorts of book lists to use as guides. If you find your child is particularly enamored of one book, you could then invest in a copy for your home.

If you are interested in a child's encyclopedia, ask the children's librarian at your local library for advice.

Watch out for the cheapies sold in supermarkets. Many are

garish, most are poorly written. They are designed to catch the eye of the parent, not to supply a need of the child. Not included in this category are the new paperback versions of hardcover children's books. These are excellent money-savers.

Other guides to choosing children's books are the annual awards. The Caldecott Medal goes to the best *picture* book and is awarded to the illustrator; the Newbery Award goes to the best overall children's literature book. And runners-up are named and honored.

A poor guide to choosing children's books is the age designation some books have on their covers. These are not always accurate; they are not done by an independent organization; they do not reflect a child's mental age.

If reading the same book 300 times or more is not your bag consider investing in a record player that the child can manage himself. Then you only have to steel yourself to hearing the same record 300 times or more. A wind-up toy one costs about $5 and comes with its own special records. Electric ones for the older child (age four and up) will cost $15 to $25, depending on the number of speeds available.

Craft Materials

Did you know that you can make a jim-dandy playdough for mere pennies with things you have in your kitchen? Mix ½ cup salt with ¾ cup flour. If you desire the clay to be colored, add several drops of food coloring to ¼ cup water. To this add 3 tablespoons vegetable oil. If the clay isn't easy to work, keep adding oil to it. You can't add too much. If the clay seems too greasy, simply wrap pieces of it in paper toweling to absorb the extra oil.

Once made, it will keep beautifully in the refrigerator, but allow it to warm a bit at room temperature before your child starts playing with it.

For paste, mix flour and cold water into a thick paste (like heavy cream) and bring it to simmer on top of the range, allowing it to cook for a few minutes. This can then be stored in air-tight jars in the refrigerator.

For finger paint, Wilma M. Sim, of the *Farm Journal,* passes on this recipe to me. *Ingredients:* 1½ cups laundry starch, 1 quart boiling water, 1½ cups soap flakes, ½ cup talc. Mix starch with a little cold water to form a creamy paste. Add boiling water and cook until mixture is transparent-looking. Add talc for a smoother paint. Let mixture cool a bit; stir in soap flakes. Let cool; store in screw-top jars. Stir in poster paints as needed to color it. Oilcloth makes a good surface for fingerpainting; it can be washed and reused. Glazed shelf paper's the thing to use for paintings you plan to keep. Allow each painting to dry, then press on the back with a warm iron to set the color.

For poster paint, buy it powdered and mix up small batches as you need them. Much cheaper that way.

For painting surfaces: don't invest in good paper. Either buy pads of newsprint, or make up your own pads out of regular newspapers (naturally, you won't use the colored sections). Beginning painters are more interested in putting paint on something than in painting a particular thing.

Tricycles

Another toy that you will probably find to be a necessity is the tricycle. If you find your child falls off it a great deal, don't think he's clumsy. He's not. The standard tricycle with its seat high up above the ground is not designed for stability. Far more stable is the low-slung plastic type that has the child practically sitting on the floor.

However, it is almost impossible to keep your child from being exposed to the normal tricycle. So it might be to your best interest, and to your child's physical advantage, to let him learn to ride one in an area that is safest to him: the carpeted areas of your house. Push back furnishings that might catch the wheels and tip him over. Stay with him so that you can catch him.

As to the tricycle itself, if you're going to buy one, don't get the smallest size; you'll just end up buying another one. Look for one with the widest possible rear-wheel base. Be sure the handles are padded. Don't add on that bicycle bell or the special horn. Any protrusions on the handle bar might hurt him when he falls. See if you can lower the seat as much as possible. Note which way the seat tilts—some practically push the rider forward as if he were on a slide. And take your child along to buy the tricycle to be sure his feet reach the wheels without needing blocks added. A surprise gift can fall flat on its face if the recipient can't use it.

Another favorite toy is a form of tricycle—the tractor. In the government's product safety performance tests, it showed excellent stability, a maximum straight speed of six miles per hour (less than the 14" and 20" tricycle), and unlimited steering motion freedom. It offers the playability of a trike combined with the glamour and pretendability of a pedal-car.

Bicycles

A startling number of bicycle-related injuries require hospital emergency-room treatment each year. Many, if not most, are caused by the negligence or faulty judgment of the rider, but some are the fault of the bicycle itself. Here, again, the Product Safety Commission has regulations in the works.

In the meantime, you can look for certain things:

The right height for your child. Determined by seat. At its lowest height, it should allow rider's feet to touch the ground on both sides.

Boy's bike or girl's bike. The crossbar on a boy's bike adds stability to the bike, an important factor for a beginner. In these days of unisex dressing of young children, the crossbar would not be an impediment for girls, who no longer wear long, cumbersome skirts. But, is the child—no matter what sex—old enough to sling his leg easily over the seat to mount and dismount (front-dismounting on a boy's bike causes accidents)? If not, buy a girl's bike for him and sacrifice a little stability for a lot of safety.

Training wheels. A necessity for all mothers, not all children. They add stability and prevent accidents and maternal anxiety. Buy them at same time you buy the bike (to be sure they'll fit), and make sure the metal struts are *strong,* the wheels as big as possible.

Reflectors. Six two-inchers, red at rear, clear in front, amber on each front side, red on both rear sides.

Pedals. Skid-resistant surfaces to prevent shoes' slipping due to wetness.

Fads. The banana seat, the weirdly curved handlebars, the sissybar, etc.—avoid as long as you can. They may be "in," but too often they are injurious.

Multispeeds. You have a choice of three. The three-speed, fine for countrysides with gentle inclines or for using for errand-running. It costs $60 and up. The five-speed, which starts at $85, is good for serious touring and low hills because of its light weight and easy pedaling. The "superbike," as Orien Reid, Consumer Reporter for KYW Newsradio (Philadelphia), calls it, is the ten-speed, built for cross-country touring. However, as she is quick to mention, "the first five speeds on the superbike are identical to those on the simple five-speed. Gears six through ten don't make uphill climbs any easier—contrary to wishful thinking and popular opinion. What they *do* do is to eliminate the need for constant braking—and make for lighter pedaling on long straight laps." For that, you'll pay anywhere from $100 to $500.

Toy Chests

The government warns that toy chests have trapped and smothered small children. So be wary before you buy one. Check to make sure the lid is lightweight, preferably padded so that when and if it falls on your child's head, the bump will be minimized. There should be no automatic locking devices. Check for air holes or other means of getting air into the interior. Watch out for the hinge action; could those hinges catch, pinch, or squeeze small hands and fingers?

Or take the lid off. That solves all your problems, but doesn't get the clutter out of sight.

Educators suggest that in lieu of a toy chest, you use a set of bookshelves. That way toys are out in sight where they may fascinate their owner over and over again. Mothers prefer toys *out of sight,* however. So, if you go for the bookcase idea, you might want to put doors on the front so that the clutter may be hidden from company on occasion.

Playground Equipment

Start with the sand-tire, as already described (page 194) unless you want to just dump a pile of sand in a corner of your yard or set aside a section of the yard for mud and water play. Frequently children will prefer the ground to sand. However, just as frequently mothers prefer sand to mud, since the former is easier on clothes and children alike.

In addition to the sand-tire, you'll probably want a swing. Again a tire is the traditional one. However, you might want to suspend it horizontally instead of vertically—that way more children can ride on it at once, and the child will be able to get into it earlier on his own.

Instead of a tire you might want to use a sling-swing—a piece of heavy rope or chain fastened to each end of a piece of heavy canvas. The child fits better since the sling conforms more closely to his body. Also, there is no chance of someone pushing the seat of the swing out from under him as can happen with the normal rigid-seat swing.

You'll also find that children are slower getting to their feet and standing up in a sling-swing. Instead of the canvas, you might try a piece of fire hose (call your local fire department and ask them to save you a piece if they are repairing or discarding a hose)—this you can thread through with chain and needn't be concerned about fastening it securely at both ends.

For more ideas on salvaging odds and ends, look for Paul Hogan's book *Playgrounds for Free* (M.I.T. Press)—he makes a business out of building playgrounds and playground equipment out of junk, recycled and discarded materials, telephones poles, railroad ties, etc.

However, if you are not a do-it-yourselfer and intend to go out to buy playground equipment, the Product Safety Commission people recommend that when you purchase new equipment, you can prevent knocked-out teeth, permanent disabilities, and even fatalities if you'll check to see that the equipment includes:

• No exposed ends such as screws, bolts, and footrests. They should be tightly covered with caps or plugs. If you can't find a set with covered protrusions, cover them yourself with heavy tape.
• Anchoring devices that will insure the stability of the set. It is very important for playground equipment to be well anchored to the ground. Never install playground equipment over concrete, brick, or other hard surfaces. Install the set at least six feet away from fences, walls, or other obstructions.

If possible, avoid:

• All open-ended hooks, especially S hooks on swings. If your set has S hooks, take a pair of pliers and pinch the ends of the hooks in tightly.
• Pinch or crush points, such as glider hinges. Teach your child not to play with these joints.
• Sharp edges or rough surfaces. Cover them with heavy tape or cloth.
• Accessories such as rings that measure more than five inches but less than ten inches in diameter. Children can catch their heads in rings of these dimensions and hang themselves. If your playground set is equipped with rings of this size, remove them.

Maintain your child's play equipment by:

• Checking twice monthly during the active play season to make sure all nuts, bolts, and clamps are tight.
• Removing plastic seats during cold months.
• Oiling all metallic moving parts monthly.
• Checking swing chains and seats for wear or rust, and replacing these if necessary.
• Sanding and repainting all rusted areas on tubes.
• Replacing rusted hardware (nuts and bolts).

Playhouses
It used to be that all playhouses were treehouses. But that's not true for most children anymore—nor is it a particularly safe idea for your young children. However, the fun of playing house can be his in other ways:

(*a*) You can cover a card table with an old sheet. If you cut a slit for the door and flaps for windows, you've made your child a mansion.

(*b*) You can get a large cardboard carton, the kind appliances are shipped in, and cut holes for windows, a moving open-and-closable door, etc.

(*c*) You can buy a dog kennel for the future use of your dog-to-come. (Please, no puppies in a house with a child under three—not fair to dog or child.)

(*d*) You can buy a playhouse.

(e) You can buy toddler gym-type equipment that includes a covered area that could be a house.

(f) If you don't mind having an abandoned car in the middle of your backyard (minus windows, doors, engine, etc.), you could paint it gay colors and make an ideal plaything (a British double-decker bus is one of my friends' dream toys for her kids).

If you do already have yourself a playhouse, you may find you need equipment for it. Try a cardboard carton for a play stove or sink. Or make a "stove" out of a wooden box, complete with hinged oven door and painted-on burners, but with knobs that turn "on" and "off." A matching sink would have a hole cut in the top just big enough to take a plastic bin, and old faucets from a junkyard make it a real thing. The refrigerator is just as easy to make. It is merely a shelved cabinet with a small door up top and another, larger one underneath. A set of old ice-cube trays gives it the aura it needs. Of course, you can buy all these, but the prices are unreal. Figure $35 apiece and up.

For dishes, use jar lids and plastic lids; old pots and pans will do just fine. Plastic silverware, glasses, and cups will cost you less than a dollar, and the child will love them.

WHAT TOYS NOT TO BUY

1. Don't buy toys with many small pieces that are essential to the operation of the toy. When one piece is gone, the toy is shot.

2. Don't buy toys with many small pieces that are not essential to the operation of the toy *if* you are a fussy housekeeper. Those little pieces will end up in the strangest places.

3. Don't buy toys that are too old for the child. Games, for example, are wasted on the preschool child if the game involves rules. Children at that age don't know the meaning of rules, much less abiding by them.

4. Don't buy toys that can only be played with a certain way. For example, the wind-up toy loses its fascination once your child has mastered the mechanics of winding it up.

5. Don't buy the toy that requires more than one child to play with it if you have an only child. I'll never forget an enormous toy cannon we bought for David. But what use is a cannon without an army to back it up, or to attack?

6. Don't buy toys that overpower children. The doll that was

the same size as Julie wasn't the one she liked; she liked a small one that she could mother and boss and spank and kiss. The big doll wasn't good for any of that.

7. Don't buy toys in lieu of sports equipment to save money. An example is the "sports helmet" that looks like a motorcyclist's helmet or a football player's, but it doesn't protect the way the real things do.

8. Don't start buying toys that are advertised on TV. Once you do it, you've got a running battle on your hands every time a toy commercial comes on (which is practically every five minutes all day long). It's "I want that" and "Buy me that" and "Gimme" and sometimes even "Please?" Many TV toys are gimmick toys, ones that are new this season, like the toy cannon I mentioned. The old standbys that sell and sell and sell are not advertised on TV—they don't have to be. If you decide to break this rule, let several weeks or more go by so that the connection between TV and buying isn't made obvious.

9. Don't worry about the weaponry toys. The best play gun in the world is a pointed finger with a mouth that yells "Bang!" or "Pow!" If a child is bent on having a gun, he'll make do with sticks and twigs and things. Since you can't prevent that, there's no point in making up "no gun" rules that you can't enforce.

10. Don't buy toys to use as bribes, rewards, or ersatz mother-substitutes. However, a "surprise" is nice now and then. And on "what do I do now?" days, having a toy hidden away somewhere could be a godsend.

Chapter 14

Preschool Schools

There you are, a mother-to-be, sitting with your feet propped up high—and does that feel good!—with this book balanced precariously on that inflated bookrack you call an abdomen—and you turn the page to a chapter on schools. Schools? Schools. Now, if I were you, I'd be tempted to flip some pages and get on to the more pertinent things. But, as it happens, *I* know better.

I know that if, three years from now, you wish your heir to go to the best preschool school in your area, or even the only one in your area, you may have to enroll him the day he is born, or soon after. I kid you not. Some nursery school waiting lists put those of Harvard and Smith to shame, and it can be easier to get into either of those than into a good nursery school.

So don't wait until your child is ready for school to look for the right school for him, you may then have no choice.

You have three *basic* types of schools to choose from: the private academic; the play-teaches; the Montessori. And there are variations and combinations of each. The names are somewhat misleading but do reflect a basic attitude or philosophy, which one nursery school director expressed as: (*1*) structured learning/ teacher-oriented, (*2*) open classroom*/teacher-facilitating, (*3*) open classroom/teacher-facilitating, using highly structured materials.

Private Academic
Here, education is spelled with a capital *E, D, U, C,* etc. The emphasis is on curriculum, on mathematics, science, social studies,

---
* Open classroom refers to a teacher's method of treating her students and their day (its meaning is identical to "open to new ideas") and does not describe a way of building schools in which walls are movable and removable—that's an open-*space* school.

geography, on art and music appreciation, on the introduction of a foreign language leading to bilingual abilities, and especially on early reading. Or, as they put it, on *reading-readiness*.

The private academic school may stress straight memorization (not very popular today; it's considered too old-fashioned). The in-thing is a form of phonetics, which requires the use of the Initial Teaching Alphabet—I.T.A. This is a special alphabet composed of "sounds," rather than the twenty-six letters we know, and used only in special I.T.A.-written books. Later, of course, the child must unlearn this and switch over to orthography (reading as we know it), which usually takes an extra year of schooling to do.

Or the school may offer a combination of phonetics with memorization of certain sight words that do not lend themselves to easy phonetic sounding, such as "the."

The really high-class, expensive, not necessarily good, academic school may offer all, or two, or one of these. Their motto seems to be "the more the better," and you are welcome to interpret that as you please.

In addition to having an educational program, they stress testing. And especially testing to determine maturity levels, since they pride themselves on placement of children on the basis of maturity rather than chronology.† It should be pointed out that such testing, when done by those who have a financial stake in the outcome, can be misleading.

Allow me to explain: In the two years that I taught at a very expensive private school, not one child entering the school was advanced or skipped a grade, a few were kept at their chronological grade-level, and many, many were held back a grade. It should be noted that with the last group, the school could look forward to one extra year's tuition. If you find yourself in such a position, it might be cheaper in the long run to apply (forfeiting if necessary the registration fee) at another school to get a second opinion.

The whole concept of maturity placement is questionable. Supposedly, going to a private academic school buys you a low teacher-student ratio—one that should make it possible for a terri-

† Although they may stress it, all do not actually do it. Watch for this.

bly bright child to be stimulated, and, at the same time, a rather slow child to be encouraged to perform.

Therefore, whenever the teacher-student ratio is one teacher to ten or fewer students, maturity placement is not as important as chronological placement. Because, whether you like it or not, chronological age does determine physical development.

The genius who graduates from high school and goes on to college at age twelve has some major problems to face, one of which is the maturation of his voice box, which his compatriots have already undergone. If the mature child is a girl, she's still learning about bras and menstruation at a time when her best friend may be doing some experimenting.

The Private Academic that Isn't all that Academic

Just because a private academic school offers preschool classes, it does not mean that those classes are watered-down imitations of the regular academic classes. Not at all. Many schools believe that the years under the age of six should be devoted to learning from experience, not from educators. For this reason, they do not subscribe to reading-readiness, they do not have workbooks for number concepts, they do not have sit-down work at miniature desks, they do not set academic goals and measure their pupils' progress toward them.

Although art, music, counting, languages, dancing, even nature may be taught, they are taught through imitation, not by rote-learning.

Of the many schools like this—and you have to do some detective work to find them—those that base their preschool education on the work done by The Waldorf Schools, founded in 1919 in Europe, come the closest, in my experience, to giving your child an educational experience within an academic setting without formalized learning.

To find the Waldorf school nearest you, write to The Waldorf Institute of Adelphi University, Garden City, Long Island, New York.

Play-Teaches

Here, the emphasis is on learning from play—not from toys per se —but from play in which the teacher acts as coordinator, facilitator, guide, assistant, helper, motivator—but not taskmaster, leader, or authority figure. The teacher in a student-oriented school can never be described as BOSS.‡

However, one nursery school director explained.

> I found it works great to have one teacher who presents a very strong Mother appearance: round, jolly, and full of touching love. The young, shy children need her to hold onto when they are tired or they feel sad or hurt.
>
> We use this person in our free play area and it works out fine. She is the one who goes to a child who has been corrected for undesirable behavior and who is feeling really sad. She puts her arms around the little one or sits down beside the child and says, "I can see you really feel sad that you threw the sand and that Mrs. D. had to ask you to leave the group for a while."
>
> The child then has a chance to verbalize his feelings or even explain that the circumstances had been such and such. By the time he has had his chance to use this mother-figure as a sounding board [notice she is neither approving nor disapproving of what he says, but more a warm, round security blanket], the teacher comes to get him and to ask if he is ready to rejoin the group.

"Is there nothing," asked one mother, "but play, play, play in such a group?"

"It doesn't sound like a school to me," agreed another.

Of course it's a school. Have you ever watched a group of children play? Or even joined in such play? It can be exhausting. That's because children play at 100 percent capacity. If they're moving slowly, it's only because they're giving 100 percent of their attention to a bird, or to a stream of ants on the ground, or to what that man over there—five houses away—is doing. In fact, there will be times when you're embarrassed at just how observant your child can be.

The Montessori School

As one Montessori directress put it, "A Montessori school is as different from a traditional play nursery school as night is from day." The typical Montessori school offers a three-hour, five-days-

---

‡ The good teacher accepts a child as being special and important and an individual with a right to be an individual. Although she must be firm so that a child does not initiate behavior that will hurt himself, his peers, or his environment, she is not out to mold your child's personality her way.

a-week program for children from two and one-half to six and one-half years old. The Montessori School does not stress maturity placement, nor chronological placement, because an assortment of children of all ages will be in the same room.

Within the room, the ground rules are simple. A child is free to select any work that has been previously demonstrated to him by the teacher. He removes it from the shelf, works with it as long as he chooses, and returns it to its proper place on the shelf before going on to another thing. He may not abuse any equipment, nor may he interfere with another child's work. The classroom itself is basically five areas: the area of practical life, sensorial work, language, math, and the humanities.

Practical life. Children participate in scrubbing floors, polishing shoes and silver, carrot cutting and more. I must confess the idea of spending money to have my son taught to scrub a floor or polish various items gets to me—especially since I have floors of my own that could use a good scrubbing, not to mention shoes and silver that need polishing.

Sensorial work. Available to the child is a smelling exercise, for example, that includes six jars with three sets of familiar fragrances. The child is asked to match them in pairs. You might want to try this at home. Another exercise includes a large mystery bag. With his eyes closed, the child is asked to reach into the bag and recognize a familiar object by touch and so name it. You could do the same with an old handbag and five or six familiar but very differently shaped and textured objects such as a ball, a cube, a jar lid, a key, etc. As the child masters these, add more related items, such as an oval, a rectangle, etc. It all reminds me very much of the program Rudyard Kipling devised for the training of a spy in *Kim*. Much the same could be done to teach textures using squares of silk, carpeting, vinyl, fur, and so on.

Language. The letters of the alphabet are cut out of sandpaper and glued to cards. As he learns the phonetic sound of the word, the child sees the shape and feels it with his fingers.

Math. Number rods represent quantities of one through ten. With the teacher's help to begin with, he learns to count the colored bands on each rod and then to arrange the rods in a step-like sequence.

Humanities. Learning of the world around him can be very descriptive and illustrative when the learning of "island," "peninsula," "isthmus," for example, is taught through the use of clay formations around which water can be poured.

And these are but a few of the many, many materials a Montessori student may work with. Are you impressed? I am. But those materials are designed to be used one way, and only one way. Couldn't that stifle creativity? Obviously, using such materials would be of great help to the mentally retarded or the physically handicapped or those from experience-deprived areas—such were the children Dr. Montessori developed her methods for—but I wonder just how much ingenuity and experimentation are sacrificed in normal children in the name of self-discipline.

Since some Montessori schools bill themselves as A.M.I. schools, and others as A.M.S., and others as neither, you might want to know the difference. To begin with, all Montessori teachers must be college graduates and preferably have their degree in elementary or preschool education. Those schools that say they are A.M.I. schools mean that all of their teachers are also graduates of a course offered under the auspices of the Association Montessori Internationale. This is a nine-month course that includes attending classes and observing at Montessori schools. It is the most expensive course. Therefore, in some people's eyes, it is the best. (Remember?)

The A.M.S. school has only teachers who have been trained in an American Montessori school. Under this training program, the student spends three months in school and then undertakes a nine-month internship in an American Montessori school. Since the internship is a paid position, this course costs less than the A.M.I. course—but on the other hand, it is the longest.

Those schools that do not describe themselves as A.M.I. or A.M.S. can have teachers with either (or both) training—as well as a third type of training—that offered by the St. Nicholas Training Center in London. It is a six-months' correspondence course, followed by a three-week workshop. Since it is possible to hold another job while taking the correspondence course, this method of learning Montessori is the least expensive—and remember, if most cost doesn't mean best, least cost doesn't mean worst.

Test Yourself! Which School Is for You?

1. Is it important to you that your child learn to read as early as possible? Ninety-nine percent do, you know, and some will do so without any formal training at all.

2. Will you feel more confident about your child's abilities when they are defined for you in terms of numbers and test scores?

3. Do you wish your child to have a private school education as opposed to a public school education? (*Note:* Enrolling your child in a private school's preschool classes can automatically guarantee him a spot in the regular school. It also gives him an advantage over those who enter at the kindergarten or first-grade level. Since he knows his classmates and has made friends, his adjustments to group and school are already completed.)

4. Do you wish the atmosphere of an academic school without its formalized, highly structured curriculum?

5. Do you wish your child to enjoy his childhood to its fullest, and to learn from it and his experiences with classmates who will, like himself, probably utilize the schools for which you are paying all those school taxes?

6. Do you wish your child to have access to a vast variety of playground equipment, which the average family can't afford, but which will foster the development of large muscles and bodily coordination?

7. Do you wish your child to have playmates his own age with whom he must cope, adjust, and even fight if necessary?

8. Do you wish to expose your child to a group in which some are his own age, others younger perhaps, others older?

9. Do you wish your child to develop self-discipline and perseverance even if at the expense of creativity—to learn to respect the work of others and not to intrude upon it without specific invitation?

10. Do you wish your mentally or physically handicapped child to have an education that will enable him to develop to his full potential through the use of repetition and highly structured materials?

11. Do you wish your child to have the experience of living in a

world where the toilets are the right size, the basins within his reach, the furniture of a height where his feet don't dangle?

12. Do you wish your child to be given an educational experience of a new and different kind while you are given some time to be by yourself, so that you can enjoy the times when the two of you are together?

Yes to questions 1, 2, 3, 6, 7, 11, 12—the private academic education school

Yes to questions 3, 4, 6, 7, 11, 12—the private academic Waldorf-type school

Yes to questions 5, 6, 7, 11, 12—the play-teaches school

Yes to questions 8, 9, 10*, 11, 12—the Montessori school

Yes to questions 11, 12—almost any school will do for you.

There is another factor that will influence your choice of type of school and that is cost. And one of the major determinants of cost is the financial purpose for which the school is operated. Is it out to make a profit or just to recoup expenses?

The Profit-Makers

Proprietary. These schools are owned and operated for the purpose of making a profit. This can mean that the owner acting as a teacher gets some reimbursement for her time, or it can mean that the owner is supporting a family from the profits of the school (a good sign of this is that the wife acts as headmistress and the husband is in charge of maintenance and machinery—in other words, he mows the lawn and does the janitorial work).

(1) *Private academic*—which particularly lends itself to profit-making if the owner combines the school with her home and utilizes the grounds all year round either in the form of school/summer school or school/day camp.

(2) *Montessori*—which in an area of high competition may manage to make a profit only by substituting the owner as teacher and saving the $5,000 to $7,000 salary that hiring such a teacher would mean.

(3) *Play-teaches, church-related*—you might think that if the

---

* Although not all Montessori schools will accept handicapped children.

church is involved, you are dealing with a charitable organization. No way. The church-related school often merely rents the church facilities, in which case it's a business like any other.

Franchised. This is something new to education, and so far is confined to Montessori-type schools. Some parents may find it repugnant to put preschool education in a class with fast food, employment agencies, car washes, art galleries, and you-name-it franchising. But it works like this: A person† buys the right to operate a Montessori school under the mother organization's name. In return for this right, most of her equipment is packaged for her and sold to her at a lower price than she may be able to get it for elsewhere. She may receive training, she may receive suggestions on how to operate her school most profitably, she will get some support from national advertising, publicity, etc. In return for this, she pays the franchiser a percentage of her *gross* receipts each year and every year.

Now obviously anyone who is out to make a profit under these circumstances must either charge more than the competition does, or cut corners somewhere, or offer something different from the offerings of other nonfranchised Montessori schools. On the other hand, if the franchising method contributes to more ready availability of Montessori-type schooling, it should be a good thing.

The Non-profit-makers

Accidentally so. These could have been created "for the purpose of making money" (a government stipulation of the I.R.S.) but, due to high operating expenses, etc., are failing to do so.

Deliberately so. Normally such a school is incorporated within the state as a nonprofit organization so as to take advantage of property-tax breaks, as well as making contributions to it income-tax deductible. The nonprofit school never hesitates to admit the fact.

(1) *Private academic:* Most of these schools are in the nonprofit category. However, their charges for tuition will depend

_____
† Although many men own or subsidize the purchase of such franchises, most have women managers and/or instructors.

to a great extent on their endowment. Since they try to provide a good teacher-to-student ratio (one to ten is normal), their salaries for teachers may take away the advantages they have in not paying property taxes.

(2) *Montessori:* Because of the large start-up expenses and the high teacher salaries, many Montessori schools start out accidentally non-profit-making and then become deliberately so in order to remain competitive with other nonprofit Montessori schools.

(3) *Play-teaches, church-sponsored:* When the church, as a means of helping the community, actively sponsors a preschool, it must, as must all other church-sponsored events, be non-profit-making. This does not mean it's free. Nor that it doesn't pay its teachers. Nor that its student body is open only to members of that church or that denomination or that religion. It means only that the church has elected to offer this service.

Cooperative. In this type of school the parents donate their services in lieu of paying *high* tuitions. They still may have to pay something to cover salaries, equipment, rent, and/or utilities.

(1) *Montessori:* Classroom participation is out, but parents can and do provide maintenance, take care of administration and bookkeeping, act as a board of directors or trustees.

(2) *Play-teaches:* The parents pool their labors and skills, providing a specified minimum amount of time to the school. In addition, they may participate in making policy decisions either through elected officers and/or a board of directors. That could be the extent of their involvement, or they could have fund-raising responsibilities, too, in which case they will be called upon to contribute time, energy, and goods or to buy tickets to various functions, such as bazaars, bridge parties, dinners, etc.

Of all the types of schools mentioned, the cooperative is the only one feasible for parents to begin on their own (the government estimates more than $1,000 will be required to buy the necessary outdoor play equipment, motor-activity-related toys, and manipulative toys,‡ which does not include books, phonograph

‡ Don't buy these if you can help it. It's more important to have toys different from the ones the child has at home, and to have creative toys. For outdoor equipment see Paul Hogan's *Playgrounds for Free.*

records, supplies, etc.). Because the above looks and sounds cold-blooded, a sort of tit-for-tat financial arrangement between parents and school, and because the cooperative offers you the most economical way to get a play-teaches education for your child—because of all this, allow me to go into more detail.

Under a cooperative, the mother is expected to donate at least one morning a week to the school. At some schools, she will be in the room that her child is in, at other schools she'll be in a different room. The father is expected to help build school furnishings and equipment, to take toys home to be repaired, and to help with the annual spring or fall cleaning.

What does this mean to the child? It means that the school is not "my" school but "our" school, that the transition from home to school is eased for him—that he's with his mommy, that he can get the facilities and toys normally available only at expensive schools, that the teacher is free to spend more time with each child since she has mother-helpers, that the child can take pride in saying, "My daddy fixed that swing," or "My mommy did the bulletin board."

And what of the parents—are they just getting a financial break? Not according to the director of the first cooperative play-teaches school on the East Coast, who says,

> Mothers, by coming once a week to work with a group of preschoolers, derive valuable learnings which they can then apply to their job at home.
>
> Wise methods of handling little children are best taught by example; and in the relaxed atmosphere of play school, free from the tensions of home, a mother gains new insights into the needs and characteristics of all little children. She learns little things. How to make papier-mâché, how to handle a paintbrush.
>
> And she learns big things—how to separate fighting children without adding to the total grief; how to lead children gracefully from one activity to another. For years, mothers have been telling us how much their mornings at Play School have helped them in their daily lives.

Are there disadvantages to such schools? Obviously, if spending one or more mornings a week working with fifteen to twenty youngsters doesn't appeal to you, that's a disadvantage. If you're working, you have to find alternative ways of serving the school—and some schools won't accept this. And, being in the same room as your child can create problems. Your child may remain too dependent on you. You may find yourself resenting the time the teacher spends on other children as compared to your own. You may have to fight the urge to intervene if your child is corrected by the teacher. Not being in the same room solves these problems, of course, but in the beginning it may mean you're running back and forth from your child's room to your room trying to prevent the blues. Many nursery school teachers will tell you that the crying child's tears are quick to dry up once Mommy is gone. Knowing Mommy is in the next room may not be as effective. It all depends on your child.

Then, there are always the possibilities of teacher-helper conflicts, especially in the area of the mother taking directions in how to handle children, situations, and problems. If you're a strong-willed lady with opinions of your own, you may find yourself biting your lip many a time.

But, under the right circumstances the cooperative school can offer you and your child a unique experience at a big financial saving. Which brings up the matter of cost.

Although tuition fees literally vary all over the map, the following are presented in the usual order of cost, most expensive first, with the exception that in those areas where Montessori schools are not widely available, the franchised Montessori school will probably be the most expensive.

Proprietary Academic
Nonprofit Academic
Franchised Montessori
Proprietary Montessori
Nonprofit Montessori
Cooperative Montessori
Church-related Play-Teaches
Church-sponsored Play-Teaches
Cooperative Play-Teaches, no fund-raising responsibilities
Cooperative Play-Teaches, with fund-raising responsibilities

In addition to the tuition charges, you should be aware that whatever the type of school, there are extras you may face:

1. A registration fee that is nonrefundable. This may be as low as $5 or as high as $50. It is an attempt on the school's part to

prevent no-shows caused by parents' doing multiple enrolling of a child or changing their minds between time of enrollment and school's starting.

2. Tuition-reimbursement insurance. Many schools require that you sign a contract that will guarantee that you will pay a full year's tuition no matter what (but don't sign one that has no escape clause based on your being transferred to another location). For a small sum, a percentage of the tuition charge, you can get insurance that will, in case accident or sickness prevents your child from attending, pay the tuition for you.

3. Accident insurance, to cover costs of setting broken bones, etc. The school should carry liability insurance.

4. Transportation charges. At some schools, this is a flat fee, at other schools it is based on zones (i.e., how far away from the school you live). And these transportation charges can be steep. Would you believe they can cost almost as much as the tuition?

5. Supplies charge. To cover the cost of paper, pencils, paints, paste, etc.

6. Snack charges. To cover the cost of the milk and cookies or juice and pretzels.

7. Lunches. If the school day covers the lunch period, you may be charged for meals, or you may have to invest in thermos and lunch box, and pack lunches.

8. Special-trip charges. Especially if the school must rent a bus to use, or if an admission charge is involved.

9. Class photos. Both individual and group. These are brought home for approval and need not be purchased. But the pressure from your child and your own pride is tremendous. Fortunately, the charge is usually reasonable.

10. Special clothing may be required. You may need to buy dance shoes, a smock,* a blanket or sleeping rug, special boots to

* Make your own out of Daddy's old shirt. Remove the collar by cutting it off at the neckband, or open the neckband and remove collar, then resew the neckband. A short-sleeved shirt may be just the right length for your child, otherwise cut a long-sleeved shirt to wrist length, allowing enough material to turn a large seam. Put elastic through the hem of the sleeve to draw it tight. With the garment on, cut off the shirttails so that the smock comes to just below the knees. Machine-stitch the hem, or finish with pinking shears. Oh, by the way, the shirt is worn backwards, the teacher buttoning it up the back.

keep at school in case of wet weather, a complete change of clothing to be kept at school at all times.

11. Check and double-check your charges and/or bills. Some schools have amateur bookkeepers. (I know of one who can't work in decimals; she rounds everything off to the *next,* not nearest, dollar.)

How can you know whether you're getting a good school for your money? I asked a group of nursery school directors, administrators, teachers, presidents, etc., as to how they would evaluate a school. Here's what they said:

Physical Plant

1. Is it spacious? (Thirty-five square feet of free space per child indoors, seventy-five square feet outdoors.) Is there room for vigorous play as well as quiet activities? Are there various areas for different kinds of play, such as a housekeeping area, a puzzle area, a quiet area to be off by one's self for a while?

2. Is the room well-lighted, both from windows and overhead lighting? Is there adequate provision for heat during winter, ventilation or air-conditioning during summer?

3. Is the artwork on exhibit the children's or a teacher's? The former is preferable.

4. Is the equipment in good repair? Has it been chosen to offer a variety of experience, is it sturdy, is it flexible, is it sterile, or imaginative?

5. Do toilets and washbasins appear sanitary? Is there one for every fifteen children enrolled? (Count them, check the enrollment, divide.)

6. Is the school safe? No unprotected stair wells, no uncovered radiators, no kitchen area left unsupervised at any time?

7. What about dangers from automobiles when outside? Is there a fenced-in play yard?

Personnel

1. Are all teachers certified by the state?

2. Will there be at least one teacher and an assistant for every group of children?

3. Will class size be limited to no more than twenty per group, fifteen preferable?

4. Is there a school nurse or a person with first-aid training available?

5. Will there be male authority-figures on the premises in a position to talk to or correct your child? What is their background? A minister or priest can be of benefit to your child, a janitor can be detrimental, a male teacher can offer a new experience.

Attending a Session

1. Do the children seem involved, happy, comfortable? Or are they frustrated, bored, and submissive? "Turned on . . . or turned off," as Gwen Robinson of the Valley Forge, (Pa.) Presbyterian Co-Operative Nursery School put it.

2. Is there an atmosphere of love and respect between adults and children?

3. Is there an acceptance of differences in the classroom?

4. Is there evidence of respect for the rights of others?

5. Is the teacher allowed to be flexible or must she follow a schedule?

6. How does the teacher head off or handle an argument?

7. How does the teacher—literally—handle children? Does she encourage them to climb in her lap? Does she shove or use force to get them to do things?

8. Is the teacher so obviously in charge that children wait to be told what to do and constantly turn to her for approbation or direction?

9. Will she be given in-service training (workshops, etc.)?

What You Should Avoid in a Nursery School

1. A school that discourages visitors, especially parents.

2. Noncertified teachers.†

---

† These are people who do not have either the educational background or —in some states—a required amount of practice teaching and/or in-school training. Admittedly, certification does not guarantee a gift with children. Many noncertified teachers are by nature better with children. But it does make sure that the teacher has the background to know what to do when. And equally important, what not to do. About toilet-training or table manners or three-year-old negativism or whatever. The certified teacher may not be exceptionally helpful for your child; the noncertified teacher may do irreparable harm, even to the extent of ruining your child's love of learning for the rest of his life.

3. Schools that are not licensed, registered, or approved by the state.

4. Schools that are accredited by the state or regional association of private schools; in some states, however, no proprietary school can be accredited because it is so difficult to assess their financial stability and responsibility.

How to Find a Nursery School

How do you *find* a nursery school? Beatrice B. Szalai, president of her local cooperative play-teaches school in southeastern Pennsylvania, suggests the following:

1. Consult the directory of the National Association for the Education of Young Children.

2. Consult the directory of the American Association of Nursery Schools.

3. Consult the local phone book.

4. Ask neighbors.

5. Ask your minister.

6. Ask your pediatrician.

7. Ask the local kingergarten or first-grade teacher.

Another nursery school director suggested the Chamber of Commerce, the County Superintendent of Schools, the State Department of Education, and don't forget The Waldorf Institute.

Part 6

Maintenance

Of each dollar spent raising a child, 14 percent of it will go toward maintenance in one form or another: 5¢ toward shelter-related expenses, 9¢ for personal care.

Of course, shelter-related applies only to homeowners or those renters whose leases require them to maintain—paint, repair, mow, shovel, etc. If this is not the case with you, you'll have an extra $10 a month for the next eighteen years to spend on other things, like higher rent, for example.

If you do own a home, your cost will be for electrical work, redecorating, furnace repairs, gardening, etc. The etcetera includes such child-related maintenance costs as calling a plumber to retrieve a flushed teddy bear or other goody you cannot extract yourself.* (Relax, it happens to everyone at least once. The knack is in not having it happen twice.) It also includes the upkeep and repair of any appliances you use to try to beat the high cost of maintenance, such as a washer, dryer, or sewing machine, but not the cost of buying them.

The other 9 percent of maintenance costs covers hair cuts,

* Use a coat hanger (although a more flexible wire would be better) and open it. Sharpen the end and make a hook there. Then use this crude toilet-problem extractor to avoid calling the plumber unnecessarily.

drycleaning bills, toothpaste and toothbrushes, deodorants and hair sprays and so on. It includes feeding utensils and diapering needs, replacement of linens and the cost of their laundering, the paper you write your shopping lists on and the pencil you use to write them, but not the cost of getting to the store. It also includes reading material, such as this book, plus any other items that will cost less than $5 on a regular basis over the years.

In other words, maintenance is the great budget catchall. It can help you or hurt you budgetwise depending on your flexibility and your willingness to do it yourself.

When making out your budget, remember that shelter-related maintenance costs are highest the first two years, gradually drop to a low point during the preteens, and then go up as gradually as they went down, but never again reaching the heights they did in the beginning.

You should also remember that this is not true of personal-care maintenance. It starts out steep, drops dramatically at the toilet-training stage of the game. Then, freed of the necessity of diapering, it remains low until school enters the picture. At this point there is an even more dramatic rise in maintenance costs, but they then hold steady and under $200 per year until your child enters seventh grade (or junior high school). Again there is a plateau until the time when dating escalates costs again.

You will find that the personal-care portion of maintenance costs will average out to approximately $200 a year, but beware of setting that as your goal right from the beginning. Maintenance costs go above $200 the moment your child steps foot into the teens and discovers cosmetics and acne lotions, and toiletries.

There is one thing missing from all this, and that is the dollar value of the work of the maintenance-workers: you and your husband. According to a study done at Cornell University, Ithaca, New York, by Kathryn E. Walker and William H. Gauger, the work you will put in for one child over the first eighteen years would, if reimbursed at the going wage rate that would have to be paid to others for the same services, be worth $96,300. That's right, ninety-six thousand, three hundred dollars. And the average husband will contribute some $25,000 worth of services over those same eighteen years.

Chapter 15

At the Diaper Station

Somehow, some way, you've come up with something to use as a changing table. On it, in it, above it, or below it go the following:

DIAPERS

As sure as babies cry, you'll need diapers. What kind you use is up to you. You can use fabric or disposables. Or both, since each has its advantages.

Disposables

Statistics tell the story here. Disposables have grown from around 5 percent of the total diaperings in 1968 to over 30 percent in 1972. And a look at the sales charts shows a continued upward trend. Additionally, more than 80 percent of American mothers use disposables at least part of the time.

It's interesting to note that disposables were invented in Sweden, according to the American Paper Institute, and for the past twenty years their acceptance has been so great there that cloth diapers are not now available.

Why such a dramatic acceptance? A study conducted in a leading Midwestern hospital might be illustrative. When records were kept of the launderings in two nurseries, one using only fabric diapers, the other disposables, it was found that the disposable diaper nursery had used 19.4 percent fewer diapers, 36 percent fewer crib sheets, 47 percent fewer blankets and 20.8 percent fewer baby shirts.

Certainly such statistics are dramatic and of special good news to the laundresses, but it should be pointed out that the differences would not have been as significant if disposable diapers, with their built-in waterproof pants, were compared to cloth diapers plus such pants.

As for mother, whether disposables cut down on her other baby laundering or not, they do eliminate all diaper washing.

And since a new diaper is used each time, the chance of diaper rashes, due to a buildup of urea in cloth diapers over many home launderings, is eliminated. That's why when diaper rash happens, many pediatricians tell mothers doing their own cloth diapers to switch to disposables, at least temporarily.

Yes, that kind of diaper rash does not happen with the throwaways. But another kind does; it's called DDR, or Disposable Diaper Rash. And its cause is that nice waterproof outside sheet that keeps the urine from getting the bedding wet, and that keeps you from noticing that baby is wet. Thus, urea can break down inside the disposable and cause diaper rash just like waterproof pants can.

Which, some say, is the fault of the mother, not the diaper. And I agree, so long as the mother is using disposables as an alternative to cloth diapers, not as a means of using fewer diapers of any kind.

In other words, any savings coming from the use of disposables should come from saving on laundry costs and supplies and saving on the need for a large wardrobe, on the savings on diaper pins (with pretaped disposables)—but not from using fewer diapers.

In fact, those pretaped disposables may cause you to use more disposables after a while than you would cloth diapers. It happens when you discover baby isn't always all wet. With the pretaped ones, once you rip off that tape, which you have to do to see whether or not the diaper's wet, one side of the diaper is ruined. Trying to reuse it, if dry, by pinning the side back together doesn't work. Also you are letting yourself in for leakage. Presto—sheets need laundering.

What do disposables give you for your money? Freedom and convenience and, for some, even safety. Freedom from carting diapers to the washer . . . spinning the first load semimoist . . . running them through the longest cycle . . . going back for another rinse and spinning. Next, into the dryer. When dry, there's folding and smoothing to do. Then back they go to the diaper station. Multiply all that by 75 to 100 times or more in a year, depending on how many cloth diapers you own, and you'll see why mothers love disposables.

What about the woman without access to her own washer and dryer. If she must use a coin-operated machine, that's $20 a month out of her pocket. If the machines are in her building that means a trip up and down for each stage in the operation, a minimum of three trips, if she's not going to stay there the whole time. Where's baby all this time?

The woman who has to go to a public laundromat may be able to combine doing the washing with doing errands, but not always. Staying there for the whole operation could mean spending one to one and a half hours, two or more times per week, waiting for diapers to be laundered. What's happening to baby all this time?

What about the possible dangers inherent in basement laundry rooms, or in public laundromats. Then there's theft to think about. And the chance of a blue sock being left in a washer: abracadabra, baby blue diapers.

For these mothers, disposable diapers mean money well spent. But the wise mother will keep a dozen cloth diapers on hand just in case. Just in case she runs out of disposables. After all, there's no way to reuse a diaper that's been flushed down the drain.

Speaking of which, don't be taken in by the term "disposable" diaper and think: unfasten, pull off, drop in toilet, and presto! one disposable diaper disposed of. Uh-uh, it doesn't work that way. Take the directions printed on one manufacturers' box. They go something like this—of course, "Britches" is not these diapers' actual brand name.

1. When it is time for a change, remove Britches by tearing down through the tape fasteners where they join the Britches together.

2. Take the end of the Britches with the tape fasteners and separate the plastic backsheet from the pad at both corners. Now, starting at the corner, pull the plastic from the pad. DO NOT FLUSH PLASTIC.

3. Rinse the Britches by dipping it up and down in the toilet until most of the absorbent pad separates from the inner liner and falls apart in the water. If the Britches is soiled, be sure the inner liner is rinsed extra thoroughly.

4. Wrap the rinsed inner liner in the waterproof outside sheet, along with the tape fasteners, and discard in the wastebasket. Then flush away the absorbent material.

Now that's not exactly what I'd call work-free. Nor 100-percent disposable.

Although toilet-disposables work well for those who have sewers, others beware! The man who unclogs septic tanks charges $25 and up, a rather costly proposition.

One of the ideal times to use disposables is when visiting. Watch it! Step carefully! Don't, I beg of you, if you value your friendships, don't put a disposable down a friend's toilet. You can't tell the condition of the plumbing from the lack of the pull chain that lets down the water from an overhead tank. But flush a flushable, and you find out in a flash. Then there's *real* cleaning up to be done! The only thing worse is the plumbing bill you will either gallantly insist on paying or find in your mailbox anyway.

So when visiting and a change becomes necessary, it will be much easier on you if you wrap that disposable up in a plastic bag and toss it in a trash can. Which is what most disposable-users do *all* of the time.

That raises the question of the ecological costs of disposable diapers. To begin with, according to William V. Driscoll, of the American Paper Institute, disposable diapers do not introduce any new or dangerous materials into our environment. "All the materials used in disposable diapers have a long history of use in many different kinds of products."

He says, for example, that the absorbent pads are made of cellulose. So are cotton and rayon and linen and acetate—materials that can be as safely and easily incinerated as a sanitary napkin. The plastic backsheet will burn up completely and harmlessly, giving off only carbon dioxide and water vapor—the same gases formed when you burn bread in your toaster or wood in your fireplace.

In the case of a landfill, the absorbent pad will biodegrade, while it's conceivable that the plastic backsheets help to stabilize the landfill. It's also conceivable that the bag you use to hold the plastic backsheets is more dangerous ecologically than the whole of the disposable diaper.

As far as its effect on the sewage system is concerned, well . . . you get varying reports. One group will tell you that introducing 4 billion (number of disposables used in 1972) anything into a sewage system will have serious consequences. The estimated load of 171,000 tons of waste paper and 43,000 tons of sludge (solid waste) will cost somebody—you the taxpayer—something to dispose of. In a city with a population of 100,000, the amount of paper diapers used—if all were flushed—would result in the same amount of normal sludge produced by 1.1 million people.

Another group will tell you that even if disposable diapers were used exclusively on all babies, and the pads were all flushed, they would account for no more than 3 to 4 percent of the total load currently being handled by sewage-treatment plants.

Both will tell you, however, that most of any environmental problems could be minimized, if not eliminated, if mothers would simply follow those flushing instructions just given above for "Britches."

Speaking of which, that's about a dozen flushings a day. With the maximum tank capacity 6 gallons of water, you're talking about using 72 gallons of water a day, over 500 gallons a week. Depending on what your water company charges for water, you just find your water bill going up a dollar or two a month—just for flushing diapers.

And based on national averages, you'll have used more water to flush disposables than you would have used to wash cloth ones!

Which brings us to the great alternative.

Cloth Diapers
You have your choice of four styles of cloth diapers:

1. The most popular is the prefold, which is a rectangular piece of material folded and stitched in such a way that there are extra layers of material in the central section.

2. The preshaped are basically formed into a figure-eight or hourglass shape. These you buy in various sizes, for newborn, six months, etc. They fit the baby the best, but cost the most because periodically you have to replace them.

3. The square diaper is meant to be folded into a triangle. This is the one favored by cartoonists because it shows the pin in the middle—and I distrust it for just that reason. I don't trust two diaper pins to stay closed, much less putting all my faith in one.

4. The rectangular diaper was the one that your mother used and is nothing more than the prefold unfolded—you do the folding. A lot of work, repeated week after week. Of course, there's no law against folding and stitching it down.

The diaper services will give you your choice of styles and allow you to change styles at any time if you wish, but do-it-yourselfers will need to make a choice. Faced with approximately 10,000 changes in the first two years of motherhood, you are wise to choose a preshaped or prefolded diaper and save hours and hours of folding time. Although the shaped ones do fit better and are less bulky than the prefolds, they only come in sizes up to 27 to 30 pounds. If your baby is a big one, you may have to change over to prefolds during the second year.

On the other hand, the prefolds put the most protection where it's needed: in the middle. One catalog company offers a prefold with an eight-layer center panel compared to the normal six-layer and guarantees the diaper for the diapering life of your infant.

Naturally there's a difference in price. The rectangular and square diapers cost less compared to (a) the prefolds, which can cost from 50¢ to $1.75 a dozen or more depending on quality, and (b) the preshaped, which start at $1.50 more than unfolded and go up to $3.25 or more for a snap-on style. My recommendation: the most expensive prefold, the one from the catalog company.

How many? That depends on your access to laundry equipment. For the first month or so, a baby may need ninety to one hundred changes a week. However, the maximum number of diapers you can do in the normal twelve-pound-capacity washing machine is six dozen, so you might as well make up your mind that you'll have to do at least a load and a half a week (or one every four to five days) for the first two months, and at least one load a week after that. But by six months, you'll be using about seventy diapers a week, and the number you'll use will gradually decrease until at the end of the first year, five dozen will see you through a normal week. But six dozen is safer. However, I've known mothers to make do with less than two dozen diapers on hand—but those diapers were washed daily. And that's one to one and a half hours a day doing diaper laundering.

Diaper Service
A diaper service is one answer to saving time as well as preventing ecological problems (cotton diapers, having had at least seventy-five washings, are sold as reusable rags or recycled into paper. I can't vouch for the paper, but the rags are great).

The advantages are many. For example, you usually get a free diaper pail with vastly greater capacity than you'd normally use, complete with free deodorant cakes and plastic liners. All you need to do is take the diaper off, plop it into the pail, and once a week take the plastic liner out, fasten it some way and lug it outside (no heavier a burden than your own diapers or a bag of disposables).

Within hours, those dirty diapers are replaced by beautifully clean, practically sterile diapers. And you pay not for what you think you will use, but for what you actually do use.

Therein lies the problem. Determining how many you have used. The mathematician and record-keeper will do it handsoff scientifically, the mother with money will let the diaper service figure it out, the rest of us take the simple way, the pungent way. We count out those diapers ourselves. Which comes as close as you can imagine to washing an oven with ammonia while keeping the door partially closed.

The man on the other end, receiving your bundle of joy, also does some counting. But he's not apt to be as thorough as you, which is why double-diapering sometimes results in up to 50 percent fewer diapers coming back than went. Of course, that also means you only pay half, but the system is self-defeating for you, since you soon run out of diapers. When you try to explain that to the diaper service, you'd better have on hand an accurate count of what you sent.

HOW A DIAPER SERVICE WORKS ON THE BASIS OF 100 DIAPERS

	Received	Sent	Have on Hand	
1st week	100	—	100	(total number received)
2nd week	100	95	105	(total number received less returns, or 200 minus 95)
3rd week	95	90	110	

As you can see, the fewer you use the more you have on hand, until theoretically, at the end of your diaper-service life, you will have 200 diapers on hand, the exact number you were advanced over the first two weeks.

But life doesn't work as simply as that. Things happen.

Example: The fourth week, you go to visit your mother for a few days and use disposables instead. Whether from the change in drinking water, or from an infection, or whatever, the fifth week, upon returning home, the baby gets diarrhea. Here's what happens then:

	Received	*Sent*	*Have on Hand*	
1st week	100	—	100	
2nd week	100	95	105	(200 minus 95)
3rd week	95	95	105	(200 minus 95)
4th week	95	45	155	(200 minus 45)
5th week	45	150	50	(200 minus 150)

At this stage, if the runs continue, you will run out of diapers before you get those 150 diapers back a week later.

Aware of this, many diaper services give you more than your base 100 contract, such as 125 diapers the first and again the second week. Then your Have-on-Hand figure would be based on 250 diapers advanced. Other diaper services will give you your base contract at the time you sign up for diaper service, and then the first week give you still another contract worth. This makes your diaper-advance 300.

Check this feature out when you are determining which diaper service to use. The one with the largest advance is your best bet, in terms of not having to worry about running out. On the other hand, storing several hundred diapers can be a problem. But one I can live with very happily.

Which brings up the whole subject of cost. The table on pages 234–35 shows various costs for various types of diaperings at various levels of usage.

These levels were based on recommended usages as set by both the disposable and the diaper-service people and on the actual experience of an average person: me.

The rates themselves came from various sources, such as institutes and companies and diaper services and consumer shopping reports. They are 1973 *national averages*. Diaper-service rates, for example, would be higher in New York City and lower in Chattanooga. Home laundering will be affected by utility rates, etc. However, in most cases, the relationship between the costs of doing-it-yourself, diaper-servicing, or disposing will remain the same.

Why put together such a chart that may be outdated with every increase in the consumer price index? For many reasons. First, because I am not so sure it will go out of date that fast. Competition has kept the prices down before, and probably will again— especially with a declining birth rate. Thus, the costs of disposable diapers have remained relatively stable over the past five years, with certain prices going up as little as one fifth of 1 percent per diaper, and others going down as much as 1¢ per diaper.

The same has held true, *nationally,* of the diaper services. Prices have been creeping up, rather than skyrocketing; in my area, for example, they've gone up for 100 diapers only 5¢ a week per year. And although their costs have gone up, automation beckons, which should further stabilize the picture.

Another reason for the chart is that I want something that would compare costs *objectively,* with bias neither toward nor against diaper service, disposables, or do-it-yourself. Depending on whom you talk to, you will hear "disposables are 40 percent cheaper than diaper service," or "diaper services cost 20 percent less than disposables," or "home laundering is the most expensive." To be fair, these people take into consideration the cost of your labor. I didn't. That pleasantly surprising do-it-yourself $136.43 figure does not include 7 hours a week of washing, drying, folding, etc., or 364 hours the first year alone. And 208 the next, and 52 the last. That's 624 hours you've donated to the cause of saving money on diapering. Tell that to your husband next time he complains about costs. At $2 an hour—and you're certainly worth that—you've invested $1,248 of your hard labor.

And that figure really isn't that accurate, since it does not include extra rinses, bleaches, presoaks, etc.—the things you'll need to do the first year when diaper rash is a problem, at least for the first six months. A case of diaper rash can wipe out all the do-it-yourself savings in a flash by requiring a changeover to diaper service or disposables. It can add to your work load timewise by forcing you to boil and sterilize diapers to undo what has been built up.

At the same time, ointments and medications may be needed, the baby may have to be undiapered for long hours (with result-

Time Period	Quantity	Do-It-Yourself
		(*Usual way*)

YEAR ONE

13 weeks	90 per	$ 19.31
13 weeks	80 per	17.16
13 weeks	70 per*	15.02
13 weeks	60 per*	12.87
Total Diapering Cost for One Year		$ 64.36

* Double-diapering normally occurs at night after age six months; keeps number used higher than would be expected.

YEAR TWO

52 weeks	48*	$ 41.18
Total Diapering Cost for Two Years		$105.54

* Reflects a gradual decrease from 5 dozen to 3 dozen over a year.

YEAR THREE

52 weeks	36	$ 30.89
Total Diapering Cost for Three Years		$136.43

Do-It-Yourself	Diaper Service	Disposables
(*As diaper service does it, complete with boiling, antiseptics, etc.*)	(*With a base rate of $3.75 per week for 90 diapers, less 18¢ average per 10 or less*)	(*Beginning with small sizes and graduating to larger sizes*)
$ 46.80	$ 48.75	$ 58.50
41.60	46.41	62.40
36.40	44.07	50.83**
31.20	40.43	51.87†
$156.00	$179.66	$223.60

** Switching to extra-absorbent nighttime size at night will decrease number of disposables needed but increase the price per nighttime diaper (56 diapers at 6¢; 7 at 7¢ per week).

† Switch made to overnight size at all times, the increase in cost per diaper offsetting the cost of fewer overall diapers.

$ 99.84	$152.36**	$174.72†
$255.84	$332.02	$398.32

** Adjusted to reflect rates normally done in progressions of 10 or less, but not 12.

† Continues to reflect the lack of double-diapering, and is figured at the rate of 42 per week.

$ 74.88	$138.34	$131.04
$330.72	$470.34	$529.36

ing cleanups of his room), he may require special healing-light treatments, he may require visits to the doctor. He may require all of these. But at what cost the hours of screaming and fretting and hurting? Compare the agony you've suffered from the worst sunburn you've ever had, and you'll only feel a portion of what a baby feels from diaper rash. So, let's be realistic and substitute the greater of the do-it-yourself figures, noting as we do that such treatment takes more of your time than the other in terms of laundering, not in treating diaper rash.

The difference between that form of do-it-yourself and diaper service is only $24 a year, or $2 a month; the difference between do-it-yourself and disposables is $68 a year or around $5.50 a month.

But explore those figures a little further, and you discover that for the first six months at optimum, most diaper-rash-preventing usage, the cost of having diaper service over do-it-yourself comes to less than $7. Seven whole dollars. The first week of do-it-yourself will require about seven hours of work on your part. Multiply that by twenty-six weeks, divide into $7—and you're being reimbursed at the rate of 4¢ an hour for doing your own laundering.

RECOMMENDATION: DON'T DO-IT-YOURSELF FOR THE FIRST SIX MONTHS. Return enough baby gifts to make up that $7 difference, and use diaper service.

The next thing to notice: The difference between the most expensive do-it-yourself and disposables the following year is almost $75, and between the same do-it-yourself and diaper service almost $54. But the difference between cheap do-it-yourself and disposables is $131.54, and between cheap do-it-yourself and diaper service is $101.18. Now that is a lot of money.

RECOMMENDATION: DO-IT-YOURSELF-CHEAP THE SECOND YEAR. Do you realize that your savings the second year from doing-it-yourself over disposables would pay for a third year of using disposables? Now, that makes sense. If you did your own diapers for year two, you could put your child into disposables during year three for free. And would that take the drive out of toilet-training! With a year's free use of disposables, you could take your time toilet-training, realizing that the lack of it was costing you nothing. Shrinks will tell you that too early or too forcible toilet-training may make you feel more powerful and godlike, but it can also cost your child in terms of ego and self-esteem. Relax, use disposables. The toilet-training will come of itself.*

NOTE: *if you plan to toilet-train between ages one and two, don't do it yourself, go directly into disposables.*

RECOMMENDATION: DISPOSABLES THE THIRD YEAR. Why didn't I suggest you go back to diaper service? Because, although the final figures for year three are only about $7 apart, at the end of the year diaper service is costing you much more than the equivalent in disposables. Even on a diaper-for-a-diaper basis—forgetting the lack of need for double-diapering with disposables—at the national average rate, twenty diaper-service diapers will cost you $2.39 a week, the exact same number of disposables $1.40.

NOTE: *if bed-wetting is a problem, it's much, much cheaper to keep your child in disposables at night until four, five or six years old or even longer than to launder bed linens every morning.†*

DIAPER SERVICE: HOW TO
SAVE MONEY DIAPERING

Another look at the example on page 232 reveals something else. Although you have contracted for 100 diapers a week, what you have done is to use less three out of four weeks. Those three weeks, your charge should be lower, too. The following week, when you used a greater number, your charge would be higher. (But you must keep track of this to make sure.)

These charges may be determined on a base rate—set by your contract—with X number of cents subtracted or added per every 10, more or less, that you use. Or the charges may be based on a sliding scale, with 61 to 70 one price, 71 to 80 another price, 81 to 90 still a third price, and so on.

Usually, they equalize. But not always—so get rates from com-

---

* Ten percent of all eight-year-olds are bed-wetters, but less than 2 percent of eighteen-year-olds still have the problem. Among such older bedwetters have been famous athletes.

† And much cheaper than using drugs to solve the problem. Most don't; those that do frequently work only temporarily. Moreover, the use of imipramine-hydrochlorides, such as Ciba-Geigy Corp.'s Tofranil had been blamed for deaths due to overdoses: the drug looks identical to those heart-shaped candies we used to call "red hots."

petitive companies. You may find it cheaper to contract for a higher number than you had originally planned. And take advantage of the correspondingly lower rate.

Diaper services do, however, have one thing in common. They charge in multiples of five, seven, or ten. Act accordingly. If you find you have need for four extra diapers, use one more for free on the five-rate, three on the seven-rate, six on the ten-rate—and I leave the how-you-use up to you. If in counting you find you have used only one or two or three diapers more than the base number, hold those back until next week.

By wisely using and counting and adjusting the number of diapers you return each week, you can save enough to pay for an extra two or more weeks of diaper service per year.

Another saving that should be explored is the possibility of a long-time or multiple-week rate. This involves committing yourself to the use of diaper service for X number of weeks, but not X number of diapers. You may use less if you choose.

DO-IT-YOURSELF OR DISPOSABLES

Another source of savings with any type of diapering pertains to your diapering habits. Some mothers must diaper a baby the moment they pick him up no matter how loudly he's protesting. Others won't change a diaper until the room reeks. The first concept costs money; the second saves little or nothing because it causes diaper-rash problems that are cured only expensively.

There is a happy medium. It involves a bit of knowledge about the physiology of infants. In young children, when food goes in one end, expanding the stomach and passing the message on to the large intestine as well as bladder, it comes out the other in the form of urine or feces. Thus, to change a diaper *before* a feeding is to waste money. Either before or while you're burping your baby, his depository system is at work.

What this means to the mother who is coping with six feedings a day is an extra forty-two diapers a week either to care for or to avoid. If, in the name of conscientiousness, you feel the baby should be changed before his feeding, this could cost you almost $15 for disposables over six weeks, $5 for diaper service, and $2 to $3 for home laundering.

You figure it out over a yearly basis. It's formidable in terms of cost. It is also not so kind to your child. There he is, trusting soul that he is, and he calls for action to fill his stomach. Here she comes, the angel in denim, and she picks him up. In expectation he trustingly stops his cries. She rewards his trust not by feeding him but by carrying him to the changing table and . . . but you get the picture.

A small investment in lap pads and quilted pads will enable you to teach your child that life can be satisfying and rewarding. At the same time, enabling you to save some money. So, if you have an instinctive feeling that you must immediately cleanse this child of his dirty diapers, you may take deliberate satisfaction out of the fact that your not-so-immediate, no-time-for-diaper-changing feeding is probably much more psychologically and physically satisfying to him.

DIAPERS, ETC.

Speaking of instincts, there are such involved in using a diaper service. After all, each week you get somebody else's diapers. What if the other baby had a disease, such as prenatally induced gonorrhea, or a more common yet devastatingly dangerous infection of staphylococci—a known baby killer—what then?

The National Institute of Infant Services will tell you that the *accredited*—their emphasis—diaper service uses such high water temperatures plus bleaching agents that it will almost always destroy germs such as those causing venereal disease and all other pathogenic bacteria.

Moreover, an accredited diaper service will offer diapers that meet the following specifications: elimination of bacteria normally found to be pathogenic, finish to the pH of normal skin, impregnation with a safe bacteriostat to retard the development of ammonia while in use, sufficient softness to prevent abrasion, adequate absorbency, whiteness retained for aesthetic reasons.

So there you have it, three alternatives to choose from: disposables, do-it-yourself, and diaper service. You have the prices, the advantages, the disadvantages. You should from these be able to determine which is the best for you. But only if you level with yourself.

How able are you to deal with the problem of stool and urine?

Can you see yourself swishing dirty diapers around in a toilet? Can you face counting out a hundred reeking, visually sickening, rented diapers? Can you do load after load of diapers, have them come through stained, and, rather than subject your child to the bacteria that must be where the stains are, can you do the whole wash again?

Like breast- versus bottle-feeding, these are questions only you can answer. But ecology must be considered. After all, you hope the child to whom you've given birth will have at least as good a world as the present one.

If you have a septic tank, you shouldn't flush the disposable diapers—at least at the rate of ninety to one hundred a week. It creates a sanitation problem.

If you are really uptight when it comes to stool and urine, a diaper service won't be. You may have to take pains to separate double diapers before putting them into the pail, but they'll take care of everything else.

If you can't count them out because of the stench, you'll find most diaper services err on the side of too much instead of too little. A call to the headquarters will have your future loads double-checked and even an emergency requisition to bring your current supply up to standard. The problem doesn't exist with disposables.

Can you wash and wash and then rewash? If you can't you'd better be prepared to switch to one of the other alternatives. Otherwise, you'll spend your $40-to-$95-a-year savings for boiling diapers in a pot on the stove, for chemical diaper-purifiers, for tube after tube of A & D ointment, Desitin, Diaperene, or whatever the latest diaper rash-cure is.

I shall not, can not, recommend one alternative over the others. I have used all three; I have found all three had advantages and disadvantages that seemed to cancel out. You must decide for yourself, but this quiz might help.

TRUE OR FALSE QUIZ ON DIAPERING

1. T F The least amount of distasteful work in terms of swishing diapers within toilets occurs with diaper-service diapers.
2. T F The best time to change baby is just before feeding him.
3. T F A better diaper would be made of no-iron, permanent-press cotton-polyester blend. The best of 100-percent miracle fiber.

4. T F If your baby gets diaper rash, it's your fault, since you haven't changed the diapers frequently enough.
5. T F Teething, according to old wives' tales, is a cause of diaper rash.
6. T F Children in countries where neither diapers nor anything else is used never suffer from diaper rash.
7. T F You can always tell when children are wearing disposable diapers because of the bulges.
8. T F The use of oil instead of water to cleanse baby after a bowel movement prevents diaper rash.
9. T F A baby needs to be bathed at least daily to prevent diaper rash.
10. T F A baby is uncomfortable when his diaper is wet.

ANSWERS:

1. *True*. The greatest amount of time is spent on disposables. It is for this reason that a vast majority of mothers elect not to flush their diapers. The next most time is spent on do-it-yourself diapers in hopes of preventing stains and problems during laundering. Although the diaper service would hope you'd dump large amounts of stool in the toilet, the soiled diaper can be put directly into the supplied diaper pail without rinsing—the deodorant cake will prevent your being reminded of the fact odoriferously.

2. *False*. A baby should be fed first, changed later, in order to avoid washing an extra diaper per feeding per day per week. The reflex action of the large intestine, which is triggered by feeding, is the reason that many people feel a cup of coffee and a cigarette are laxative in effect. It is also the reason that children may stop in the middle of a meal and claim a bellyache. They are feeling the intestine in motion. If excused to have a bowel movement, they'll be able to eat normally afterward.

3. *False*. The more polyester or miracle fiber present, the less absorbent the diaper. Both regular diapers and disposables are made of natural and cellulose fibers, for one main reason: absorbency.

4. *True*. Diaper rash *may* be caused by too infrequent changing of the diapers, which results in the buildup of ammonia in the diaper. It can, however, also be caused by chafing. Or by an allergic reaction to a disposable diaper or to the chemicals used in cleansing the diaper. Or by diarrhea.

5. *False*, according to doctors who debunk the whole idea. True, according to mothers who will swear on the Bible that teething causes diaper rash. I am one of them. A possible reason is that teething causes extra salivating and thumb-sucking—both of which can increase intestinal action. Presto: diarrhea!

6. *False*. They do not suffer from diaper rash caused by contact allergens, by chafing, by ammonia. They do suffer from diaper rash caused by food allergies and diarrhea. Only the diaper rash is confined to the immediate vicinity of the anus.

7. *False*. Disposable diapers don't bulge as much as specially folded cloth diapers. But you can tell, every time, when a child is wearing disposables—he rustles.

8. *False*. Oil, in fact, can cause diaper rash by setting up an allergic condition. Also, oil is messy to use and can cause cotton strands to adhere to the skin. Oil makes a baby smell good and your hands slippery. Other than that it is of little use. Water is the one *safe* thing to use in terms of avoiding allergies. Anything with alcohol in it must be avoided.

9. *False*. In fact, doctors have done research that shows that people, when bathing, wash off helpful substances that resist illnesses. They have recommended that a Saturday-night bath—as the old saw goes— may in fact be the healthiest treatment. As for your baby, if you wash off the urine or fecal matter after each change and make sure his face is clean of drools and spittle, you do not need to bathe him more than once a week, unless cooling him off is the reason.

10. *False*. A baby is very comfortable when his diaper is wet. It keeps him warm. Only when diaper rash becomes a problem will you find a baby complaining because his diaper is wet. Many won't even complain of a soiled diaper.

Accessories

Diaper liners. "Oh, no," you say. "Don't tell me there's a difference in liners, too." Oh, yes, I do so say. Some are white and paperlike, coarse and scratchy and a waste of money. The other kind is made of a nonwoven fabric and printed with green or blue dots or waves. Feel them. Where the first kind is stiff and scratchy and crinkly, this kind is soft, gentle and flexible.

All serve the function of keeping the bowel movement close to the baby and away from the diaper, which is of dubious benefit to the baby but great for the mother who is a do-it-yourselfer.

Almost all claim to be medicated, and may be. Medicating also can be an irritant to baby.

All claim to be flushable, and some may be. After all, it's your plumbing, and it may even be your septic system.

Some even claim to be dissolvable (I hope so, for your septic system's sake—or the city's, as the case may be), but I don't believe it.

If you're at all interested in ecology, a flushable, nondissolvable diaper liner isn't going to be your dish of tea under any circumstances. Not even a flushable, *maybe* dissolvable one. As for me, I have faith that one loaded diaper liner a day (from about age four months on) isn't going to tax my septic tank any more than a little toilet paper would—so hi, ho, I flush away.

But that's not really why I use diaper liners and wouldn't be without them. Not the ones that look and feel like tissue paper, nor the ones that pop up out of their box like one-ply toilet tissue and are about as strong. No, for me, I want the ones with the blue-and-white diamond pattern that are folded neatly in a neat little box with a window and go through the washer whole and fluffy. I use them in a thousand and one ways besides as a diaper liner. For example, wet a couple, stuff them in a plastic bag, and presto! washcloths for traveling. Or for bathtime, or anytime, for that matter.

And hand me a box of soft diaper liners everytime I run into a loose stool. They're strong enough to clean up most of the mess on the first wipe and will do a better job than a dozen cotton balls, which also take a dozen wipes.

For another thing, for the first few days a male infant, if circumcised, must be protected with a gob of petroleum jelly smeared on a 4"×4" gauze pad, which in turn is placed against the sensitive area. Have you priced 4"×4" gauze pads recently? Don't. Save yourself some money. Smear that petroleum jelly (Vaseline to the uninitiated) on a nice soft diaper liner. The box costs less than a dollar. By the way, you'll save cents by buying "petroleum jelly" by its generic, not a brand name.

Bar of soap. To act as a pin cushion for your diaper pins. The soap makes it easier for the point to penetrate the diapers, and it keeps the ends of the pins sharp. The bar should not be a thin, guest-size souvenir from a motel or hotel. It could be a bar of your regular soap, cut in half. When the bar begins to deteriorate, use it for washing by hand—the crumbling helps the soap dissolve.

Cotton somethings. I say that because every list you see calls for cotton balls. I find cotton balls a nuisance, a mess, and a costly expense. You need to use three or four or more once or twice to clean a halfway messy stool, double that for a big load. They stick to the baby, they stick to your fingers. I heartily recommend that you use small cotton rectangles, about 1½"×2½". They have character. They clean up a wide swath, can be doubled in half and used on at least half the other side. They stick to themselves and not your fingers. Inexpensive, too, compared to wasteful cotton balls.

Oils and lotions. Oil is preferable. Lotions, because they are complexes of ingredients, are more apt to be allergenic than simple oils. Some people believe that using an oil to clean the genital area at diaper-changing time is easier on the skin than water. However, many pediatricians believe that oils left in the baby's creases may irritate the child as they decompose under heat from the baby's skin, especially vegetable-based ones. Why then do mothers buy them? A major company conducted an in-depth survey, complete with various product testings, and came up with this reason: because oils and lotions make baby smell like the mother thinks he should smell. Sad, isn't it?

If baby oil is not needed for cleaning up at diapering time, nor after every bath, why then should you have a bottle on hand? For cradle cap, a form of seborrhea that commonly happens to infants' heads. To loosen the crust formed you use baby oil.

Powders. Powder is used to absorb any moisture left on the skin. The nonmedicated, nonperfumed ones, while not contributing anything extra to your sensory perceptions, will be 100-percent okay for most children. However, the others may cause allergic reactions. Cheap alternatives put forth include cornstarch or baking soda when applied with a regular salt shaker. However, some pediatricians feel the possible inhalation of these substitutes is so potentially dangerous as to outweigh any possible financial saving. Dr. Frederick W. Rutherford, M.D., in his book *You and Your Baby,* suggests flour, browned in the oven. He doesn't give a recipe, but I should like to point out that if you decide you don't like it on baby, it will make an excellent brown gravy.

Swabs. These are used for cleaning out babies' ears and nostrils. They are dangerous, but safer than homemade alternatives. Use sparingly and with care. It's better to put nothing into the ear than to put too much of a swab. And any baby over the age of two months will fight you like crazy, making it even more difficult to control the swab. When in doubt, don't.

Tissues, pop-up. They do the light jobs almost as well as diaper liners, but cheaper. Keep on hand for cleansing your hands as well.

Water bucket. I look at list after list and can only imagine that 99 percent of all changing areas are complete with little bar sinks, and mine is the only one that isn't. It's the only imaginable explanation for why you aren't asked to supply a container of water, replaced fresh at least once a day, in order to clean up BM's. Oil is much more expensive, you know. A cut-off half-gallon plastic milk bottle does fine.

Waste Bucket. Another, matching cut-off half-gallon milk container, so you can throw the waste cotton balls, etc., into a *handy* container. Unfortunately, your instincts are such that if you drop a soiled swab on the floor, without thinking you'll stoop and pick it up—and there falls baby. Used breadwrappers can line it, as can small paper bags, if you're fussy. Unlined, it washes fine. After a few months, a waste paper basket is a necessity. Either one that can be lined, or a plastic one.

Gauze squares. Use liners, they're cheaper.

Rectal thermometer. Nine out of ten hospitals will give you the one they used for baby. As noted earlier, it's cheaper for them to buy a new one than to sterilize the old one.

Nail scissors/clippers. The former are the more dangerous, yet the more usable over the long run. Blunt ends are necessary. Preferably get ones that fit in a case for protection from busy little hands.

Diaper pail. If you don't use a diaper service, get the tallest one you can that will hold a large plastic trash-can liner, with overlap around the edges. This will work equally well for disposables that aren't flushed.

Hamper. The word makes it sound large and solid, but it could be a real diaper *pail,* or a bucket, or any other container with a handle. A detergent bucket could be perfect.

Chapter 16

Cook, Bottle-washer, Laundress, Etc.

SEAMSTRESS: A STITCH IN TIME
TAKES TIME—YOURS!

Don't get me wrong, I am not anti-sewing. Quite the contrary. But sewing all of your children's clothes, for example, is economic foolhardiness. There are times when it costs you more to make a garment than to buy it. Take Jesse Hutton's word for it (she's the Director of Sewing Education at the Singer Company). She'll tell you that AS A RULE OF THUMB, ANY MASS-PRO-DUCED, UTILITARIAN, READY-TO-WEAR GARMENT IS CHEAPER TO BUY THAN TO MAKE.

See? And she can't be accused of being pro-buying, anti-sewing. Examples of what she's talking about? All clothes for newborn children and those up to the age of one, men's pajamas and shirts, crib sheets and towels, and more. ("Sewing baby clothes is for grandmothers," according to Miss Hutton.)

Disillusioned? Don't be. You can save money, lots of it, making clothes. For example, a woman who is a reasonably steady sewer, who makes most of her own clothes as well as clothes for her older two children, and does mending and darning as well by machine, can save $375 to $400 a year. Since the average sewing machine, Singer claims, should last twenty years, this would save the family budget over $7,000 in its lifetime. That's a lot of money in anybody's budget.

But you have to be selective about your sewing. For example, many little girls' dresses sold in the $9 to $22 range are more distinctive for the frills and frou-frou on them than for their workmanship. Using the same basic materials and general style, you can make the dress for one-third to one-half the cost of the ready-to-wear dress just by eliminating gingerbread.

The simpler the dress, the easier to sew. Let me warn you here, that if you're just learning to sew—having a baby is a good incentive for starting sewmanship—the way to learn is *not* on children's clothes. I know from experience, and Jesse Hutton backs me up, that children's clothes are harder to make than adult clothes for the nonexpert seamstress. Why? Because every step you take in making a dress for yourself, you duplicate in a child's dress—only in much less space and with less margin for error. Example. Once I elected to salvage a little girl's dress out of my yellow organza high school graduation dress. Well, I worked and I struggled and I sewed and I ripped and I resewed, and finally the dress was done. But when the big day came for a pretty little dark-haired girl to wear my dress, DISASTER! It wouldn't go over her head—the neck opening was too small. In my desire to be extra particular about this dress, I had made one teensy little error. I had sewn on the inside of the seam line, decreasing the neck opening by just a fraction of an inch all around. That little bit less meant the garment wouldn't go over her head.

And that's what I mean by less margin for error.

So, in learning to sew, start with an adult-sized garment, then apply what you've learned to a child's garment. Sewing, while not difficult to learn, does require patience and planning. As such, it's a good idea to sew ahead of your child's size. That way, as you sew, your child is growing into, not out of, the garment.

There's another way to avoid losing that race against time. And one of the best reasons I know for making children's clothes.

Sew Special Growth Features into the Garment

Overalls—make the straps two to three inches longer than called for.

Jumpers and short-all suits—make snap shoulders instead of regular shoulder seams, include extra fabric at the shoulders for eventual letting out.

Dresses—those without waistlines can have two lengthwise tucks both front and back that can eventually be let out for needed width; sleeveless dresses can have extra-wide side seams to be let out when needed, elasticized waistbands can be substituted for fitted ones, thus incorporating growth room right from the start; extra-long hems and cuffs will allow for letting down later, and a horizontal tuck at the waistline will do more of the same.

Shirts—an inverted pleat at center back will allow room for spreading later. Make front pieces ½" to 1" wider (doing it at center front) so buttons can be moved later for more width. A tuck above the cuff will allow sleeves to grow.

Pants—boxer-types already incorporate growth room. Make the side seams wider on pants without a waistband. Add ½" to a waistband to allow snaps or buttons to be moved, which will spread the zipper a bit but add weeks more wear to the garment.

Additions and Subtractions to Make Clothing Grow

Salvage tops or bottoms of dresses by removing the worn area and adding a cotton camisole top to the skirt (to be worn under overblouses later), or a cotton half-slip to the top, which can be used as a blouse with skirts.

Jackets can be made into vests by removing sleeves and enlarging armholes.

Ruffles and flounces can be added to the bottoms of full and flared dresses to allow more growth. Making a sleeved dress into a sleeveless one gives extra room across the chest.

Money-saving Ideas for Home Sewers

1. Buy basic patterns and enlarge them to fit your growing child. Example: a pair of classic pants in size 2 can be converted into a size 3 by: slashing it lengthwise down the center of each pattern piece (not the garment, otherwise crotch will be wrong) and spread apart to add width. Repeat horizontally ½" above the crotch line to add length in the seat, again at the knees for leg-length. Spread pieces farther apart to make the pattern into a size 4.

2. Buy basic patterns and use them over and over again. As Barbara Hulse, head designer of Simplicity Patterns, tells it, too many people don't. Instead, more than half will make only one garment from a pattern and do that in exactly the same color or print in the illustration shown in the pattern book. (She tells of the time for example that a woman chided her about not including a polka-dot dress in the latest Simplicity pattern book.) Her point

about reuse is well made. Buying a new pattern for each garment you made adds 85¢ or more to the cost of the finished garment, and takes more, rather than less, time to make because you're not familiar with the instructions.

3. Choose simple patterns and use trims to change their appearance. Example: An A-line pattern made up in a solid color with a white piqué Peter Pan collar . . . becomes a different dress in another color with rows of rickrack around the hem (or braid or appliqués or whatever) . . . without sleeves it becomes a jumper . . . inserts of lace or smocking at chest height give a yoked effect, and more of the same at cuffs or hem would vary the pattern more . . . two vertical rows of buttons marching down the front could clean out your button jar and give a unique effect to that same old pattern. If you have a buttonholer on your sewing machine, give each button a dramatic buttonhole. But don't go as far as to slit the fabric the way you would for real buttonholes. Just sew the buttons in place. Such ideas are endless because, as Miss Hutton notes, "Trims give you a lot of effect with little effort!"

4. Make simple styles reversible, giving you two outfits in one.

5. Cutting the cost of the fabric will add to your savings on a garment. Naturally, shopping the remnant counter can pay dividends; so can shopping discount fabric stores and mill outlets. Just be sure, in the case of the latter, that the material isn't irregular, with for example, the grain not running true up or down. This is a major problem, especially lengthwise. However, sometimes stretching and pulling on the bias will eliminate crosswise problems.

6. Save the findings (zippers, buttons, trims) from your own clothes and clothes your child has outworn. Appliqués can be reappliquéd on another outfit; good buttons can jazz up a run-of-the-mill plain blazer; an oversized zipper from a man's jacket becomes the center front seam on a girl's dress.

7. Make new garments for your son or daughter from your or your husband's old, unused clothes.

Do-It-Yourself Permanent Press Isn't!
There are those who love ironing, and then there are those who don't. Those who do need read no farther; those who don't should.

Permanent-press or *durable press* or *wash and wear* or *no-iron* are all terms for a process that retains creases and keeps out wrinkles. However, there are differences in the no-iron qualities of ready-to-wear and home-sewn garments. Garments you buy have their no-iron finish pressed in or baked in after the garment is made. Thus whatever was included in the garment—pleats, creases, seams, hems—they're all permanent. Clothes you make are made from fabrics that have not been high-pressure pressed or baked. Which means, to be frank, that pleats, creases, seams, hems *you* put in are *not* permanent.

This can be to the good. For while it is almost impossible to shorten or otherwise alter a permanent-press ready-to-wear (RTW, from now on) garment, this is not true of home-sewn garments. What is also true is that home-sewn, permanent-press garments are not truly no-iron. They have to be touched up, more or less, every single time you wash them.

To some, a mere touching up after washing is infinitely preferable to a total ironing. To others, the very thought of getting out that Rube Goldberg of a machine, the continually cumbersome ironing board, is enough to drive them to a store, any store, to buy no-iron RTW.

But what if Junior or Junioress is not long enough to fit into that stunning, new no-iron slack set? You can either return it, or you can put it aside in hopes that eventually the child will fit the garment, or you can attempt to make the garment fit the child.

The latter, according to Robert Spain of E. I. du Pont de Nemours & Co., is rather difficult since permanent-press garments are deliberately—not maliciously—engineered not to take any new creases. Otherwise, every time you washed them and forgot to remove them at exactly the right moment from the dryer, you'd have one or more new permanent creases, and not always where you wanted them.

But Mr. Spain is only partially right. It is possible to put a new crease in, especially at the bottom of little boy's pants. The crease may start out soft, but soon abrasion sharpens it until it's as neat a crease as you could want. That's when the axe falls. By the time abrasion has set a knife-sharp crease for you, that's the time that you're ready to let the pants down and to remove the crease again. Now you have a white line where the crease was. Good luck.

Here are some tips for dealing with permanent-press clothes, either homemade or ready-to-wear:

TIP ⚹1: With permanent-press RTW, decide how to hide a crease before attempting to make one. Try rickrack, decorative stitching, soutache braid, bias tape, embroidered tape, tucks, hand embroidery, or a piece of fabric from the garment itself.

TIP ⚹2: With any home-sewn garment, prepare for a white fadeline where hems were and are no more. See tip ⚹1.

TIP ⚹3: Use vinegar to remove an unwanted crease. Vinegar works on cotton or rayon blends, because they are cellulosic and thus susceptible to acids. This is why cottons are readily bleached, and why hem marks in fabrics either entirely or predominantly cotton or rayon will come out with the mildly acidic vinegar. Vinegar rinses will also remove some slight stains from those clothes that are supposedly unbleachable.

Obviously the problem with home-sewn garments is just the opposite of RTW: how to get creases in, not out. The easiest way is to avoid them. Rather than a pleated skirt, choose a ruffled skirt. Use rolled hems and edges rather than sharply creased ones. Do frilly blouses rather than hand-tailored ones. Use button-closings rather than zippers (the placket gap doesn't stay flat). Choose darts that are on a bias. Make gored skirts rather than straight skirts so seams lie flatter.

And, of course, be prepared to touch up those garments after every laundering, or make up your mind to have soft creases rather than hard ones.

There is another problem in sewing with permanent-pressed yard goods. Permanent-press yard goods are permanent in the bolt. No amount of pulling or pressing or steaming or pinning is going to change the grain line of such a fabric. To do so is a major project involving cutting off selvages and aligning threads and—take my word for it—it's a mess. For the beginning sewer it comes down to this: If the fabric isn't square and true when you buy it, it cannot be made right later. That makes buying permanent-press fabrics more hazardous than buying other fabrics.

TIP ⚹4: Never buy a piece of permanent-press yard goods without double-checking the grain lines.

TIP #5: Never buy a remnant without insisting on opening it to check the grain lines.

TIP #6: Never cut out a single piece of a single pattern without double-checking that it is straight on the grain lines.

I think you have the point.

Next, you must accept the fact that sewing with permanent press is not the same as sewing with ordinary cotton.

TIP #7: "Permanent" includes everything. Therefore, a row of stitches will appear as a row of holes after being torn out. Baste loosely first to make sure that stitching that goes in stays in.

TIP #8: Use the right thread, either 100-percent man-made fiber or a cotton-polyester blend. If you don't, you'll have puckering, and puckering can't be pressed out.

Since permanent-press doesn't shrink or stretch, it's important that the bindings you use with it neither shrink nor stretch.

TIP #9: All interfacings, underlinings, and regular linings should be preshrunk at least once, preferably twice. Otherwise use types recommended for permanent-press, or use permanent-press fabrics themselves, such as more of the same fabric for interlining and lining.

TIP #10: All bindings and trims must be preshrunk to prevent puckering later. Zippers, for example, should be soaked in very hot water for ten or more minutes and allowed to air dry without stretching; then do it again. "Otherwise," suggests Simplicity, "wash and dry the zipper in automatic washer and dryer." Which says something for today's laundry equipment and how hard it is on clothes.

TIP #11: In the "always a silver lining" category, one of the more beautiful things about permanent-press remaining permanently pressed is that seams do not need finishing. You are being extra cautious if you pink.

General Pointers on Home Sewing and Its Costs

Open any book supposedly on general sewing and you will find a list of the most extraordinary needs one must have in order to sew. Examples? "Glass jars, with tops painted in gay colors, are great for buttons and small notions." I have never had a glass jar, much less a glass jar with a gaily painted top, for my buttons. Since buttons come on cards or in little envelopes, shoe boxes are the answer. Glass jars are for lost buttons.

I'm splitting hairs. I admit it. So what do you need?

Needle. A hand-sewing needle—and a thimble if you have any pity for your poor fingers. Don't know how to use one? Try to learn. It could save you the cost of a tetanus shot.

Sewing machine. Franklin Kolyer, Education Director of Singer, points out that the cost of a good machine could be recovered in the first year. But you don't need the biggest and the gadgetiest. He gave his newly married daughter her first machine, and it was nowhere near the top of the line. As she used that one, she was saving toward another, more versatile one. The beginner does not need a zigzag machine that will do everything but sign your name to each garment.

Scissors. Or as they're called in the sewing game, shears. Scissors are small and dainty. Shears are rugged and determined. I love bent-handled shears for cutting fabric. I also have to admit that better than three fourths of all the garments I've cut out were cut out with whatever *sharp* shears/scissors were available.

Pinking shears. They cut a zigzag edge and prevent the need for further finishing of a seam, unless it is one that frays terribly. "Never use them for cutting out the garment," says Simplicity's Sewing Book. And with good reason. It's more work. The pinking throws off your seam allowances. Those must be marked on the fabric by hand. You won't be able to save time by using the seam gauge on your machine. I must confess I have never owned a pair of pinking shears. Why? Because it's just as easy to run a row of stitches along the edges of the seam, something you sometimes have to do inside the notches of pinked seams to prevent further fraying.

Seam ripper. I use a straight-edge razor blade or half a safety razor blade with part of a match book folded over the top. But I'm careful.

Scalloping shears. They're probably delightful and very handy. I can't tell. I've never even seen a pair, much less used one.

Cutting board. Nice to have providing it's wide enough. Otherwise use your dining-room or kitchen table. The floor, preferably uncarpeted, does fine, too.

Measurers. Musts in my book: a sewing gauge (a six-incher with movable indicator) . . . a tape measure (sixty inches long is standard) . . . a yardstick, of immeasurable help with flat goods . . . a skirt marker that's supposedly a do-it-yourselfer, but works best with anyone else, even your husband, manning it.

What else? Straight pins. Definitely a necessity. And tailor's chalk, which, however, can be dispensed with by a lass who can handle a needle and do tailor's tacks. You can use a plain lead pencil, too, but only on medium colors, wrong side, and washable fabrics. My husband, who has read this far, chides me. He reminds me that having an iron and ironing board is necessary to sewing. You do have one, don't you? Good. I'm off the hook.

HOUSEKEEPER: MAKE ROOM IN THE LINEN CLOSET, HERE COME BABY'S THINGS

Bassinet Needs

For the mattress, use a blanket folded up and enclosed in a zippered plastic pillow cover, or a pad of newspapers sewn into a heavy plastic bag, or buy an inexpensive plastic pad. Just don't use a pillow, no matter how great the temptation; it's too soft compared to the bone and buoyancy your body has provided.

But pillowcases are just the right length to use as sheets in a bassinet or cradle. (You'll need three or more, and they needn't be new.) To make that pillowcase fit as wrinklefree as the best fitted sheet, do as the nurses do in the hospital. Put your makeshift mattress in the pillow case. Hold the case lengthwise, letting the mattress slide down to the far side. Without disturbing the position of the mattress, set it, case and all, on a flat surface. Then fold the pillowcase in on itself, in the form of a pleat that will extend lengthwise over half the width of the mattress, but does so on the inside of the case.

Cradle Needs

The same as above in the case of a truly oldfashioned, straight-sided, solid cradle. The cradle that's made with slats, or worse, with spindles, will require a bumper. A bumper is a form of padding that folds to conform to the interior of the cradle. It's tied in place with ribbons at every corner. A bumper is useless with a solid-sided crib—there are no places to tie it.

As well as protecting him, the bumper constricts the child's point of view. For many babies, especially those kept in cradles only during the day, the bumper may not be needed. For the rest, the bumper will prevent those frightening, but not dangerous, red marks on the head. It will also prevent some children from slipping feet-first through the rungs. But not all. In some cases, the child may become trapped between bumper and mattress. That can be injurious, too.

Lap-Pads and quilted pads. With the exception of those mothers using disposable diapers, these pads can cut laundering in half—at least in terms of crib needs—and save your own clothes all kinds of wear and tear and urine.

The lap pad is a piece of waterproof material, usually with cotton flannelette bonded to both sides. It is a water barrier, not a sponge. Thus, if too much liquid comes along for it to handle, the liquid spreads over the pad area. That's why you need quilted pads, which are not waterproof but are absorbent. They look like miniature mattress pads. You'll need half a dozen of each.

Which reminds me. Does your own bed need a new mattress pad? Buy one and cut up the good parts of the old one into squares about 14″×14″. The edges will have to be bound securely with bias tape. (You can make do with several rows of stitching plus a pinked edge to prevent serious unraveling. But there will be lots of lint at the bottom of your washer and in the lint traps of your dryer after every laundering.)

What are the pads for? To protect the sheets and mattress from baby. Put the quilted pad directly under baby, the lap pad under that. When baby wets, the padding protects the bed and you needn't remake it six or seven times a day. You just change pads. Picking baby up to feed him? Pick him up, lap pads and all. While protecting your clothes, you won't get a wet reminder that what goes in the top end seems to come directly out the other.

Blankets. Receiving blankets do just fine for his small bed. You'll need three for sleeping, the fourth—the bath towel one—can be held in reserve just in case. Rarely will you use more than two in a night, with one more typical, at least for girls. Not so for boys, who have a habit of directing their geysers upward and blanket-ward.

Pillows. A waste of money. Not needed. Dangerous.

Crib Needs

Mattress. See Chapter 6 for a complete discussion of the buying of crib mattresses.

Mattress protectors: A vinyl cover isn't really necessary on a waterproof mattress; it can even interfere with the ventilating holes. But in the event urine manages to penetrate the stitching or you find one of your I-didn't-mean-to-stick-the-diaper-pin-in-there holes, you may find that you and your heir are living with a constant pungent odor of urine in the room. A plastic cover prevents that, and it's cheap. But, please, *do* avoid sticking pins in the protected mattress. It defeats the purpose of the cover.

Mattress pads. Anachronisms. They protect the sleeper from bumps, dips, buttons, and crevices that today's mattresses don't have. What's worse, they soften the mattress that you've just gone to such trouble and expense to buy as firm as possible.

Sheets. Although there are fitted top sheets on the market to lure the overly conscientious mother into spending more, only bottom sheets are needed. These should be—and 99 percent of them are —fitted sheets. A baby is too hard on his bed for tucked sheets to stay tucked.

Of these fitted sheets, you may choose from 100-percent cotton and cotton-polyester blends. Of the two, the cotton is the more absorbent; the blend is less likely to start an allergic rash.

Lambs and calves and ponies and butterflies frolicking about the sheet are nice to look at, but they're for you, not your baby. He is farsighted to begin with, and those decorations are wasted on him. However, they hide the souvenirs of his spittings up.

It has been said that money can be saved by making your own fitted crib sheets. Here are the specifications you need to make fitted sheets for a 6″×27″×52″ mattress:

In width you need 47″
(½ +3½ +6+27+6+3½ +½)
In length you need 72″
(½ +3½ +6+52+6+3½ +½)

The ½″ allowances are for hemming, the 3½″ for underlapping the mattress. Once this 47″×72″ rectangle is cut, it will have to be fitted on the mattress itself or boxed on the corners. To box: mark ½″ beyond the 27″ measurement, or the 52″ one. But only in the corner areas.

Draw a line from each outside corner to the inner corner, which is ½″ from the actual mattress corner, and slit the line from corner to corner. Now finish either the sloppy way or the expert way. With the sloppy way, you turn each raw edge under, and stitch to finish it. Then slide the two finished edges across the other until they are equidistant from the original line. Pin in place and wait until you put the elastic in to finish them.

The expert way calls for putting those slitted edges together and marking a seam line straight down from the inside corner. A seam is then sewn, and the long excess triangle of material is cut off. Now you have a really well-fitting box. But the bottom edge still needs finishing all around. Just turn up the ½″ allowance.

For a good fit, the end should be elasticized—from 6″ above the corner on both sides, across the entire end of the sheet. If you measure this distance, subtract 25 percent (or more, if your elastic is old and not very stretchy) and you know how much elastic you'll need per end.

Before stitching, mark the sheet at several equidistant points across the end (at the one-quarter-, one-half- and three-quarters-way points, for example. Do the same to the unstretched elastic, but don't include the 4½″ needed at each end to extend beyond the corners and up the sides. Now pin, with the elastic under the sheet, matching marks and stitch.

You now have a reasonable facsimile of a store-bought fitted bottom crib sheet. You also have spent a great deal of time and energy on the project and will need to repeat this at least two more times.

What have you saved? Buying the cheapest permanent-press material available (a regular twin-bed sheet), which will make two cribs sheets, I find I can save less than 25¢ per sheet (not including the cost of the elastic and thread nor the bias tape that purists believe should finish off the elasticized edge) over the cost of buying a permanent-press fitted crib sheet.

Naturally, if you were to use one of your old twin-bed sheets, you would not need to buy material, just thread, elastic, and bias tape. But first make sure your sheet is in condition to take two or more washings a week for three years. Few are. Especially in the center.

Number of sheets for baby? Depends on whether you elect to go top and bottom or—better—just bottom. The rule is: one in use, one in the wash, one on the shelf. And it works. If—and that's a big if—if you make some attempt at protecting the sheet from its user.

Lap-pads-grown-up. Do you buy waterproof sheets in crib size, 27″×50″ or 27″×52″? These, at about $2.50 per, are a waste of money. What you need is the cheapest size that turned lengthwise will fit over the crib crosswise. Example: The crib is 26½″ wide with a 4″-thick mattress. A 36″-long, flat portable-crib sheet, at $1.50 per, will cover the head area if your child is a spitter, or the genital area if your child is a wetter, or both if your child is less than 30″ long. There is no point in protecting those areas of the sheet not exposed to trouble. So, for the first year or more in the crib, place the lap-pad-grown-up on top of the sheet to protect the sheet. After that, lengthwise and underneath.

NOTE: Save these lap pads for use at age three or four and up when bed-wetting's a problem.

Bedspread. An extra. A crib does not need one under any circumstances. A youth bed might, then again it might not. A colorful blanket and a well-made bed are completely acceptable in lieu of a bedspread. Consider starting to use one at the time your child is capable of helping you put it on as symbolic of his growing up and with a view to his taking over the bed-making. This is certainly not before the age of four.

Blankets. Of most importance is the fiber of which they are made. Wool and cotton, the traditional ones, are also the most allergenic. Avoid them, just in case, at least for the first few years of the child's life.

The warmth of a blanket depends not on its weight but on its nap—the thickness and resilient qualities it has—which traps the air in thousands and hundreds of thousands and millions of cells. A good blanket is relatively light in weight. It captures body heat within its countless air cells. To determine this, examine the nap. It should be of good depth, fine, even, springy. This may seem to be true of cheap blankets, too. Try rubbing the blanket against itself; if pilling occurs, there will be shedding sooner or later, and the blanket will neither wear, wash, nor warm well.

Frequently you have no choice in the blanket you use—it is a gift. If the blanket is 100-percent wool, I would try to take it back, citing the fact that "the doctor says I can prevent asthma now by avoiding wool," and you'll be telling the truth. However, the typical gift blanket is usually more—quality wise—than you really need. So receive it joyfully. By the way, the cheaper thermal weaves are not as warm, according to laboratory tests, as the traditional blanket. So judge accordingly.

NOTE: Once your child has moved up to a large bed, save the crib blanket for use elsewhere: in the family room or living room for unexpected naps . . . in the car for same . . . on the lawn for picnicking . . . in the cedar chest for remembering.

Pillows. Still no need of pillows. The baby in a crib not only doesn't need one, he is safer without it. The chances of his smothering are minimal, but real. If you are given one, use it in your changing area to cushion his head.

Transitional Furniture: "Youth" and "Junior"

Mattress protectors. Depending on the mattress you choose, I suggest you put the cost of a mattress pad into getting a better mattress. But if you're going to use a hand-me-down mattress that is so firm it's boardy, then mattress pad to the rescue; it provides needed cushioning.

However, it is wise to have something waterproof between the geyser and the mattress. This usually takes the cheapest form: a vinyl cover.

Lap-pads-grown-up. And temporarily grown out. In the beginning, there's no confining a child to any given area of the bed, thus the helpful waterproof pads are not as protective as a vinyl mattress cover. Eventually, your child will adapt to sleeping near the head of the bed, and the lap pad can go back under the sheet. It's also a handy thing to have when staying with friends or in a hotel.

Sheets. Here is your first chance to choose between fitted and unfitted bottom sheets. The way I see it is that if you had the money to buy a "youth" bed, or if you were lucky enough to be given one, you can afford fitted sheets, but only on the bottom, only in white, only the cheapest they have.

As for the top sheet, look for twin-size flat sheets. Wonderfully colorful ones have really small prices. Especially if you realize that that inexpensive sheet will fit the youth bed for three years or more, then the regular bed for five to six years (or until "I'm no baby" forces you to buy other sheets). Again, observe the rule of three: one on bed, one in laundry, one in reserve—and this applies to both top and bottom sheets.

Pillow. If he is aware that you sleep with a pillow, he may demand one. Give in—to the extent of buying a very flat, very soft, absolutely nonallergenic, cheap pillow. You will probably find that he sleeps nowhere near his pillow for the first couple of years. Which is all to the good.

Pillow covers and cases. A cover really isn't necessary unless you are using a pillow whose fiber content concerns you. In that case use a zippered pillow cover. Never use a dry-cleaner's bag. Too many children have suffocated from these. As to number of cases, again it's one in the wash, one in use, and one in reserve.

Blankets. Get the twin-size version of a crib blanket. You'll probably need a pair because of urps and spills and night wetness.

Adult Furniture

Do as you do for other beds in the house. Remember that the top sheets, the twin-size blanket, the pillow and pillow cases used with his youth bed will continue to see service here.

Now you shall probably want to invest in a bedspread. Look for one that will be sturdy and hide shoe prints and jelly marks. Even big girls have been known to make a mess of a bedspread.

One other new purchase would be in order: another pillow for use when your child is reading and/or playing in bed. Somehow, being sick doesn't seem so bad when the patient can be propped up to see what's going on about him.

Some Points to Consider When Buying Linens

No-ironability. The difference in cost between permanent-press and non-permanent-press sheets and pillow cases has become so minuscule—especially when you consider the cost of the iron you'd have to buy to press the non-permanent-press—that you should never buy anything else. Unless it's a knit crib sheet, but that is also no-iron.

"Seconds" and "irregulars." Good buys—providing you take your handy-dandy little tape measure with you to make sure that the size is accurate. (It usually is, but with my luck, I hit the sales in which the sizes are off.) Well, then, if the sizes are the same, what's the difference between the two? The term "seconds" used to be used by fastidious manufacturers to denote minor, very minor, flaws. "Irregulars" meant serious ones. Not any longer. Now the terms are synonymous.

Possible flaws? Irregular selvages, slubs in the fabric, crooked seaming, deviations in patterns, and inaccurate—but not by much —sizes. And have you noticed there are fewer and fewer sales of "seconds" and "irregulars"? That's because women have learned they are better and better buys.

White sales. Although crib sheets and such are not usually found during the traditional White Sales held in January and August, you sometimes will find them in the baby sales held in September and March. However, since sheets are such staple items, having a sale on them is the exception rather than the rule.

This is not true of cot sheets and twin sheets—especially those with fantasy prints on them. These will definitely be available in the White Sales. You should be aware that the patterns on sale are usually discontinued ones. So if you wish to buy sets, do it then. You may never see another matching pillowcase.

It is at the White Sales that you should look for bedspreads and quilts, if you desire them. Sometimes the savings will be great— unfortunately, it is usually impossible to use a twin-size bedspread on a youth bed. The width is too great. Nor does a quilt work well —its length is too great. The necessary tucking in creates lumps around the edge, gullies in the middle. If you can't find a suitable spread, consider using a colorful sheet on top of the blanket. But watch out for sheets with design motifs that have a definite top and bottom. You'll find the design on the upper section of the sheet has been reversed and is upside down. That's so it will be right side up when the sheet is folded back down over the blanket. It's a fooler. And sometimes you can't tell this the way the sheet is packaged. So, don't buy without opening that package and checking.

Towels. Continue to use receiving blankets for the first two years. Then use adult-sized towels, the bigger the better. Never buy towels for your youngsters at any time but White Sale time.

Different towels for different people is the rule at some houses. Each member of the family gets a different color in the way of towels and face cloths. Why I don't know, unless some mothers don't believe that laundering gets linens sterile enough. Then again, if you indoctrinate each child in this way, you immediately know—the towel will tell you—who didn't wash his hands thoroughly before wiping.

LAUNDRESS: A LOAD A DAY KEEPS YOU BARELY AHEAD OF THE GAME!

Or at least so it will seem.

Diapers. Remember, the diaper services or disposables save you this.

1. Urine-soaked diapers go directly into the diaper pail.
2. Stool-covered ones need rinsing out. (If you stop using the

soiled diaper to clean up the baby—use tissues or other throwa-wayables—your laundry problems will be lighter.)

Use the toilet, dipping the diaper up and down to loosen as much as possible. Then holding the diaper securely—*very securely*—flush the toilet. The swirling of the water will do most of the work for you. It will also carry any insecurely-held diapers down into the pipes. Hello, Mr. plumber!

Wring the diaper out sufficiently to keep it from dripping all the way to the pail (they have a special diaper wringer that fits on the toilet for fastidious mothers; reports have it that the thing isn't too successful), and into the diaper pail it goes.

3. Be sure the diaper pail is lined with a plastic bag. In the old days, a diaper-soaking solution would be mixed up and used in the pail. Carrying the full pail from nursery to laundry was not only hard work, it could also mean a sloppy trail behind you. Today, use a plastic liner to keep the moisture in and the diapers from drying out. You'll know how well it works the first time you take the cover off.

4. Dump the diapers into the washer.

5. Spin to remove as much moisture as possible from them.

Expensive option: fill washer with water, add enzyme product to presoak. Then spin dry.

6. Set washer on heavy-duty or longest cycle.

7. Add soap, and a water conditioner if your water's hard. Otherwise you may find that there's been a wedding in your washer: between soap and minerals.* The result, a curd deposited on clothing that creates that tattletale gray, hangover-dirt, ring-around-the-collar look.

Possibly expensive option: bleach may be added during the wash cycle to keep diapers white and more sanitary. However, to be sure that diapers are free of bleach after washing, use at least one extradeep rinse at end of cycle. Otherwise, you'll have a very, very unhappy baby.

A handful of baking soda added to the next to the last rinse will keep the diapers as soft and fresh-smelling as the most expensive fabric softener.

---

*Detergents and minerals remain unwed, but detergents often cause rashes since they irritate the skin.

If you find you have a case of diaper rash on your hands, you can buy chemical sterilizers to use on your diapers. They're added to the last rinse. They're also very expensive. They have been known, in rare cases, to make the diaper rash worse because of a reaction to the chemical itself. This even happens with the bacteriostats used by diaper services. (Notified of this, the diaper service will do your diapers separately and leave out the bacteriostat.) Old-fashioned boiling is better.

8. After running your diapers through the entire cycle, put them through the last or deep rinse again. This is to make sure you've removed all the stuff you used to remove the soil on the diapers.

9. Into the dryer they go. If you can regulate the temperature on the dryer, turn it to hot. Heat sanitizes the diapers and rids them of the last traces of chlorine bleach.

Keeping diapers white and fragrant and soft is only part of your goal. The balance is to prevent their causing troubles on their own. Thus, the fewer chemically complex laundry aids you use, the less chance of diaper rash or even chemical burns. Detergents cause trouble because they are hard to rinse out. Products added to the last rinse are the first you should eliminate if diapers may be causing rash problems.

Baby clothes. Don't wash along with diapers: they may absorb the urine and ammonia from the diapers. Put them in a hamper and treat separately. This is no problem and rather a dream compared to caring for diapers. About your only major concern is ordinary food stains. Enzyme presoaks are one answer to this. Washing with detergents is another. And our good friend bleach will come in handy. Although wash-and-wear garments are uniformly labeled "Do Not Bleach," it's no longer true 99.9 percent of the time. It once was when some finishes on wash-and-wear garments were (notice the *were*) chlorine retentive. This meant that chlorine in such bleaches as Clorox was retained by the fabric. When heated, the chlorine was chemically converted to an acid, either tenderizing the fabric, or yellowing it with little or no obvious deterioration. Originally, this phenomenon was caused by the high heat of an iron. Unless you plan to iron your permanent-press garments or use *strong* concentrations of chlorine bleach, you need not worry about this prohibition. Besides, according to du Pont, the resins used today to make garments permanent-press are not susceptible to such problems—at least in home laundering. Commercial laundering is another story.

But manufacturers are not as brave as they might be. Thus, they do not label their garments as bleachable. You, knowing this, are braver—or are you? I certainly am not. I didn't go around bleaching garments for the sake of bleaching them. I have, however (which is how I discovered all this) accidentally bleached something. The result? A very nice, attractive, not-yellow-at-all, not-holey-at-all, stain-free, clean shirt.

When I questioned du Pont, they said, "Of course." Since then, I have, as one of the world's most consummate cowards, resorted to bleach when I was at my last resort. When the shirt or top looked like a map of the sacred, hidden treasures of a clan of pack rats, I would force myself to pour that bleach in. I have always been surprised at the result: a clean, wearable shirt; often a shade or two lighter than before, but not always.

However, the do-not-bleach prohibition does apply to commercial washing operations in which strong bleach and high temperatures can turn a garment yellow. Or so du Pont says. Also, chlorine bleach used in conjunction with enzyme presoaks has a deleterious effect on clothes. They disintegrate. Or so says the owner of a 104-piece set of a pair of shoelaces.

Sleepwear. The Department of Commerce's new flammability standard for sleepwear for infants and children (i.e., Infants, Babies, Toddlers, and Children) went into effect in 1972. It required that all sleepwear be made of *naturally* flame-retardant fibers. (The miracle fibers, for example, melt rather than burn, a fact home economists have used for years to test the fiber content of a fabric.) If not naturally flame-retardant, fabrics must be so *treated*. It is these garments, 98 percent of all sleepwear made so far, that present a problem. These garments must be washed, according to the cleaning directions attached to each, in high-phosphate detergents. Otherwise the flame-retardant qualities may be washed out.

What do you do if your child has a contact allergy to clothes washed in such detergents, or if your own personal philosophy makes using phosphates onerous to you? Well, you can quit smoking, stop using your fireplace, give up your gas range. In short, eliminate all obvious fires from your house—that means matches, too. Or, you can wash the garments your usual way and discard before the flame-retardant qualities are completely washed out—after approximately fifty washings.

Laundry Tips for Getting Best Results and Most Wear

Remove permanent-press clothes as soon as the dryer stops to prevent new wrinkles from forming.

If you're too late, dry another five to ten minutes. When the clothes are rewarmed, they come out surprisingly wrinkle free.

Many synthetics are better removed while still damp. In fact, you save money if you turn your dryer off too soon or have a sensor device that automatically turns the dryer off when clothes achieve a certain degree of dryness. The dryer retains enough heat to continue to dry clothes long afterwards. Which is why wrinkles in many garments seem locked in. So keep your dryer set, if you can, on the moist side.

Wool and wool-blends can go into a dryer until no longer moist (on a blanket, check the binding—if it's dry, the blanket's ready to be removed). Then remove and block into shape. But it's a tricky business—a little too long in the dryer and . . . SHRUNK!

Sorting

Sorting is a necessary evil if you buy inexpensive clothes that may run. The accidental inclusion of a red sock in a load of white underwear turns everything a permanent pastel pink—which girls may like, but boys think it's sissy. Unless you can do a great many clothes at one time, you will find sorting such clothes into stacks of whites, pastels, medium hues, darks (all reds go here, always) results in too many small loads, which take too much time, too much soap, water, gas, or electricity. In the long run, you would have saved money if you'd bought the more expensive colorfast clothes to begin with.

If you have already done so, cast a cynical eye on the load of colorfast clothes before you. For appearance's sake, which must look their best? Right. The permanent-press. So put everything through the permanent-press cycle. Semiannually you may have to do the whites by themselves and use a little bleach, too, but think

of the time, work, and money saved every other wash day of the
year.

To Launder or Not to Launder

There are three times in a child's life when you will be faced
with this choice. The first happens somewhere around age four,
when your child becomes less messy than you had thought possible. But, by this time, you're in the habit of throwing his clothes
into the hamper the moment they come off. Don't. Steel yourself,
take a good look at them. Surprise! Some might do for another
wearing.

The next happens when a child grows attached to what he's
wearing. So attached in fact, that it's almost impossible to pry the
dirty underwear or old shirt off his back. You'll know you've
reached this stage when you go to get the week's dirty clothes and
find the hamper empty. At this point, you'll have to insist that certain clothes get washed at regular, designated intervals.

Just when you get this stage under control, along comes the ul-
traclean, just-to-look-at-a-blouse-makes-it-dirty stage. Now, you
have twice as many clothes to wash as you had before. At this
point in life, I suggest you abdicate as family washwoman and in-
struct your infant on how to run the washing machine and dryer.

Ironing

If you always buy knits and/or permanent press, you needn't iron.
So don't. I have now gone three years without touching an iron
other than when sewing. I think that's great, and as a busy parent
you probably will too.

If you must iron, you or your husband might want to make a
new top† for your ironing board that will clamp on when you're
doing large objects. This is the fast, easy way to iron adults' shirts,
for example, or tablecloths and other flat things. I only hope
you're not in the habit of ironing sheets. That may be fine for
Jacqueline Onassis, but for the new mother it's out of the question.

† Make it of wood or hardboard; cover with some sort of padding (an
old, badly worn blanket will do); use a bleachable, 100-percent cotton sheet
on top as the ironing surface.

ARE YOU A CHIEF BOTTLE-WASHER . . . OR A CHOCK-FULL BREAST-LEAKER?

To be the former, you need a sink, water—cold, it's cheaper and more effective—and a bottlebrush. If you don't want to buy a succession of brushes, make sure the first one has a wire spine securing the bristles in place. More important, the spine should not protrude beyond the bristles, nor should the bristles slant back up toward the handle. If either happens, the bristles won't be able to get into the crevices at the bottom of the bottle to clean out the stubborn milk ring. Buy—don't skimp—your bottlebrush carefully. It will clean out thousands of bottles for you, and continue doing so long after your baby is off formula feedings.

As for you, breast-feeder, don't laugh at your bottle-feeding sister's problems, you'll need a bottlebrush, too, for supplementary bottles—only yours need not be as sturdy. You have troublesome milk containers of your own to worry about. They may leak. Lots. It's normal. Especially during the first month or so of nursing when the milk flow isn't regulated, and even after that, at night. You won't find it at all unusual to wake up in the morning to find yourself—literally—taking a milk bath.

What you need are pads. You can buy disposable nursing pads, but they cost about 5¢ apiece, and at night you may need two or three per breast. Another solution is to buy disposable diapers and cut each into large squares (at least 4″×4″), retaining as much of the plastic backing on each square as possible. These will cost you less than a penny apiece, and you can change thicknesses going from Newborn to Toddler, as your nursing progresses. To use with these, and strictly optional, are washable quick-dry nursing pads, that are shaped to fit you and your bra. You can stuff them with as much or as little padding as your milk flow requires. They cost less than $3 a pair and *may* be available from your local La Leche League, or Childbirth Education Association chapter. They are definitely available from the Childbirth Education of Greater Philadelphia, P. O. Box 8741, Philadelphia, Pennsylvania 19101.

An alternative to pads are milk cups. These are made of plastic —the heavy, boilable kind—and come in two sections that snap together securely. An air hole in the top keeps the cup deflated, when empty, so you won't look like you've had a silicone treatment of your breasts. The hole in the rear section fits over and around your nipple. What these cups do is solve the excess milk problem, relieve engorged breasts, protect you and your clothes from leakage. And not by absorbing the milk. The cups collect it. You can then use this milk with baby's cereal or save it, frozen, for use in a supplementary bottle. The cost? Depends on where you get them. The original version from Sweden cost about $3 apiece, an American version costs less than $3 *a pair*. Where do you get them? Again maybe through La Leche or your local CEA chapter. The American ones are definitely available from the Childbirth Education Association of Greater Philadelphia. For more information, call them at (215) MElrose 5-5045. Tell them Carol Knight sent you; she's the one who told me about them.

PURCHASING AGENT: PENNYWISE; EIGHT-POUNDS, THREE-OUNCES FOOLISH

In the name of your baby, you're apt to overspend rather than underspend. You've already proven you're a conscientious buyer by buying this book. But there are other things you can do to help increase your wise-purchasing power.

Consult *Consumers Reports* and *Consumers Bulletin,* both monthly and annuals, before buying. But don't take out a subscription to either. After all, you are buying wisely, not constantly. Therefore, to buy an issue that features soft contact lenses, peanut butter, depth sounders, toaster ovens, saber saws, tire gauges, road tests of the AMC Matador, Chevrolet Chevelle, Concours-Ford Torino, Plymouth Satellite Custom, as well as a zigzag sewing machine is great for non-peanut-butter eaters (those who aren't already addicted) and for sewing machine purchasers. But what about you who have used forethought and purchased a regular sewing machine? You don't need to spend $7.20 a year on magazines that *may* be of aid to you, and that will, with the introduction of new car models and new sewing machine models and new peanut butters, become outdated. Use your library card instead.

Contact your utility companies about buying appliances for which you might be in the market. Many, if not all, have booklets prepared that will guide you to the wise buying of most appliances. If such booklets are not available through your local companies, contact Electric Energy Association, 90 Park Avenue, New York, New York 10016, or American Gas Association, 1515 Wilson Boulevard, Arlington, Virginia 22209. What will you receive? A buying guide for automatic washers and dryers, or refrigerators, food freezers, and combinations, or electric ranges, or portable appliances. They also have books on the wise utilizing of such appliances, including recipes that freeze well, design ideas for planning your lighting, and more.

With all this high-pressure, profoundly knowledgeable talent on hand to either guide you or warn you of pitfalls, I have no business opening my mouth. Yet, taciturnity has never been one of my virtues. The most desirable appliance from the novice buyers' point of view is usually the impressive one with the most gadgets and/or options available. The most desirable appliance from the seasoned owner's point of view is the one with the least gadgets and/or options that need repair by a hard-to-find, hard-to-pay-for service man.

Since that is the case, you ought to take into consideration, before buying an appliance, whether or not the store, or company, or organization offers repair service. If they don't, you may have a problem; sometimes other firms will only service what they sell.

It's not always cheapest to call the store from which you bought an item for service. Frequently, a local repairman can do the same job for less (remember that before signing a service or maintenance contract), but in times of desperation, when parts can't be found, it is well to have the store from which you bought the appliance the one you appeal to or cuss at or threaten loudly.

It is this hard-to-find-a-reasonable-repairman concept that has spawned the myriad of portable appliances. The ones that do in miniature twelve of the same jobs one big one does. Understandably enough. In most cases, the whole range doesn't fall apart at once. A burner goes, or a broiler goes, or the oven thermostat goes, or whatever. If you're using an electric skillet instead of a range, you might find it cheaper to scrap the skillet and buy a new one than to pay for the service-call, labor, and parts needed to put a new burner in your range.

Looking this over, I feel like a shill for the electric company. Not so. In most areas of the country where electricity is not subsidized by the government, using gas appliances will save you money. And not just in the cost of the utility alone. The basic gas range, as compared to a basic electric range, should have fewer major repairs. For example, the gas range rarely has a burner that needs replacing; electric range owners know that isn't true of electric burners.

CHEF: "HUNGRY MEN THINK THE COOK LAZY"

You may or may not have indoctrinated your husband into the concept of eating frozen dinners on a nightly and weekly basis prior to the baby. If you have, you have no problem. Just stock your refrigerator-freezer or your freestanding freezer.

If you have not trained him thus, and if you, in fact, don't believe in such dinners, you have an adjustment or an accommodation to make *before* the baby arrives.

Becoming a mother is the most traumatic, dramatic thing that will happen to you, at least it will seem so the first time. Once the baby comes, you're on twenty-four-hour duty. You can't sleep late, you can't sleep for more than three hours at a clip (that every-four-hour feeding includes one half hour or more—usually more—for the actual feeding, plus the changing, and burping, etc.).

If you are one of those lucky people who can fall asleep instantly upon hitting the pillow, fine! You're in luck. For the rest, you will have to find your sleep where and when you can get it. That means taking enough naps during the day to replace the sleep lost at night. But if colic strikes, strike the nap.

Under these circumstances, no graduate of the Cordon Bleu could operate successfully. Or inexpensively.

So, unless you want to live on franchised foods or takeouts from pizza parlors and submarine shops or expensive quickcooking steaks, chops, and such, something must be done. Before the baby comes.

This: Utilize the freezing space you have to precook dishes. Not dinners per se, but entrees. Example: a beef roast in your sixth month of pregnancy could yield several dishes of leftovers: a roast beef hash, a shepherd's pie, a pepper-steak casserole, roast beef sandwiches, to name only a few. Making stew? Double the recipe and freeze half. Making sauce for lasagna? Triple the recipe to yield a freezable spaghetti sauce and chili casserole. The idea is to have those leftovers during the first six weeks of motherhood.

Limited in your freezer space? Just half a dozen of these emergency meals could be the answer to caring for baby and daddy simultaneously.

BARBER: ALL IT TAKES IS A BOWL AND SOME SCISSORS

If you're out to save the cost of a hair cut by doing your own barbering, that's fine. But if you're not good at it, invest in one professional cut—around age two is usual—to have the pattern set for you.

To avoid the tearful scenes cartoonists love to portray, have your child accompany you or his father to the barber shop or hairdresser's when you're having your own hair done. After a few visits (could be as few as one) the fear should be eliminated along with the newness.

You can save some money by checking to see whether the hair cut is cheaper if not combined with a shampoo. If so, do your own shampooing at home. But for fewer sniffles' sake, let the hair dry before going to get the cut.

Improvise your own shampoo-sink in the kitchen. Put a small hand towel or dish towel, rolled into a compact wad, on the edge of the sink. Then, lay your child down flat on his back on the adjacent counter to wash his hair, with the towel under his neck.

To wet and rinse, use the sink sprayer attachment if you have one, always making sure the water is just barely warm. Since, as any shower-lover can vouch, water temperatures fluctuate so, it is important to check the temperature each time you go to use it. For those with old-fashioned sinks, a cup works fine. If you get used to holding the cup, not by the handle, but with a finger inside it, you have an automatic temperature gauge with each refill of the cup.

This method, which is really only a modification of the standard head-washing procedure used with young babies—the counter replacing your cradling arm—can be used for so long as the child fits the counter or submits to this less than dignified position.

One great advantage of it over other methods is that the child can remain fully dressed, with less chance of being chilled or catching cold.

Shampooing in the shower is not for young children, who can't keep their eyes closed during the rinsing. If you wish to change from the lying-down method to the bending-over-the-sink method, do so gradually. And the way to do this is to do your own hair that way for a couple weeks, allowing the child to help you rinse (don't let him control the water temperature, though—that can hurt). Then, have the child kneel on a chair, give him a face cloth or towel to hold against his face to ward off the suds, and get the shampoo over fast! This first time is not the time to do the double sudsing followed by the triple rinses, followed by the conditioners, etc. If you don't want shampooing to be traumatic every time you do it, then do make this first one a fast-over-lightly, which he will remember as being not too unpleasant or uncomfortable.

By the way, although there are shampoos on the market that promise not to irritate children's eyes, most do, according to consumer tests. One of the best ways to prevent such irritations and save money at the same time is by either using less shampoo than you would normally or diluting it fifty-fifty with water.

Part 7

Transportation

Over the next eighteen years, your baby's share of the transportation costs of your family will amount to 16 percent of the total cost of raising him, or enough to buy you a deluxe station wagon. Those figures are predicated on the basis that you do not end up buying him or her a car of his/her own at age sixteen or seventeen—that is extra.

These figures are based, like those for shelter, on a per capita share of the total costs of transportation for the family as a whole. Which will seem ridiculous to the new father, who can't for the life of him figure out how his stay-at-home infant will cost him several hundred dollars the first year of life. Is he in for a surprise! For one thing, there's the equipment you'll need to convert your car into a child-transporter: infant seat, child carrier, car bed. Then there are the extra trips to the store for the little one's food, to the doctor, to the drugstore. Since carrying a child can be heavy work, short trips will be driven instead of walked.

And then, a few years later, the chauffeuring really begins: to school, to lessons, to activities, to friends' homes. This lasts forever, it seems, but only until drive-it-yourself age, and then comes the car-borrowing period.

That's not all. Everything, especially vacations, will cost more to get there, whether by train, car, bus, or plane. So take my word for it, your transportation costs are going up and on and on.

Chapter 17

Getting from Here
to There

VIA CAR

On the way home from the hospital with that surprisingly heavy
little creature, you will, if you're like most mothers, hold that child
protectively yet gently in your arms. Let's hope that that is the last
car trip your child will make riding in such an unsafe manner. I
don't care if you're a weight-lifter by profession, or a professional
bull-dogger, you are not strong enough—nor are your reflexes fast
enough—to protect or hold your child in case of a crash.

So, as the first step in getting from here to there, do it safely.

An infant carrier is your best investment. One that will be held in
place on the front seat by the vehicle's seat belts (it should have
seat belts one and one half inches wide to fasten the child in
place), that will be high enough to protect the infant's head, that
will be lined for energy-absorbing protection, and that is designed
so the child faces the seat, not the dashboard.

The latter has several advantages in addition to the safety feature: for one thing, it is easier for you, when driving, to keep a
wary eye on your child without having to take your eyes off the
road for more than a second, or having to turn your head very far.
When you are not driving, you can, from your own seat, play with
the child easily or give a bottle if it's feeding time. You can even
shovel in the food while remaining comfortably seated and seat-
belted yourself.

As of this writing, General Motors' infant carrier has been the
only one to not only meet federal standards but also tests conducted by several independent testing groups. It costs less than

$15 and is available from GM or Chrysler dealers, or write to General Motors Corporation.

Car-bed. For longer trips—not just a few hours, but for a full day or more—you may wish to invest $25 or more for an infant car-bed that will be used in addition to the infant carrier. You need both because the infant car-bed does not provide protection for an infant who's sitting or standing.

Here are some points to remember regarding the car-bed;

- It should be designed to be positioned crosswise in the vehicle, not lengthwise.
- It should be designed to be fastened at its base (not by the handles) by the car's safety belts.
- The interior should be lined with special padding materials—which pretty much rules out all those mesh types unless you add padding.
- It should be constructed and designed to withstand collision forces—which again definitely rules out those mesh models. And pretty much rules out most other car-beds on the market, especially the ones with slats, unless a padded lining is available.
- It should have netting or straps over the top to prevent the infant from being ejected. You can add this yourself if necessary.

Some parents have found no need for a car-bed since their young ones seemed more than happy to fall asleep at a moment's notice in the reclining infant carrier. However, in the event of a long trip, investigate renting such a bed.

Car-seat. The child over nine months of age, or twenty pounds, should graduate from the infant carrier to a child car-seat. And at this stage, the choice you make may be literally one of life and death. Although the government set safety standards and made those standards law as of April 1, 1971, many consumer groups believe that the federal standards are not rigid enough and should be upgraded.

As of this writing, only the Ford Tot-Guard has been approved by all such groups, including that of Dr. Verne L. Roberts at the University of Michigan; the Action for Child Transportation Safety (ACTS) group of concerned mothers; Ralph Nader's Center for Auto Safety; Consumers Union. It costs less than $30 and is available from Ford, Lincoln/Mercury dealers, or by mail.

However, GM has entered the market with a "Child Safety Seat," which is being tested by all the various concerned groups.

Because of this, and because federal standards may be upgraded, and because manufacturers are upgrading their products (Klippan, for example, received an acceptable, but poor, rating by Consumers Union in 1972 for its $50 model; the company promptly turned around and started publicizing an "improved" model, which may or may not be improved), I seriously recommend that you go to your local library and check out the latest, most up-to-date test ratings for car-seats. Then and only then should you buy. Remember, more than 1,000 children die each year as the result of automobile accidents—and many of those victims were lovingly strapped into "safety seats" or "safety belts."

Child-restraint harness. As of late 1973, Sears is the only one to come up with a winner in the harness-race, but the word is that others are challenging. The government suggests that in selecting a harness system, you give preference to those that either attach directly to the vehicle's floor, or to the vehicle's seat belt, not to the seat back, nor over the seat back. They also suggest that you "choose the type which, in the width and type of belts used, distributes the crash forces over the widest possible body area." Which is nice to know, but I must confess my own inability to make such a distribution judgment. Again, I suggest you check consumer magazines for their ratings.

THINGS TO TAKE ALONG FOR BABY WHEN TRAVELING

• Breast-feeding is the most convenient since the supply's right there, as is the equipment, and everything's at the right temperature.
• Use the premixed, prebottled formula that needs no refrigeration. If you will be switching to this for the trip, make the switch several days before the trip to make sure the baby will (*a*) take the new formula, and (*b*) not adversely react to it.

- Make up your baby's regular formula, refrigerate until chilled, then wrap it in several layers (the more the better) of newspaper, which will act as the best possible inexpensive insulation.
- If feeding warm formulas, include a bottle-warmer that plugs into your car's cigarette lighter. For the child on cold formula you won't need this.
- If you're doing the blender-bottle routine, you can make up his meals and handle as you did the formula. If not, the various canned foods are a wife-saver. Chill those you normally serve cold and wrap in newspaper. Store others at room temperature and warm when necessary, using the bottle-warmer.
- Diapering—disposables are the only sane things to use here. Take along a supply of moisture-proof bags to place them in (save the plastic bags bread comes in; they're long enough so that you can tie the end in a knot, keeping both moisture and odor inside).
- Cleanups call for a box of tissues. They are a must for spitups and runny noses and such. Something stronger and wetter is necessary for sticky hands or messy bottoms. Although there are many premoistened products on the market, they're expensive. Try wetting diaper liners and carrying them along in a plastic bag.
- Litter bags of any kind or description.
- Playthings. A favorite toy is a must—if you have a new one, take it for a surprise. Never forget his "Lovy," and/or security blanket.
- A first-aid book and a first-aid kit (homemade, if you're cost-cutting) should be in your car's glove compartment.

THINGS TO TAKE ALONG
FOR OLDER CHILDREN

- Appropriate food, finger or otherwise, depending on age.
- Snacks and something cold to drink.
- A piece of candy appearing as if from nowhere is an effective bribe, to be resorted to in case of emergency.
- Cups, bottle openers, plastic spoons, knives, napkins, etc.
- Toileting—if the child is still in diapers, continue as you have been doing. If trained or partially trained, bring along the toilet

seat or potty chair you've been using. Some children won't go otherwise. A roll of toilet paper in the car is cheaper than tissues for cleanups.

• An extra set of clothing is a must—between spills and crumbs and accidents, your beautifully dressed, neat little child may arrive looking like a refugee from a mud puddle.

• A blanket and pillow for napping.

• Cleanup equipment. At this point, we switch over to those disposables that pop up one by one and stay forever moist in their container. They're kept in that trash container that sits on top of the drive shaft hump in the front seat area of rear-wheel-drive cars.

• Toys. Toys that the child can play with by himself, toys you can play with together. I keep the color-forms type just for this purpose, and they are used only for car trips so that their novelty doesn't wear off. A favorite book—or a new book, one that has some relationship either to traveling or to your destination—can be a time-spender.

• Games can while away time, too. Learn Pat-a-cake, Here's the Church, Itsy-Bitsy Spider, Peas Porridge Hot, Thumbkin, This Little Pig; bring along string to work a cat's cradle; play I Spy. Later, for the older child, you can expand this to more sophisticated games, like "Count how many cars go by before you see a Volkswagen," and "See how many things you can find that start with first initial of your [the child's] name." And you always top whatever he says by "And one more" until he figures out you're talking about him.

VIA MOTHER-PROPELLED WHEELED EQUIPMENT

Prams/strollers. Unless you live near a large city park or belong to a group that perambulates, the pram is an anchronism. Those women who have them tend to use them more indoors than out, as second cribs.

Strollers, however, serve a more necessary function and you should check them for sharp edges, dangerous hinges, and spaces where two metal tubes come together. Remember, the stroller's collapsibility, which makes it an improvement over the pram, is also what makes it more dangerous.

There are certain places where a stroller is a necessity (unless you have arms of steel that never tire)—but that doesn't mean you have to *buy* one. The zoo, for example, rents them. Call and reserve one to be sure. Shopping malls, like certain stores, have strollers for hire. Supermarkets have their own version of the stroller, and it's for free—the shopping cart. For a baby use the infant seat cross-wise in the child's-seat area. The young child can sit in place if you buy all your soft goods—napkins, toilet paper, paper towels—first and prop them around him to support him. For an older child the shopping cart can also be used within a shopping area strictly as a stroller. The basket will carry more than the parcel area of your stroller; the child is up higher and less apt to have a door slammed on him; there's no need to wrestle with that octopus of chrome and vinyl to get it out of the car, or back into it. And remember, it's free.

What of those places where there are no shopping carts, yet you need a stroller—like flower shows and dog shows, carnivals and circuses, visits to museums and botanical gardens? Rental could still be the answer here. For a couple of dollars you can rent a stroller for a weekend. If you find you really like it, then go buy one. But remember, the child who has mastered walking is not always happy riding. In fact, you may find that rather than ride in the stroller, he'd like to push it. (Montgomery Ward has a splendid one, by the way, that folds up like an umbrella. And its cost is at the low end of the stroller scale. Sears has one, too, but it is not as inexpensive.) By age four, most children won't ride in them.

Alternatives to Prams/Strollers—Front-Packing or Back-Packing. Of the two, the latter is most convenient for you, the former safer for baby. That's because you can't see behind you—a quick turn may give clearance to your shoulders but not to the burden on your back. Doctors will tell you there are all kinds of psychological advantages to the child in your carrying him on your person and keeping him in close physical contact to you. Of course, there is one problem: it takes a strong back on your part—especially as the child grows. The carrier that can be used fore or aft is a better buy than a strictly back-packer, unless you take week-long hiking trips.

However, you may be in for a shock when you discover just

how much these carriers can cost. The nationally advertised one, for example, costs over $30. The catalog companies have deluxe models that run between $15 and $20, and economy models for around $10. There is also an inexpensive front-cuddler for under $10; however, it is only usable during the first three months—and, in my book, that makes it rather expensive. (The Childbirth Education Association, either your local chapter or the Greater Philadelphia Chapter, P.O. Box 8741, Philadelphia, Pennsylvania 19101, has a young baby sling-carrier that is comparable in every way to the most expensive baby carrier with three exceptions: it is sturdier, it does not have a built-in diaper bag, and it costs only $8.)

VIA AIR

Before deciding to go anyplace served by several carriers, check each to see what they offer for your child, and what their rates are. For example, in 1973 the child under two rode free if he sat in his mother's lap. When he reached age two, by federal regulations, he must occupy his own seat. However, his rate, depending on the carrier, may be much less since he can fly under a family plan.

All airlines will warm bottles, but you bring your own. Some airlines carry a supply of disposable diapers "just in case," others don't. Some offer you a child's meal if you order in advance; even for that freeloader under the age of two you can get one at a reduced rate. As well as books and puzzles, blankets and pillows, most planes have first-aid equipment available. Some have lounge areas that make for convenient diapering; in others you can do it at your seat (provided your seatmate doesn't object). In some of the newer, bigger planes there is a let-down, diaper-changing shelf in the restrooms. Other flights offer a stereo sound track just for youngsters that includes storytelling. On some flights toys are given away; on others coloring books and crayons. And most have storybooks and children's magazines there for the looking.

Certain airports provide special child-size playrooms with their own television sets. Strollers are available at most airports, but you must request them in advance.

Although you may be asked to hold your freeloading child in your lap if the plane is full, on most planes mothers with babies get extra-special treatment. Stewardesses will rearrange seating so that a mother can have an unused seat for her child; if there are several unfilled seats, a sleepy child may find himself stretched out full-length across two or three of those seats.

And there is one other benefit that concerns pregnant mothers: most stewardesses have been given some training in emergency childbirths; what bus driver or train conductor can say the same?

VIA TRAIN

Once upon a time, just decades ago, the train was the *only* way to go. With the coming of planes, many train rides became obsolete. But the shunting aside was only temporary. The long-distance luxury liners are back on the track.

If you're traveling with a child under five, you may find the train *the* way to go. On all trains except Metroliners and Turboliners you can take one child free for every adult ticket bought; this automatically entitles him to a seat. On the Metroliners and Turboliners you may take one child free if he sits in your lap; if two children can sit in one seat, you may reserve a seat for the two of them by paying half the fare for that seat.

On long-distance trains, between Chicago and Los Angeles, for example, you can have the use of a roomette for $15 less than a first-class ticket on a plane. It might be a little crowded, but it is quiet, it is private, it is less nerve-wracking. If you wanted a bedroom for yourself and a child, you would have to pay for the cost of the bedroom plus half of one base fare (the railroads charge a base fare and add on a surcharge for the bedroom or other accommodations).

If there's a passenger service representative on your train, she'll make arrangements to warm bottles and heat foods, etc. If not, the snack-lounge or dining-room people will do so. On short runs you are probably best off to carry a thermos of warm formula with you.

What else can you expect going by train? Depends on the distance you travel. Some trains will have lounge cars where you can amuse your child, some will have coloring books, all have aisles for children to run up and down (as I did when I was young, and as your grandchildren will do some twenty years from now). In the future, there'll be a special car—it's on the drawing boards right now—that will be a game room for children during the day-time and convert into a night club for adults after dark.

The pros and cons of train travel? Well, it's faster than by car, but slower than by plane. However, the scenery is more interesting on the ground, and the accident rate is lower, too.

VIA BUS

Like the railroads, bus companies let one child under age five ride free per adult ticket. This doesn't guarantee him a seat in princi-ple, but in practice on certain bus lines it works out that way. Whenever a bus line has a policy of no-standees, such as Grey-hound has, the bus driver controls the loading of the bus. He can, if he chooses, stop the loading at any point and call for another bus, thus giving children seats. Those turned away who have paid for seats are often better off on the second bus—since as few as three or four (although in practice it could be one) would have a whole bus to themselves, and they'd arrive only minutes later than they would have originally.

However, if it looks as though you may have to hold your child, you can, with those bus lines that require no advance reservations or tickets, scoot back into the terminal and pay half fare to guar-antee your child a seat.

Although all interstate and intercity buses are equipped with lavatories, there are no facilities on the bus to warm bottles or food, so come prepared. And, unless the bus is partially empty, there is no place to change diapers.

Although luxury coaches will have reclining seats, tinted win-dows, and climate control, you furnish your own amusements. On those routes where V.I.P. service is available (Greyhound calls it Bus-Plus) for a slight surcharge, there is a hostess on board who will serve hot and cold beverages, snacks or lunch, help out with children, provide reading material, etc.

CAR, MOTHER-POWER, PLANE, TRAIN, BUS—
WHICH IS CHEAPER THAN WHICH?

Mother-power comes free. You're the cheapest. After that, it all depends. That sounds like a cop-out, but it isn't. It depends on the length of the trip. For example, take the trip from New York to Washington; it's a distance of approximately 220 miles. By car, you can figure on a cost, at 12¢ a mile (the government's allowance in 1973), of $26.40, plus tolls of about $5. Let's round that off and call the trip a $30-, four-hour trip by car.

The same trip by bus will take slightly more than four hours (because of rest stops), and the fare will be approximately $11.

The same trip by plane will take about one hour at a cost of $35. However, you must include travel time to and from the airport, plus taxi fares or parking charges.

Again, by train, conventional that is, the trip will cost you $13 and take a little less than four hours. By Metroliner, it will cost $19 (and remember, the child doesn't get a seat unless you pay half fare) and take three hours.

But there are other factors that affect your decision. For example, you can take as many passengers in your car as it—and traffic laws—will allow, and there is no increase in costs. With the bus and train, one child under age five rides free per adult. With the Metroliner, a seat for him costs half fare. By plane, a child over age two must pay half fare.

Generally speaking, on trips under 400 miles a bus is the cheapest for one person, a train next, a car next, and a plane the least. But when you need to transport two or three people, the car becomes as cheap as or cheaper than the bus, the trains and planes bring up the end.

On longer trips, the time factor becomes more and more important. You'll find children under the age of two are long on fussing and short on patience. Thus, with an unhappy baby aboard, long bus rides, even with their rest stops every two and one half to three and one half hours, can be a nightmare for all passengers. At least in a car only the immediate family gets the message. A train, depending on the accommodations you choose, can be a shorter version of either car or bus. The airplane offers you a fast trip, but the waits at either end can be long. There's no way to foresee that. And remember, planes are more subject to weather inconveniences than all of the others.

In trying to decide which way to go, take the following into consideration: The costs of driving a car remain the same regardless of the number of passengers, AND—unless you are going to pack all your meals and drive straight through—the costs of meals and lodgings can make such a trip, say from coast to coast, more costly than the most luxurious alternate method.

On a train trip of several days, you pay nothing for lodging, but you do have to pay for meals.

Part 8

Financial

From a federal-income-tax point of view, your child makes you money since each dependent is worth $75 dollars or more (depending on your bracket) off your taxes. That's because as of 1973 you get a $750 deduction per dependent, beginning with the year in which he's born.

And your social-security payments remain the same since they are governed by how much you make, not how many dependents you have, yet your benefits under FICA (Federal Insurance Contributions Act) are vastly expanded. For example, you would have to have over $100,000 invested at 6 percent interest per annum to provide the annual cash benefits social security could pay a widowed mother with a baby.

Other costs, such as legal services and insurance, are entirely up to you. And as such they cannot be charged against the cost of raising a child, just as savings can not be allocated. Whether or not you save is up to you. *But* if you think college is in your child's future, saving makes sense . . . starting now.

Chapter 18
Dollars and Sense

Studies show that the one period in life that requires more changes and more adjustments by individuals and couples than any other is the one in which you have your first baby. In my opinion, it also offers more satisfactions than any other.

Be that as it may, this is the time, traditionally, that a couple moves from apartment to house, changes from sharp sports car or motorcycle to sedan or station wagon, and decides whether the mother-to-be shall leave her job temporarily, semipermanently, or permanently.

It is also the time to assess your financial situation and make plans and set goals for the future.

Where do you start?

FINANCIAL PLANNING

If you already have a lawyer, you could start with him. (By the way, nothing in this chapter is intended as legal advice; for such help you should consult your lawyer.) If you don't have a lawyer, get yourself to the nearest or best or largest full-service bank in your area and avail yourself of their financial-planning experts. What will that cost you? NOT ONE SINGLE RED CENT.

Your reaction will probably be, "Me? Go to a bank? For financial planning? They only want millionaires there. I don't own enough to make it worth their while."

Let Frank X. Gillespie, of The Fidelity Bank in Philadelphia, answer that, "To begin with, the less you have, the more reason you have to protect it. Secondly, you'd be surprised at what you do have when you add up pension plans and profit sharing or other employer benefits, life insurance policies, assets in your house."

Let me add this. If you're twenty when you and your husband go to the bank, and your assets are practically nil, you two are showing the business acumen necessary to make the next fifty years of your lives financially productive. The bank bets that when your estate comes to be settled, that nil may have turned into a million, more or less. For example, one bank estimates that a salesman who may reach a peak salary of $14,000 could easily have an estate worth over $100,000 without doing any more than working every day, saving a bit here and there, and buying a house.

What can the bank do for you? It can save you legal fees. Not all, but some. What the bank won't do is any legal work for you. You will still need a lawyer to write your wills and/or draw up your trusts. What the bank can do is most of the costly, time-consuming preliminary thinking with you, and for free! Then, when your lawyer is called in, he can get right to work on the necessary documents.

Does this bank deal sound too good to be true? Is there a catch in it? Of course. The bank wants to end up as your executor and/or trustee. And since you will need such an executor and/or trustee, you will probably end up appointing the bank. For one thing, it has an advantage no individual can match: Banks don't die.

Where else can you go for financial planning? Many insurance companies will do it. Phoenix Mutual, for example, advertises a Personal Analysis Service to help you plan your finances. And they, too, will do it without charge. Naturally, they want your insurance business—but like the banks, you get your planning done without obligation.

A third place is at your friendly lawyer's office. He's not interested in your insurance business, nor is he interested in your depositing your funds in trust at some bank (although he may very well wish to be named as your executor). He offers you impartial, objective service—and he charges for it.

DRAWING UP A WILL

For this you should have a lawyer. Not because wills drawn up by amateurs aren't valid—they can be and have been. There are too many newspaper stories about wills written on wallpaper, or on the backs of envelopes, or embroidered in a sampler for me to argue otherwise. But, legal documents should be written by a person who speaks the language—a lawyer. Once you're dead and your homemade will is ruled invalid, you don't get a second chance.

How do you find a lawyer? Most people ask a friend. But there are other ways. The bank can recommend three or four who specialize in estate planning or are eminently qualified in this area. You can ask your doctor (doctors usually have the best possible money-minded men in town working for them); you can look up the listings of lawyers in the Yellow Pages, and pick one at random; you can ask your insurance man. Or you can make use of a lawyer referral service.

Such a service is operated by your local (or county) bar association. They are usually most unwilling to give you information over the telephone. They want you to come in and register, for which some charge a registration fee, others don't; then you will be given the name of a lawyer if you guarantee to pay a minimum fee for a specified period, usually the first half hour, of his time.

If you go to a big-city referral service, the name you're given will be that of a specialist or one especially qualified in this area (and the names are rotated alphabetically). If you go to a smaller service, you get the next name on the list, the idea being that since all lawyers must show competence in will-drawing, etc., before they can pass the bar examinations, all lawyers are thus equally able to do your will. I reserve comment.

You're probably wondering if having a will is worth all that effort? Let a lawyer answer that: "In the absence of a will the property will pass pursuant to the intestate laws of the state where the person is domiciled at death in the case of intangible property and tangible real and personal property located in the state. If the person owns tangible personal property or real property in another state, that property will pass under the intestate laws of that state."

Translation: the court steps in and handles your property on your behalf, according to the way the state's laws say it *must* be disposed.

Let's take a farfetched, but possible example of what might happen. Let's say that when you and your husband were married, your parents gave *you,* not the two of you, but *you,* a house. And let's say after you and your husband have had one child, you are killed in an automobile accident. What happens to the house? Does it revert back to your parents? Does it go to your husband? Is it divided between your husband and your child?

You couldn't care less, you say; you know if it went back to your parents, they would let your husband and their grandchild continue to live in the house and what difference does it make if your husband gets it all, or if he has to share it with your child; eventually the child would get it all, wouldn't he? Would he if your husband remarried and then died? Could the new wife end up owning your house—and your child, could he end up with nothing? Think about it.

Another example: Suppose it were your husband who died, leaving you with a small child. If he had no will, the property might be divided fifty-fifty between you and your child. You would get your share; the rest might have to be applied to the benefit of the child under the supervision of a guardian. Since the guardian would be appointed by the court, they could elect not to appoint you as guardian.

Suddenly you are having to consult someone you don't know about the care of your child in terms of money being spent. What's more, that somebody else might be a bank who would charge a fee against the estate each year. If an individual were named, he might have to post a guardian's bond, another charge against the estate. And if for some reason it became desirable to dip into the principal of your child's estate, the guardian might have to get the court's approval—that could cost estate filing fees and attorney fees.

Now, to make matters worse, let's suppose both you and your husband died in an automobile accident; however, your child survived. But neither of you had a will. Now you get all kinds of wild complications. For example, if your husband dies first, you have the situation described above. But if you die shortly thereafter, everything's got to be divided up again. And all this time, there's the problem of who is going to take care of your child? Now that's a frightening possibility!

You need a will, your husband needs a will, and both wills should be drawn up together to provide for all possible eventualities.

How much will this cost you in the way of legal fees? As little as $25, as much as several thousand dollars, depending on the complexities of your estate or your desires. The best way to determine it is to ask your attorney at your very first conference. The best way to keep it low is to go into that conference prepared. You should have a list of your assets, the names of your heirs, the executors and/or trustees, and the guardians—along with their addresses for legal identification.

How much will having a will save you in eventual legal fees? Considerable compared to the couple who dies without a will. Their posthumous legal fees could be ten or twenty times what it would have cost them to have their will drawn up.

And then there are the tax savings involved. Joint ownership, for example, while guaranteeing that an asset will pass directly to the surviving spouse, does not guarantee that it passes completely tax-free. The Internal Revenue Service sees to that. What a lawyer does, for example, by setting up trusts, is to help you avoid paying *unnecessary* taxes. Let me stress that. The government expects you to pay only the minimum taxes imposed by law, and your lawyer sees to that, and only that.

CHOOSING INSURANCE

One of the fastest ways to accumulate a large estate is to buy it through life insurance. The payment of a single premium could, in the case of accidental death, bring the beneficiary the entire face value. The problem is that the law of averages (insurance men say "actuarial tables") says you're going to do more paying of premiums than that. So the wise thing to do is to buy as much insurance as you can afford and as you need, no more, no less.

How do you find that out? A good way to start is by finding out how much and what kind of insurance you already have in the form of Social Security. For example, did you know that the widower of a woman covered by Social Security would be eligible for benefits? Certainly her surviving children would—and that coverage would continue until age twenty-two if the child were a full-time student. There's also be a lump-sum death-benefit payment (as of 1973, the maximum is $225, though).

To get this information, call your local Social Security office, or write to the U.S. Department of Health, Education and Welfare,

Social Security Administration, Washington, D.C. A booklet describing all benefits is available for 30¢ from the Superintendent of Documents, U.S. Government Printing Office, Washington, D.C. 20402. Ask for ✂1770–00101.

As long as you're writing letters, you might want to send one to Consumer Insurance, 813 National Press Building, Washington, D.C. 20004, for copies of *A Shopper's Guide to Life Insurance** and *A Shopper's Guide to Term Insurance*† ($1 each per copy), prepared and copyrighted by the Pennsylvania Insurance Department.

In each of these, the department, supervised by Commissioner Herbert S. Denenberg, compiled information and prepared rankings of insurance companies as to their premiums and cost indexes for straight life insurance and term insurance. Although the companies involved were only those doing business in Pennsylvania, most of these companies also operate nationwide, and their rates are the same everywhere in the nation. It's interesting to note that the department found a cost variation between highest and lowest of 140 percent on term insurance, and 170 percent on straight life insurance.

If you can't afford to buy both copies, choose the one on term insurance. Sidney Margolius, syndicated columnist and financial consultant, has gone on record as recommending that, "for the average young man with a growing family to protect, term insurance gives him the most protection for his money."

While you're waiting for all this literature to arrive in the mail, you might visit your public library and see if they have a copy of *Best's Review,* put out by A. M. Best Company, Park Avenue, Morristown, New Jersey 07960, or the latest edition of *Life Rates and Data,* by the National Underwriter Publications, 175 West Jackson Boulevard, Chicago, Illinois 60604.

Both of these compare costs, determine the size of the company, and tell you their financial responsibilities. This is important because as of June 1972, according to Jeffrey Adams, of Prudential Insurance Company, there were 1,829 insurance companies

---

* Refers to straight or whole life insurance that builds a cash reserve year by year upon which you can borrow or that you can cash in.

† Refers to a type of policy that provides protection only, no cash reserve, and is in effect for a specified number of years.

doing business in the U.S.A. and as of June 1973 a surprisingly large number of them were not in business.

Now, let's be realistic. The procedure described above is the best way to begin to make a decision. By far the more usual way is this: you have a friend, or a friend of a friend, who's in the insurance game. He comes to talk to you. He makes sense; you buy a policy. And that might be exactly the same policy you would have chosen after doing all my recommended reading.

How can you tell? You can't, but knowing something about this friend of a friend could certainly give you an indication. To begin with, is he a one-company insurance agent, an independent agent, or a broker. The difference? The first is either a salaried employee or a commissioned agent of a single company. All he can sell you are the policies of his company. The second, the independent agent, is authorized to sell insurance for a number of insurance companies. He gives you a wider choice of policies and may be of more aid when you try to settle a claim. The third, the broker, has no regular contract with any one of several insurance companies. He can, in effect, shop around for the best buy for you.

Actually, when you are buying life insurance, the company is more important than the agent. You're putting your money into a company that hopefully won't have to pay off for fifty or sixty or more years. Your main interest should be whether the company will be around later. One way to determine that is to look for established longevity.

However, when you shop for homeowner's or other short-term insurance, the agent is more important. Normally, when you need additional insurance of any kind, you call upon your life insurance agent first. So pick him carefully. Find out, for example, how long he's been in the insurance business. Again, longevity is important to you—it proves he makes and *keeps* customers. This can be misleading with the exclusive agent, who, if salaried, may have piled up his longevity by virtue of supersalesmanship, or by working cheap.

If your insurance salesman is holding down two jobs (such as being a realtor as well), you might wonder which commands his greater loyalty and which is his specialty. You also might wonder which is paying him the most. Generally, that which a man does best gives him the greatest financial reward.

If you have any doubts about the qualities of the man you're dealing with, ask for names of satisfied customers. Then check him out. And when you do, look for those who say he was recommended to them by someone else. Get that someone else's name, and check with him. He may have changed his opinion during the time interval. More important than that, however, he will probably have had more chances to see this agent in action.

Now, upon whose life will you put your money? In most families, the breadwinner is the only one who is insured. Which makes sense. But if the wife contributes to the family support or plans on going back to work because she must, then insurance for her is a necessity. Term insurance would seem the logical choice. But since premiums on a woman are lower than on a man, she might be able to buy a whole life policy for as little as a term policy. Check it out.

Another aspect you might want to consider, especially if you are not working, and not planning to, is what your services as mother, chauffeur, housekeeper, etc., are worth to your family. The Institute of Life Insurance, on the basis of a bank study done by The Chase Manhattan Bank, figures that back in 1968 to get someone to do a homemaker/mother's job it would have cost $159.34 a week, or $8,285.68 a year, $99,428.16 total.‡

That is, if you could find anyone to do all that work. Most people, especially housekeepers and baby-sitters and live-in-maids, like to work an eight-hour day. And do you know how much housekeepers were getting a week in 1974? You might find a fairly good one for $200; but if housekeepers are in short supply in your area, figure on more. Much more.

Now, what about insurance on the baby? Experts believe that the wisest choice is to buy a policy that has a nominal amount of death benefits (burial expenses), but has a rider that will guarantee insurability or the right to buy additional life insurance at a

‡ It's interesting to note that the 1973 study at Cornell by Walker and Gauger came up with a figure lower than this. Since the same amount of work is still needed to raise a baby, the only way a woman's workvalue could have gone down over five years (in the face of rising labor costs) is if some of her work were being done by someone else. Read husband. Women's libbers take note: You're succeeding in the home. And the Walker-Gauger study bears this out. As noted before, they say today's men will contribute about 20 percent of the labor needed to raise the child.

particular time in the future, regardless of his health condition at the time.

Or how about on the family as a whole? There are certain life insurance policies that will provide a fixed number of dollars for the father, a certain number of dollars, decreasing over a period of time, for the mother to reflect the costs of hiring a substitute should anything happen to her, and a small amount of death benefits for each child. In the case of the latter, read the fine print carefully to make sure that each child is covered from birth on, not after a waiting period of fourteen to thirty days.

It should be noted that whatever type of insurance you buy, your costs will be lower—by 9 percent or more—if you pay those premiums annually rather than on a semiannually, quarterly, or monthly basis.

Almost worse than being underinsured is being overinsured, especially if the payment of the premiums prevents you from enjoying life now. Sure, it's nice to leave your children well set up, but if *you* started from scratch, they can, too. Besides, Social Security benefits are increasing so and improving so, you can get by with much less insurance than was possible even a decade ago.

BUYING A HOUSE

Actually the buying is easy, it's the paying that's hard. To try to determine just how much money you can afford, these rules of thumb have traditionally been put forth:

(1) The cost of a house should be no more than two to two and one half times its buyers' total income, with a young couple staying on the low side.

(2) A family should spend no more than 25 percent of its total yearly income on housing expenses.

These rules of thumb are pretty inaccurate, even the experts admit.

The best way to determine how much you can spend on home ownership is to figure out what you are spending now for various expenses, such as food, clothing, medical expenses, etc., plus any fixed payments you have (car payments, insurance, etc.). Subtract the total of those expenses and fixed payments from your in-

HOW EXPENSIVE A HOME CAN YOU AFFORD*

To use the table, find your "budget allowance for mortgage," in either the monthly or annual column below. Then read across to the rate of interest which you can obtain and the number of the years the loan will run. This figure will give you the amount of the mortgage loan which your budget can finance. Add the amount of the down payment which you can make, and you will have an estimate of the total cost of the home you can afford. (The amount of the loan which you can obtain may be much less.)

Budget Allowance for Mortgage		Amount of Mortgage Which Budget Will Finance						Down Payment (after closing costs)[1]	Total Amount You Can Spend for a Home
		7% Interest			8% Interest				
Monthly	Annual	20 Yrs.	25 Yrs.	30 Yrs.	20 Yrs.	25 Yrs.	30 Yrs.		
$ 50	$ 600	$ 4,080	$ 4,315	$ 4,480	$ 3,885	$ 4,090	$ 4,220		
60	720	4,900	5,180	5,375	4,660	4,910	5,070		
80	960	6,530	6,905	7,170	6,215	6,545	6,755		
100	1,200	8,165	8,635	8,960	7,770	8,180	8,445		
125	1,500	10,205	10,790	11,200	9,710	10,230	10,560		
150	1,800	12,245	12,950	13,440	11,655	12,275	12,670		
175	2,100	14,285	15,105	15,680	13,600	14,320	14,780		
200	2,400	16,325	17,265	17,920	15,540	16,365	16,890		
225	2,700	18,370	19,425	20,160	17,480	18,410	19,000		
250	3,000	20,410	21,580	22,400	19,425	20,460	21,115		
300	3,600	24,490	25,900	26,685	23,375	24,490	25,350		
350	4,200	28,570	30,215	31,345	27,270	28,570	29,575		
400	4,800	32,650	34,530	35,820	31,170	32,650	33,800		

EXAMPLE:

Mr. W's budget shows $225 per month "allowance for home ownership." He has $5,500 for a down payment after allowing for preliminary costs. He can get a 7% loan for 25 years. How much can he spend for a home?

First, he must allow $4.50 a month per $1,000 down payment for taxes, insurance, maintenance, and improvement, a total of about $25 per month. This leaves $200 as his budget allowance for mortgage. Read down the column,

"Budget Allowance for Mortgage" to $200 a month, and across to the column 7% interest—25 years—to find $17,265. This is the amount of mortgage his budget will finance. Add $5,500 (down payment) to $17,265. This makes the total cost of the property which he can pay for and maintain $22,765.

*Home Finders Directory, Copyright 1973
[1]Figure 6% of total price.

come.† Be sure to include the various costs of your baby-to-be—these are scattered throughout this book, but summaries or ranges are found in the introduction to each section. What's left is your allowance for home ownership, your *total maximum* figure to spend per month on housing, including mortgage payments.

One other factor will determine how much of a house you can buy. That is how much of a down payment you can make. That's the sum of your savings, or the cash value of insurance policies, etc., LESS the closing costs incurred by actually buying a house. These can include: termite inspection, roof inspection, land surveys, title insurance or a title abstract, appraisal fees, insurance costs and/or penalties, legal fees (¾ to 1 percent of price, with $150 and up the norm), escrow fee, and the two biggies: a real estate transfer tax based on cost of home, plus any adjustments of taxes.

You can figure that in most states, closing costs will add 6 percent to the cost of your house. On a $16,000 house, you would need, in addition to your down payment, in the neighborhood of $1,000 just for closing ($960, to be accurate, as a national average). For each $1,000 you go over that price, add $60 to your closing-costs kitty. So subtract closing costs from savings, and you have your down-payment figure.

For each $1,000 of it, you should subtract $4.50 per month (or $54 per year, as a national average, for taxes, insurance, maintenance, and improvements to the house) from your budget allowance for housing. What is left is your budget allowance for mortgage; this determines how large a mortgage you can get, depending on the interest rate your lending bank will give you.

To determine the total amount you can spend for a home, if you know your down payment and budget allowance for mortgage, use the table on pages 300 and 301 created by Theodore Robertson for his *Home Finders Directory* (copyright 1973).

SAMPLE WORKSHEET FOR ESTIMATING HOUSING COSTS

(I have condensed this worksheet so that you might see how it works in principle. You will probably find it easier to make up separate worksheets for each category—Adult, Fixed, Flexible,

† See sample worksheet on pages 303 and 304 for a step-by-step guide to all this.

Baby, Utilities—and do one great, big subtraction afterward, to get your allowance for home ownership. One more subtraction determines your maximum monthly mortgage payment.)

Income
Monthly net income plus any
annual income divided by 12   _____

Adult Expenses
Clothing   _____
Food   _____
Medical   _____
Education   _____
Maintenance   _____
Transportation   _____
Gifts, Contributions   _____
    TOTAL: _____
    DIFFERENCE: _____

Fixed Expenses
Car loan   _____
Insurance, life   _____
Insurance, automobile   _____
Insurance, medical   _____
Household furnishings   _____
Department store charges   _____
Other   _____
    TOTAL: _____
    DIFFERENCE: _____

Flexible Expenses
Recreation   _____
Books, magazines, news-   _____
papers.
Entertaining   _____
Personal care   _____
Tobacco, liquor   _____
    TOTAL: (need not apply,
    optional)   _____
    DIFFERENCE: (if choose to
    apply)   _____

Baby Expenses

Clothing _____

Food _____

Medical _____

Education _____

Maintenance _____

Transportation _____

   TOTAL: _____

   DIFFERENCE: _____

Utilities‡

Telephone _____

Gas _____

Electric _____

Water _____

   TOTAL: _____

   DIFFERENCE: _____

OR

Your Allowance for
Home Ownership

Less $4.50 per $1,000 of down
payment _____

_____

OR

Your Budget Allowance for
Mortgage

Down Payment

TOTAL SAVED, OR ASSETS: _____

Less 6% cost of house for
closing costs _____

DIFFERENCE: _____

Add your budget allowance for mortgage to your adjusted down
payment and you have the maximum price for a new house.

‡ If they do not apply where you are presently living, call the utility companies and request average rates depending on number of people within
family and projected number of rooms.

TIPS ON CHOOSING A HOUSE

The two-story house offers you the most for your money since one floor is the roof of the next. However, with a new baby upstairs, the stair climbing can be ferocious. I counted the round trips one day, and they came to fifty-seven knee-achers.

A split-level is the next more economical, since, again, there is a dual use of building elements. But the stair climbing is almost as much as with a two-story house. The difference is that you're not as aware of that since it's only half a flight at a time.

The ranch house or one-story domicile is the most expensive to build. Here, however, you don't need changing areas on different levels, nor do you need barricades at each stairway.

The best time of the year to buy a house is when no one else is buying a house. In most areas that means an extreme of weather —summer or winter. At this time there are more houses on the market per potential buyer, and the prices may tend to be lower.

If you have enough down payment to qualify for a conventional loan (20 to 33⅓ percent or more), rather than a VA or FHA loan, be sure to take advantage of the fact that the owner will not have to pay points (penalties assessed against the seller) and may negotiate a lower price accordingly.

MOST IMPORTANTLY, IN BUYING A HOME YOU SHOULD REALIZE THAT THE REAL ESTATE SALESMAN IS *NOT* WORKING FOR YOU. HE MAY APPEAR TO BE INTERESTED IN YOU, BUT HIS INTEREST IS THAT OF AN EMPLOYEE FOR SOMEONE ELSE. THUS, TAKE WHAT YOUR SALESMAN SAYS WITH A GRAIN OF SALT—or even a truckload.

MINOR-FINANCIAL MATTERS THAT ADD UP

FORTY-THREE WAYS TO GET MORE THAN YOUR MONEY'S WORTH

1. Start sewing. Make family clothing or draperies yourself. You can save from 35 percent to 50 percent of the cost of store-bought accessories.

2. Start a hand-me-down program with your friends and relatives. When kids outgrow their clothes, just start passing them around and ask that relatives and friends do the same. You can get some nice outfits this way.

3. Try not to use frozen foods. Use canned or in-season fresh foods. And try some good, old-fashioned do-it-yourself foods instead of precooked or premixed.

4. Use a price gadget that determines cost per pound or unit when you food shop. It can tell you the best buys in a grocery store. It will help you compare prices and see whether or not you're getting cheated. You can find price comparers—simple or fancy—in your local department store.

5. Cut costs on recipes by using nonfat dry milk and water instead of milk, margarine instead of butter, skimping on the amount of ingredients when possible.

6. When shopping for canned foods, buy the house brand of your supermarket. You can save more than 15 percent this way. Buy canned fruits and vegetables that are cut in slices, chunks, or halves. They usually cost less than those that are canned whole. And when you see produce marked "small" or "mixed," buy it. It's usually a lot less expensive.

7. Forget about the milkman. Buy your milk at the store. You can save at least 85¢ a week if yours is a family using ten half gallons or more of milk a week.

8. Don't get meat on price-per-pound basis. Figure three or four servings per pound for meat with little or no bone, two or three for medium bone, and one or two for much bone or gristle.

9. Use your can opener instead of pop-top cans. Sometimes pop-tops are more expensive.

10. Buy in big amounts. Hamburger bought ten pounds at a time, packaged in convenient amounts for your family, then frozen can save you 10¢ per pound.

11. Take advantage of weekly specials advertised by grocery stores and the lower prices of seasonal products. The U.S. Department of Agriculture economists estimate this can save you as much as 6 percent on your food bill.

12. Look at classified ads before you buy new furniture. Sometimes well-off people move out of large homes into small apartments and offer beautiful pieces of furniture at bargain rates.

13. When your doctor is writing out a prescription drug for you, ask him to prescribe it by its chemical name rather than by its brand name. If a drug is available in its chemical name, you can save a good deal of money by not paying for a brand name.

14. When you plan to take your kids out on Sunday afternoons look around for free attractions. Check the entertainment section of newspapers. There still *are* such animals around.

15. If classical music is a favorite of yours, shop for it in stores that

have budget lines of major record companies. Look for names such as Nonesuch, Everyman Classics, Seraphim, Victrola.

16. Keep children's library books in one place so *you* can check for overdue books. After all, you will pay the fines.

17. If you belong to a book or record club, be sure to cancel items you don't want.

18. Examine all your bills for discounts when "prompt payment" is indicated. In some places you can save 10 percent on electricity, 10 percent on water, and 4 percent on gas if you pay promptly.

19. Save yourself 7 percent to 10 percent on heating bills by setting your thermostat down 5° at night. You can bring it back to normal first thing in the morning. But do not attempt to go down more than those 5°. It will cost you that much more in extra fuel to get the temperature back up to normal.

20. Don't use disposable items, such as paper towels, placemats, napkins, or plates, in your kitchen where possible. Throwaways cost more.

21. Cut postage costs. Use postcards instead of letters when possible and save a penny. Use regular stamps for mail going to destinations over 500 miles, because whether they have airmail stamps or not, they go by airmail. When you're sending letters overseas, use postage-paid "aero-grammes" that can be mailed anywhere. (Price: 13¢ vs. 15¢ to 25¢ per half ounce for regular overseas airmail.)

22. Save on tire and gas mileage by inflating your tires two to four pounds over the lowest recommendations in your owner's manual. But never go over thirty-two pounds.

23. When you decide to buy a new car, get one that has manual transmission with overdrive instead of automatic transmission. You can get maximum gas mileage from manual transmission with overdrive, especially if you do a lot of cross-country driving.

24. Your car manual can contain a wealth of information on how to save lots of money. Most manuals show you how to avoid over-maintenance and practice gasoline economy.

25. Stay in motels or hotels that don't charge you for your children.

26. Ignore some of the options when buying a new car. A simple thing like rolling your windows up and down manually can save you about $100.

27. When you drive to work, park farther away from the main business section. A few blocks distance from the center of town can mean as much as 50 percent off on parking rates.

28. Save on gas by knowledgeable driving. Accelerate moderately; the most gas is consumed in getting your car going. Shift to your top gear as soon as possible and stay with it as long as possible. Keep your

speed as constant as you can. Drift into stops rather than slamming on your brakes. Idle sparingly; idling uses a lot of gas.

29. Take advantage of airline excursion fares and family plans during off-peak periods. Travel during off-peak times, such as at night, when special rates prevail on some airlines. In some cases the head of a family will pay full fare, the wife two-thirds, and children ages two to twenty one, one-third.

30. Shop at cash-and-carry stores. Experts in family finance say this can save 25 percent or more.

31. Before you invest in mutual-fund shares, check into "no-load" funds. These funds have no sales commission tagged onto them. Your broker won't push these because of a commission absence, but they are the same as funds that commonly charge 8 percent or 8½ percent sales commission.

32. If enough people in a company sign up for a payroll deduction plan, some mutual funds will reduce or eliminate the sales commission on "load" funds. Whenever possible, invest and insure in a group. Health, life, and auto insurance are all cheaper when done with a group.

33. When using your charge accounts, try buying at the beginning of a billing cycle. You won't have to pay for thirty days this way, because you won't be billed for about thirty days. And, further, you usually have another fifteen days to pay without being charged interest.

34. When making charitable contributions to your church or college, don't give cash. Instead give appreciated stock or property that you had planned to sell and on which you would have long-term capital gains. This way you'll be able to deduct the full value without paying a gains tax.

35. Start an Investment Club when you plan to buy stocks. You can save on commissions by pooling money. You can also pool knowledge and take turns on doing research.

36. If your car has a low cash value, consider eliminating collision insurance, which pays costs to repair your car from accidents you cause. No matter how much insurance you carry, you won't get more than the blue-book value if the car is damaged.

37. The longer you hold funds in a bank or savings account, the more interest you earn. Don't leave checks or cash lying around.

38. Put your stocks in joint names—part in husband's name, part in wife's. This way you can take advantage of two $100 dividend exclusions on your income tax. Also, look into putting stock in your children's names.

39. Beat the high costs of baby-sitting by joining or starting a baby-sitting co-op. Parents sit for others to pay for the sitting other parents

do for them. Unfortunately, co-ops don't advertise. You may have to do some hunting around to find one, but it's worth it.

40. Teach your children the value of money early. If you're on a tight budget and can't afford "buy me that," say so and mean it. If saying so in public is too embarrassing for you, say, "It's not convenient to buy that now." The child will know what you mean, but no one else will—except the other mothers who read this book.

41. The teen-age driver, especially male, can cost you a fortune insurancewise. However, some insurance companies will make a deduction in premiums if the driver has taken a student-driving program. Such programs are often given free at public schools.

42. If you're clever, you can make your own baby announcements and make some money, too. For years, *Redbook* magazine has picked one original announcement per month and paid the authors $50 for it. They like gimmicky, inexpensive announcements, heavy on the homemade look, and tied in artwise with the parents' occupations. They also like, and print, the letter that explains it.

43. If you're going to do some regular savings, save at a savings and loan association or mutual savings bank rather than a commercial bank. At this writing, the federal government still permits savings institutions to pay higher interest rates than commercial banks.

OTHER

Recreation per se has not been included in this book, although it is, of course, quite important. The reason for its exclusion is that it is almost impossible to budget. Traditionally, what's left is used for recreation. You will also note that I have included the traditional forms of recreation for children under the section on education. It's an arbitrary decision on my part that reflects my belief that children don't just play and play and play, they play and learn and learn and learn.

Appendix: A Directory of Sources for You to Contact, Send for, or Read.

Overall. "Consumer Product Information Seasonal Index" (free), available from the Consumer Product Information Center, Public Document Distribution Center, Pueblo, Colorado 81009. *Guide to Federal Consumer Services* ($1), compiled under direction of Virginia H. Knauer, Director, Office of Consumer Affairs; *Consumer Education Bibliography* ($1), by Office of Consumer Affairs and the New York Public Library; and free biweekly list of selected U.S. Government publications, write: Superintendent of Documents, U.S. Government Printing Office, Washington, D.C. 20402.

Maternity. "Unemployment Compensation Information," Bureau of Employment Security, c/o your local office, or write to the U.S. Department of Health, Education and Welfare, Social Security Administration, Washington, D.C.; Booklet #1770-00101 (30¢), available from Superintendent of Documents, U.S. Government Printing Office, Washington, D.C. 20402; International Childbirth Education Association, P.O. Box 5852, Milwaukee, Wisconsin 53220.

Clothing. Elegance Maternelle, (money order), Department 101, Marylebone, High Street, London, W.1, England. Mothercare Ltd., Cherry Tree Road, Watford, WD 25SH, England. Rowes of Bond Street, 120 New Bond Street, London W1YOBN, England; made-to-measure clothes, $28 and up, including the John F. Kennedy, Jr., coat (coats start at $60), self-measurement chart available free.

Facts of Sizes. "How a Baby Grows" and "How to Bathe a Baby" (free), Johnson and Johnson, New Brunswick, New Jersey 08903. To get a Montgomery Ward catalog, write: Customer Adjustment Manager, Albany Catalog House, 150 North Broadway, Menands, New York 12201; Baltimore Catalog House, 1000 South Monroe Street, Baltimore, Maryland 21232; Chicago Catalog House, 618 West Chicago Avenue, Chicago, Illinois 60607; Kansas City Catalog House, 6200 East Saint John Avenue, Kansas City, Missouri 64123; Oakland Catalog House, 2825 East 14th Street, Oakland, California 94616; Portland Catalog House, 2741 North West Vaughn Street, Portland, Oregon 97210; Denver Catalog House, 555 South Broadway, Denver, Colorado, 80217; Fort Worth Catalog House, 7th and Carroll Avenue,

Fort Worth, Texas 76101; St. Paul Catalog House, 1400 University Avenue, St. Paul, Minnesota 55101.

Cuphooks and Barricades. "A Safer World for Babies and Toddlers," excellent booklet from Johnson and Johnson, including how to do mouth-to-mouth resuscitation plus pointers on water safety, baby-sitters, even sunburn.

Maintenance. For "Eco-Tips," write Concern, Inc., 2233 Wisconsin Avenue, N.W., Washington, D.C. 20007; Booklets, Electric Energy Association, 90 Park Avenue, New York, New York 10016; or American Gas Association, 1515 Wilson Boulevard, Arlington, Virginia 22209. Also, Penny Saver, Box 8699, Philadelphia, Pennsylvania 19101.

Toys. "Toy Safety" and "Banned Toy List," Bureau of Product Safety, Superintendent of Documents (⌗1712-00165, 45¢); *Guide to Good Toys* (25¢), Creative Playthings, Princeton, New Jersey 08540; *Playthings Directory*, ($1.50), Geyer-MacAllister Publications, 51 Madison Avenue, New York, New York 10010; *Childcraft Catalog*, Childcraft Education Corporation, 964 Third Avenue, New York, New York 10022; "Choosing a Child's Book" (tips and source material for getting booklists, free), The Children's Book Council, Inc., 175 Fifth Avenue, New York, New York 10010; "Growing Up with Books" (free), compiled by Eleanor B. Widdois, R. R. Bowker Company, 1180 Avenue of the Americas, New York, New York 10036.

Preschool Schools. Association for Childhood Education International, 3615 Wisconsin Avenue, N.W., Washington, D.C. 20016; The Waldorf School, The Waldorf Institute of Adelphi University, Garden City, New York 11530.

Financial. "A Shopper's Guide to Life Insurance" ($1), and "A Shopper's Guide to Term Insurance" ($1), Consumer Insurance, 813 National Press Building, Washington, D.C. 20014; *Best's Review,* A. M. Best Company, Park Avenue, Morristown, New Jersey 07960, *Life Rates and Data,* National Underwriter Publications, 175 West Jackson Boulevard, Chicago, Illinois 60604; "Everything You Always Wanted to Know about Insurance* (*but since you're a woman no one bothered to tell you)", Insurance Company of North America Consumer Service, 1600 Arch Street, Philadelphia, Pennsylvania 19101. Recommended by the Institute of Life Insurance: *The Complete Estate Planning Guide,* by Robert Brosterman; *How to Use Life Insurance in Business and Estate Planning,* by George White; *You, Your Heir and Your Estate,* by George B. Gordon; *The Planning and Administration of Estates,* by Rene Wormser; *Money and Kids: How to Earn It, Save It, Spend It,* by Mary Price Lee (Westminster Press, 1973).

For answer to specific questions, write: National Association of

Home Builders, 1625 L Street, Washington, D.C. 20036; American
Land Title Association, Box 566, Washington, D.C. 20044; American
Bar Association, 1155 East 60th Street, Chicago, Illinois 60637; Dow
Jones-Irwin, Inc., Homewood, Illinois 60430; McGraw-Hill, Inc., 330
West 42nd Street, New York, New York 10036; American Institute
of Real Estate Appraisers, 155 East Superior Street, Chicago, Illinois
60611; American Institute of Architects, 1735 New York Avenue,
N.W., Washington, D.C. 20006; American Mortgage Bankers Associ-
ation, 90 Park Avenue, New York, New York 10016. And see *Legal
Adviser on Home Ownership,* by Jerome G. Rose, published by Little,
Brown, Boston, Massachusetts; "How to Buy Real Estate," U.S. News
& World Report, Washington, D.C.; *How to Estimate Market Value
in Real Estate,* by Ray H. Arnold, published by Prentice-Hall, Engle-
wood Cliffs, New Jersey 07632.

Index